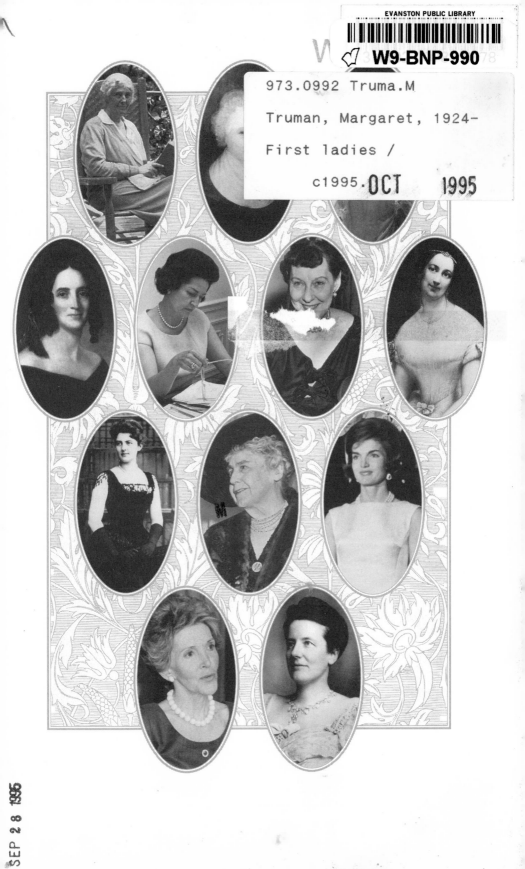

ALSO BY MARGARET TRUMAN

Bess W. Truman

Souvenir

Women of Courage

Harry S Truman

Letters from Father:
The Truman Family's Personal Correspondences

Where the Buck Stops

White House Pets

IN THE CAPITAL CRIME SERIES

Murder on the Potomac

Murder at the Pentagon

Murder in the Smithsonian

Murder at the National Cathedral

Murder at the Kennedy Center

Murder in the CIA

Murder in Georgetown

Murder at the FBI

Murder on Embassy Row

Murder in the Supreme Court

Murder on Capitol Hill

Murder in the White House

FIRST LADIES

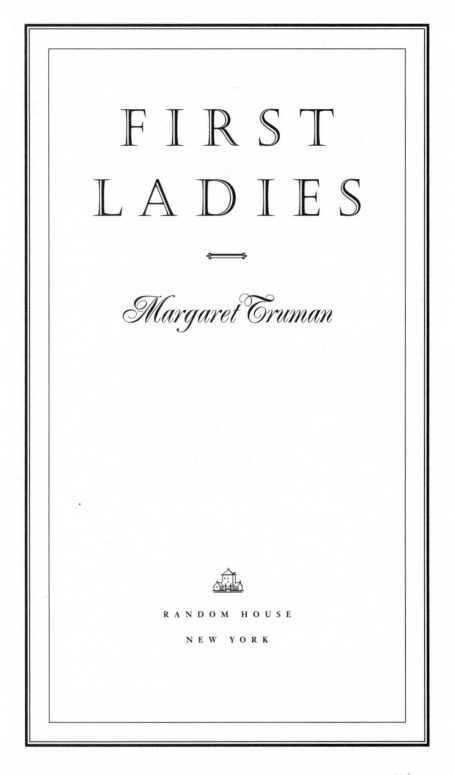

FIRST
LADIES

Margaret Truman

RANDOM HOUSE

NEW YORK

Library of Congress Cataloging-in-Publication Data
Truman, Margaret
First ladies/Margaret Truman.
p.   cm.
Includes index.
ISBN 0-679-43439-9 (acid-free paper)
1. Presidents' spouses—United States—Biography.   I. Title.
E176.2.T78   1995   973'.099—dc20   95-9713

Manufactured in the United States of America on acid-free paper
Book design by J. K. Lambert
9 8 7 6 5 4 3 2
First Edition

I hope some day someone will
take time to evaluate the true role of
the wife of a President, and to assess
the many burdens she has to bear and
the contributions she makes.

HARRY S TRUMAN

ACKNOWLEDGMENTS

A great many people have given me advice, encouragement, and help for this book. Above all, I want to express my appreciation to the First Ladies who graciously answered my many questions about their White House years—Lady Bird Johnson, Betty Ford, Rosalynn Carter, Nancy Reagan, and Barbara Bush. Numerous people at the various presidential libraries have also been helpful. I would especially like to thank George H. Curtis of the Harry S Truman Library, Linda Hansen of the Lyndon Baines Johnson Library, Herbert L. Pankratz of the Dwight D. Eisenhower Library, Leesa Tobin of the Gerald Ford Library, Dale C. Mayer of the Herbert Hoover Library, as well as Susan O'Brien of the New York Society Library. My agent, Ted Chichak, and my editor, Samuel S. Vaughan, have been warmly supportive and astutely involved with achieving the best possible book on this complex subject. Finally, I would like to thank my friend and colleague, Thomas Fleming, for his invaluable research help and literary consultation.

CONTENTS

FIRST LADIES

Chapter 1

—

THE WORLD'S SECOND TOUGHEST JOB

A FEW MONTHS AFTER BILL AND HILLARY CLINTON SETTLED INTO the White House, they invited me and my husband, Clifton Daniel, down from New York to have dinner and stay overnight with them. I said we were perfectly willing to stay in a hotel. We did not want to intrude on the rare hours of relaxation a President and First Lady have in their hectic lives. "Nonsense," Hillary replied in her direct way. "We *like* to have company."

It was one of my most pleasant nights in that historic house, where my mother and father spent eight tumultuous years and where I alternated between being full-time and part-time boarder. We slept in the Queens' Bedroom, with its majestic canopied bed, rose-tinted walls, and graceful eighteenth-century couches and chairs. A procession of reigning queens have stayed there, as well as Prime Minister Churchill and other heads of state. Its present elegance is light-years away from the run-down White House the Trumans inherited in the spring of 1945. I remember crying myself to sleep on my first night in the place, it all looked so shabby and second rate. A cadre of creative First Ladies, starting with Jacqueline Kennedy, are responsible for this transformation.

Occasionally, when the pressure got to him, my father used to call the mansion "The Big White Jail." I was amused to hear that Bill Clinton shares this salty sentiment. At one point during our evening of fine food and lively talk, he wryly suggested the place should be a line item in the budget as part of the federal penitentiary system.

Hillary smiled agreement at this presidential grousing, as Bess Truman had in her now distant days. This is the perfectly normal reaction of any two human beings who find themselves in what someone has called "eighteen acres under glass." It does not imply any lack of affection for the President's house. In fact, as we talked past midnight, I could see that Bill Clinton's fascination with the history of the place equaled Harry Truman's.

Living in the White House is a unique experience—a fantastic compound of excitement and tension and terror and pride and humility. Above all it is a historic experience. The spirit of the past is everywhere, reminding you of other men and women who have walked the corridors at midnight and morning, pondering—or regretting—large decisions.

But a President is also constantly reminded of his powers. I will never forget my awe, the first time I saw my mother and father descend the wide, red-carpeted grand staircase to lead their honored guests into the lofty State Dining Room. Dad always looked his best in white tie and tails. In an evening gown, Mother looked marvelously regal. The red-coated Marine Band blared "Hail to the Chief," the stirring march from an old London musical which was selected to enhance the presidential presence by one of our most politically astute First Ladies, Sarah Polk.

You will note, however, that the march hails only the President. In the Constitution, he is designated the chief executive officer of the nation and commander in chief of the armed forces. In the West Wing of the White House, he presides over a staff of dozens of loyal followers in a web of offices surrounding his oval sanctum. About the First

Lady, on the other hand, the Constitution is silent. No trumpets blare when she enters the State Dining Room or any other room, unless she is with the President. In my mother's day, fifty years ago, the President's wife could count her staff on the fingers of one hand. A few decades earlier, a First Lady had no staff to count. The male politicians who put together the federal government seem never to have given a thought to what a First Lady might do, thereby encouraging Congress to pretend, until recently, that she did not exist when they voted a budget for the White House.

These days, as Hillary Rodham Clinton and other modern presidential wives have amply demonstrated, First Ladies are doing a lot. But the job remains undefined, frequently misunderstood, and subject to political attacks far nastier in some ways than those any President has ever faced. It has complications as mind-boggling from a psychological or political point of view as the conundrums faced by the double-domes in the State Department or the Pentagon.

For one thing, almost all the people in Washington, D.C., are there because they want to be at the white-hot center of power. The ones with the most power, members of Congress and the President, have the added assurance that the American people have sent them there. That is particularly true of the President, the one politician who is elected by the vote of the entire nation. Few if any Presidents, including my father, did not want that unique job. Most of them have been like Bill Clinton; they have hungered and hankered for it most of their lives. Abraham Lincoln may have put it best when he said: "No man knows what that gnawing is until he has had it."

On the other hand, a First Lady, as Lady Bird Johnson has noted in her gentle southern way, has been chosen by only one man—the President—and it is highly unlikely that he was thinking about her as First Lady when he proposed. No matter how different our First Ladies have been—and as individual women they have ranged from recluses to vibrant hostesses to political manipulators on a par with Machiavelli—they have all shared the unnerving experience of facing a job they did not choose. With few exceptions, they have also shared a determination to meet its multiple challenges.

Each of them has done the job differently—yet few of them have been openly critical of their predecessors (unlike Presidents, who tend to be ferociously judgmental of those who have preceded or followed them into the Oval Office). Instead, First Ladies have, to a startling degree considering the acrimonious political world they inhabit, reached out to one another. Many have even become friends.

By a somewhat eerie coincidence, I was in Austin, Texas, interviewing Lady Bird Johnson for this book on the night Jacqueline Kennedy Onassis died. We were having drinks on the deck of Mrs. Johnson's lovely home, overlooking the winding Colorado River, when one of her Secret Service men reported they had just received word that Mrs. Onassis would probably not live past midnight. Deeply moved, Lady Bird spoke in almost biblical cadences about how much she had come to love and admire Jackie for her bravery, her grace, her generosity of spirit. She talked of how magically Jackie had captured our hearts in those thousand days of soaring hope that distinguished John F. Kennedy's administration. She discoursed even more eloquently on how Jackie's courage had held the Kennedy family and the nation together during a time of almost unbearable tragedy.

A few days after the Trumans moved into the White House in 1945, my mother received one of the nicest letters of her life from Grace Coolidge. It was full of understanding and encouragement from someone who could really empathize with her situation. Grace's husband, Calvin Coolidge, had been vice president when he was awakened at 2:30 A.M. on August 2, 1923, to be informed that his President, Warren Harding, was dead and Coolidge was now the Chief Executive and his wife the First Lady.

Mrs. Coolidge asked Mother "to accept from one who has passed through a similar experience the heartfelt expression of best wishes." She hoped Mother and Dad would be given three essentials for survival in the White House, "strength, good courage and abounding health." It meant a lot to Mother, to know there was another woman out there who had been through it all and was rooting for her—even if she was a Republican!

When Ronald Reagan was seriously wounded by a would-be assassin in 1981, Nancy Reagan received a deeply compassionate letter from Jacqueline Kennedy Onassis, who knew, better than any living former First Lady, the terror and grief and anguish such an experience evokes. Later, Jackie followed up the letter with a phone call. Nancy never forgot this spontaneous sympathy and expressed her enduring gratitude for it when Jackie died of cancer in 1994.

Along with friendship, many First Ladies have found a common bond with some of their predecessors who, on the surface at least, seem to have had drastically different styles. Hillary Clinton amazed me when she said Bess Truman was one of the First Ladies she most admired. I could not imagine two more different women. My mother would have required two divisions of Marines to drag her before a congressional committee to testify on health care or anything else.

But when Hillary began talking about the depth and intensity of Bess Truman's behind-the-scenes political partnership with my father, I understood immediately. That kind of partnership has been the bedrock of Hillary's relationship with Bill Clinton. In Hillary's case it has been a publicly declared fact. In Bess Truman's case it was a closely held secret. But for Hillary, the partnership was the important thing.

I was reminded of an almost as startling discovery about another First Lady: years ago a mutual friend told me Jacqueline Kennedy often said my mother was the First Lady she most admired. Then, too, I had to stifle my impulse to blink in disbelief. Jackie Kennedy, the quintessence of New York and Paris chic, admiring Bess Truman, with her sensible suits and flowered hats? Jackie, the woman who gave serious art and high culture a major niche in American consciousness, admiring down-to-earth Bess Truman, whose favorite reading was detective stories?

"What she admired," the friend said, "is the way your mother defended her privacy."

I nodded, much as I was to do later with Hillary Rodham Clinton, and thought: of course. A gentle, enormously sensitive woman like Jackie would understandably want to escape much of the pitiless public gaze and the occasional public frenzies that are an inevitable part of the First Lady's job.

There was another reason Jackie admired my mother, the friend said. "She brought a daughter to the White House at a very impressionable age and managed to get her through eight years without being spoiled."

I am not sure my mother (or my husband) would completely agree with that compliment. But, again, I felt an instant sympathy as I recalled Jackie's desire to raise Caroline and John in the White House without the distorting glare of publicity. She had learned that the American people tend to feel the First Family is public property, like the White House itself.

Hillary Clinton told me she did not discover this troublesome tendency until she and Bill enrolled their daughter, Chelsea, in the Sidwell Friends School. Suddenly they were under fire in a half dozen newspapers and on television for choosing a private rather than a public school.

The President and First Lady tried to explain that Sidwell was used to handling the children of VIPs and would not come to a dead stop when the Secret Service began issuing diktats about how things must be done to assure Chelsea's safety. The Clintons did not want to disrupt the lives of several hundred public school kids merely to make a symbolic statement about their support for public education. It was a poor trade-off—not to mention the likelihood that it would turn Chelsea into an isolated, unhappy young woman.

The Clintons' imbroglio reminded me of the virtual war that raged between the press and another First Lady, Rosalynn Carter, when she decided to let her daughter, Amy, come to state dinners—and bring a book to read to get through the boring adult conversation and speeches. As Mrs. Carter explained it to me, Amy had done this sort of thing when Jimmy was governor of Georgia without anyone making a fuss. The First Lady was hurt and not a little angry when the press constantly noted Amy's presence and discussed it pro and con.

Like First Ladies before her, Rosalynn Carter was feeling her way. Like them she had to learn from harsh experience that reporters love to write about the lifestyles of First Families. Frances Cleveland, Grover Cleveland's wife, conducted a running war with the journalists of her era over their coverage of her family life. White House children, from Jesse Grant to Quentin Roosevelt to Margaret Wilson to Margaret Truman, have provided grist for columnists and commentators.

Speaking of state dinners brings up the First Lady's role as a hostess. Until they got to the White House, most Presidents' wives considered themselves hard-pressed if more than a dozen family members turned up for Thanksgiving dinner. Suddenly they find themselves confronted with entertaining hundreds of VIP guests on a regular basis. All these sophisticated people expect not only to be fed well but to be charmed by discovering friends—or people with mutual interests—among their tablemates. The ninety-person White House staff is there, of course, to assist and advise the First Lady in selecting menus and seating plans. But the buck stops at her desk if something goes wrong.

A good example of how a culinary disaster can undo the best-laid plans was a dinner to which the Kennedys invited Clifton and me and my parents in 1962. It was a night of toasts and tributes to the Truman administration—a wonderfully thoughtful thing to do. The meal was planned as an elegant French feast—a demonstration of how Jackie had revamped the White House's humdrum kitchen.

Feast it was until we got to the main course, which was grouse (perfectly named, as it turned out). What the kitchen did to these birds remains a mystery. My knife glanced off mine as if the creature were titanium. On my left, Bobby Kennedy was sawing away with the ferocity of a man who never let anyone or anything, from corrupt labor leaders like Jimmy Hoffa to arrogant bureaucrats like J. Edgar Hoover, intimidate him. I leaned over and whispered in his ear: "These White House knives never could cut butter." Bobby, who seldom so much as smiled in public, burst out laughing.

The President, who had been sawing just as hard, started chuckling, too. Suddenly another guest's grouse sailed off his plate onto the floor—and a mortified Jackie ordered the rest removed. Fortunately, we were all old White House hands, and my parents told a few horror

Few First Ladies have approached Jackie's sense of style when she wanted to be regal. Here she glitters at a dinner President Kennedy gave for my parents. My husband and I were among the guests. *(Truman Library)*

stories from their early encounters with the awful Roosevelt kitchen that made the inedible fowl seem trivial.

Jacqueline Kennedy's love affair with France and European culture reminds me of another flash point in the First Lady's nonexistent job description. Jackie looked like a movie star, and she occasionally acted like one, gamboling on Mediterranean yachts with the jet set, who happened to be her friends. Some people criticized Jackie for those exotic vacations. That raises the intriguing question of how much a First Lady can be herself—pursuing and enjoying what comes naturally to her—and remain this public person, who has suddenly become a symbol of American womanhood in all its myriad guises. It is a dilemma which every modern First Lady has to face.

A painful example was one of Pat Nixon's first remarks when she prepared to take over the White House in 1968. Understandably elated by her husband's triumph, after his heartbreaking hairbreadth loss to Jack Kennedy in 1960, Pat declared that now the Executive

Mansion would be a place where ordinary people would be welcomed. "The guests won't be limited to big shots!" she said.

Her just-elected husband jokingly—and perhaps nervously—reminded her that all their friends were big shots. Dick Nixon was not about to bar the White House door to the millionaire contributors to his war chest. Pat Nixon was being herself in those poignant words—reflecting her hardworking middle-class background. For a moment she had forgotten that she was also a politician's wife.

Again and again, First Ladies, while being themselves or trying to be public symbols, have collided with harsh political realities—and with the public's often unrealistic expectations of their roles. Betty Ford found this out when she voiced some frank personal opinions about abortion and premarital sex on the TV show *60 Minutes*. The firestorm of criticism looked for a while like it might trigger a political meltdown in the Ford White House. Barbara Bush confessed in her memoirs that her opinion on abortion differed from her husband's conservative stance—but remembering Betty's experience, she artfully concealed it during her White House years.

In both their private and public lives, which have become virtually indistinguishable, First Ladies have had to feel their way along an invisible boundary between aristocratic luxury and democratic simplicity. Criticism of a First Lady's style did not begin with Nancy Reagan. It goes back to Martha Washington and has recurred with varying degrees of rancor throughout the following two hundred plus years.

Not long ago, journalist Barbara Matusow moderated a panel on First Ladies and the media at the Smithsonian Institution. She opened the discussion by stressing the importance of historical perspective in understanding First Ladies. Without naming her, Ms. Matusow described a First Lady who was incredibly superstitious and fearful for her husband's safety and who loved elaborate gowns and spent so much money on them and on decorating the White House that the bills deeply embarrassed her husband. She also had a reputation for pushing her husband around politically so often some people called her the Associate President. A ripple of recognition ran through the audience—until Ms. Matusow said: "It's not Nancy Reagan. It's Mary Lincoln."

The disapproval both these First Ladies incurred for their supposed extravagance and political weight throwing underscores a fundamental point. The American people have always wanted a First Lady to be a traditional wife and mother first. Any interests or activities beyond these spheres have frequently been greeted with criticism or distrust.

Not just from the public, I might add. Jack Kennedy was violently opposed, at first, to Jackie's plans to redecorate the White House in 1961. It took a great deal of firmness on Jackie's part to resist this presidential negativism and push ahead to the famous—and fabulously successful—redecoration. Other First Ladies, from Mary Lincoln to Pat Nixon to Nancy Reagan, have had to contend with powerful presidential aides, who saw them as competitors and were not averse to blackening their reputations.

There is another trip wire in the First Lady's path if she enters the explosive world of real politics. Bess Truman's instinct to remain behind the scenes as her husband's political partner was in part the result of her personal reluctance to face reporters and congressional committees. It was also rooted in conclusions she drew from Eleanor Roosevelt's overtly political activities. She felt that sometimes Mrs. Roosevelt's good intentions, her desire to achieve instant justice and equality between the sexes and races in America, led her into situations which embarrassed her husband—and even forced him to disavow her opinions.

FDR, one of the most popular Presidents in American history, landslide winner of a second term in 1936, could tolerate these political differences, often with a smile. As a vice president catapulted into the White House by fate, Harry Truman had very little political capital to expend, so this too justified my mother's covert style.

No one can top me (or my mother) in admiration for Eleanor Roosevelt. She was one of the great Americans of our century—and she expanded the First Lady's role as no one before her. But she should not be a model against whom all other First Ladies must be measured.

Each First Lady has to deal with the particular political climate swirling around and through the White House when she arrives. Above all, she has to consider her individual, intensely personal relationship with her husband.

Living and working together in the same house, a President and his wife often see more of each other than they have in any previous era of their marriage. The First Lady is frequently more intimately involved in her husband's political reactions and decisions than ever before. Betty Ford was one of several First Ladies who told me this in unvarnished terms. Lady Bird Johnson made it even clearer. "You and your husband suddenly look at each other and say: 'It's just you and me. Other people—our children, friends—will try to help. But in the end it's the two of us who are going to succeed—or fail.' "

Another little-understood task which many First Ladies have assigned themselves is protector of their husbands from the killing pace of the job. One out of every five presidents has died in office, at an average age of fifty-seven. Almost as many died within five years of leaving office—and these too were comparatively young men—their average age sixty. While the life span of the average American rose throughout the nineteenth century, presidential longevity declined from an average of seventy-three for the Presidents before the Civil War to sixty-three for the Presidents who followed it. My mother considered safeguarding Harry Truman from his penchant for overwork one of the most important sides of her job. Again, Lady Bird Johnson said it best: "It's up to you [the First Lady] to create a zone of peace, of comfort, within the White House where your husband can regain his equilibrium, restore his spirit."

Hillary Rodham Clinton may be able to change the public's attitude toward overt political activity by First Ladies. For her sake and the sake of future First Ladies, I wish her well. I think a First Lady should be free to make political statements and commitments—if she has the ability and is so inclined. When it comes to First Ladies, I am for more freedom, in all directions.

But Rosalynn Carter's experience suggests that politics is still surrounded by an invisible boundary that First Ladies cross at their peril.

She came to the White House determined to be Jimmy Carter's public partner. Four years later she exited defensively, explaining again and again that she never told Jimmy what to do, he was a strong person and he made up his own mind.

By now, I hope you are convinced that the title of this chapter is more or less justified. First Lady is the world's, or at least Washington, D.C.'s, second toughest job. But it can also be a fascinating job. No one else has a better view of the maddening, exhausting, frequently baffling problems of the President of the United States, the most powerful politician in the world. No one else is as likely to meet as many electrifying, controversial personalities in any given calendar year. No one else is in a position to exert more influence on the future of the world—and on the way Americans think about fundamental values.

If there is one quality that comes through vividly from studying the history of the women of the White House, it is their strength. Who else but a strong woman can live with the most unnerving aspect of her job—the knowledge that at any given moment somewhere in America there are probably a half-dozen individuals plotting to kill her husband?

More than once a First Lady has made a significant political contribution to her husband's administration. Even more often, and more difficult to discover, the spiritual strength of a First Lady has sustained a President in hours when the awful loneliness of the job threatened to overwhelm him.

No matter how political she becomes, the First Lady will always be a woman, married to a specific man (until, of course, we elect a woman President). That means there are spiritual depths in her marriage that only she understands, needs that only she can fulfill. Always, against the necessities of politics, she will balance these other needs.

Not all First Ladies have been able to achieve this wifely responsiveness. Some came to the White House with such deeply troubled marriages, they were almost forced to chart courses that were semi-independent of their husbands'—and occasionally in opposition to them. These women deserve our deepest sympathy for their struggles to cope with emotional as well as political problems in the glare of maximum publicity.

There have also been times when a First Lady has said to the most powerful man in the world: enough. He has listened, and turned away from the ecstasy and agony of power. I saw that happen in my own family when my father decided not to run in 1952. It happened again in 1968 when Lady Bird Johnson said it to her husband, the most intensely political President who ever bestrode the Oval Office.

Earlier I noted that modern First Ladies are doing a lot. I begin to think I should amend that remark. First Ladies, from Martha Washington to Louisa Adams to Julia Grant to Edith Roosevelt to Bess Truman to Hillary Clinton, have always done a lot. As symbols, wives, mothers, hostesses, and political partners, they have coped with anguish and tragedy and the temptations and illusions of power. Above all, they have borne witness, with their courage and their caring, to women's share—and place—in the shaping of America.

Chapter 2

—

DEMOCRACY
IN SKIRTS

ONE HISTORICAL OBSERVER OF FIRST LADIES HAS SUGGESTED THAT they appeal to the public's heart while Presidents appeal to the head. I resisted that idea as too simplistic when I began writing this book. But there is no doubt that a First Lady has always had a lot to do with how people feel about a President's performance. I came across other scholars who described this phenomenon as "setting the tone" of an administration.

I rather like that idea. *Tone,* my dictionary tells me, is a word with layers of meaning. It is used to describe the characteristic quality of an instrument or voice. Painters use it to discuss subtleties of shade and color. It is also used to denote a general quality, effect, or atmosphere. It includes what a First Lady says and how she says it—and what she does not say and how she manages that. It deals with the often explosive questions of class and style, attitude and manner.

Martha Washington discovered a lot of this when she arrived in New York to preside over the first Executive Mansion, a cramped, rented house on Cherry Street. (It was ripped down in the 1870s, when they built the approaches to the Brooklyn Bridge.) Her husband, our first President, was puzzled about his own role. He sought advice far and wide about how he should conduct himself vis-à-vis Congress, the title he should use, how he should receive callers. He knew he should not act like a king, but he also did not want to become a nobody. Washington was determined not to let the presidency—for which he had fought harder than anyone else at the Constitutional Convention—be diminished by petty critics and worrywarts who saw hobgoblins of potential tyranny everywhere.

It might be apropos to recall here that the Constitution and the federal government it created were by no means universally admired at birth. In New York and other states, the national charter had been approved by minuscule margins. Prominent Americans such as Patrick Henry had attacked the Constitution ferociously, claiming it would destroy freedom. Already, two political parties were in embryo: the mostly conservative supporters of the federal government, who called themselves Federalists, and the Antis, who bitterly resented being called Democrats—the worst political insult you could throw at a person in the 1790s. (The word connoted anarchy and mob rule—more than a theoretical worry in the shadow of the French Revolution.) The Antifeds tried to evade the slur by calling themselves Republicans, but they were Democrats under the skin. The word did not become respectable until Andrew Jackson's era.

From the start, Martha Washington was an essential part of George's presidential plans. When she reached the west bank of the Hudson on her journey from Mount Vernon, he brought her across the river in his official barge—forerunner of other presidential watercraft. This was a sign all by itself that the Father of the Country expected her to be something more than his after-hours companion. But Martha may have been a bit startled by the accolade she received as she debarked from the presidential rowboat: "Long Live Lady Washington!" shouted the crowd—while thirteen cannon left over from the Revolutionary War gave an earsplitting salute.

The term *First Lady*, which sounds old-fashioned to postfeminist ears, was born during that cannonade. It would take another 145 years for it to appear in Merriam-Webster's 1934 edition of their dictionary. But it would be floating through the political airwaves long before that.

So-called high Federalists wanted Martha—and half the other wives in George's administration—to be called *Lady*. The high Federalists (forerunners of Old Guard Republicans) thought only the "best" people should rule, and they wanted the unwashed masses to get the message as often as possible. Martha never used the title—though she never repudiated it either. Nor did Washington. Antifed newspapers ridiculed the notion of titles for anybody, including the President. The House of Representatives, who even then kept their ears tuned to the voice of the people, agreed with them.

Martha was not particularly surprised to discover she had a role to play. As the daughter of one of the richest men in Virginia and the mistress of Mount Vernon's 8,000 acres, she had long since mastered the arts of hospitality. She had presided over George's dinner table at Morristown and other Revolutionary War camps, where hungry

Most pictures of Martha Washington make her look like an old fuddy-duddy. I like this one because it shows her strength and intelligence.
(AP/Wide World Photos)

Continental Congressmen and foreign diplomats had to be feasted and soothed in a style befitting their stations. But she was not used to thirteen-gun salutes or the discovery that she was public property. On her first morning in New York, she awoke to find Cherry Street jammed by dozens of carriages full of curious women eager to get a glimpse of her. She became the first of a long line when she complained privately to a niece that she felt like a "state prisoner."

But she rose to the public challenge—and then some. Without her sure hand, Washington's dinner parties had drawn criticism for their lack of style. Food was served in such profusion that the diners were reduced to debating where to start. One senator went off huffing it was "the least showy [fashionable] dinner" he ever saw. Before the end of Martha's first summer in New York, another senator, one of the President's sourest Antifed critics, burped home to confide to his diary: "It was a great dinner, and the best of the kind I ever was at."

Martha did not do the cooking, of course. She had a steward and sixteen servants handling the stove and peeling the vegetables. But anyone who has ever run the White House or any other large establishment knows that the real responsibility for the success of a dinner for several dozen guests is upstairs, where the basic decisions on what to serve and how to serve it are made. "I have not had one half hour to myself since the day of my arrival," the weary First Lady told her niece, in another letter.

Callers were a much bigger problem—there were so many of them. The President and his Lady shared this dilemma. At first George thought the democratic thing to do was let anybody pop in to see him, anytime. The executive department almost ground to a halt, and he finally put a notice in the papers announcing that those who merely wanted to shake his hand should call between two and three, twice a week. Those with government business could make an appointment anytime.

To deal with the social side of his job, George decided to have a "levee" for men only, each Tuesday afternoon. This was a superdignified show, in which the President stood before a fireplace in black velvet with silver buckles on his shoes and knees, his hair powdered and gathered behind in a silk bag, yellow gloves on his huge hands. Under his arm was a cocked hat with a black feather, on his hip a long sword in a white leather scabbard. People were introduced to him, got a brief bow, and retreated to the other side of the room.

After the doors closed, the President circled the room, exchanging a few words with each visitor, and returned to his starting point in front of the fireplace. This was the signal for a general departure. The Antifeds asked each other if there was any difference between this and George III in St. James's Palace. In their anxiety to make the President important, Washington and his advisers, notably high Federalist Alexander Hamilton, were in danger of making him pretentious.

Martha rescued the situation with her Friday evening "drawing room" receptions. Dressed in white muslin, she remained seated with the vice president's wife, Abigail Adams, beside her. She chatted agreeably with anyone who approached her, and the President, sans sword and hat, soon appeared and further charmed the ladies with light conversation and the men with reminiscences of wartime heroics. A few Antifed hard-liners—the professional liberals of their day—grumbled that Martha's decision to remain seated was too "queenly" for their taste, but they swiftly became a disregarded minority.

Compliments descended on Lady Washington from all directions. Everyone loved her fondness for white. They said it made her look like a Roman matron. The color went perfectly with her fine complexion, her lovely teeth, her snowy hair. They especially liked her "unassuming manner" and "unaffected" personality. They found the President much more cheerful and easygoing in her presence. The human George Washington, who liked a joke and a glass of wine as much as any man of his era, emerged to everyone's delight.

New York was even more impressed by Martha's democratic determination to return every call within three days. This was not light work. Abigail Adams, in a letter, mentioned returning sixty visits in "3 or 4 afternoons"—and she was only the vice president's wife. New Yorkers grew downright enthusiastic about the first First Lady. When Martha took her two grandchildren, who were living with her, to a circus, the band blared out "General Washington's March" and the crowd applauded as if the President himself had arrived.

The first First Lady thus became a major player in bridging the murky gap between presidential dignity and democratic accessibility—a role other First Ladies have continued with varying degrees of success to this day. Eleanor Roosevelt's utter disinterest in style, her fondness for serving scrambled eggs at White House lunches, her earnest espousal of black equality and the trade union movement and jobs for women helped Depression-era voters accept Franklin D. Roosevelt's aristocratic bearing and Harvard accent. Grace Coolidge's warmth and cheerfulness helped dispell the chill cast by her laconic New England husband.

The greatest tone setter among the early First Ladies was Dolley Madison, wife of our fourth president, James Madison. Although his brilliant brain practically invented the United States of America singlehandedly (or mindedly) at the Constitutional Convention in 1787, Madison was not a very prepossessing man. Short, shy, addicted to wearing black suits, he was once described as always looking like a man on his way to a funeral. Without his predecessor Thomas Jefferson's vigorous backing, he would never have become President. Without Dolley, Madison would almost certainly have been a one-term failure. In those days the President was nominated—or renominated—by his party's caucus in Congress. If you did not charm the lawmakers, you did not get reelected.

Dolley Madison knew exactly what she wanted to do as First Lady because she had spent eight years visiting the White House while Thomas Jefferson was President and James Madison was secretary of state. Occasionally she served as hostess for the widower Jefferson. The Sage of Monticello had concentrated more on his wines and food than on the decor of the mansion, which was still largely unfinished when he left in 1809. One of Dolley's first and most astute moves—something succeeding First Ladies might have emulated—was to invite a select group of congressmen and senators to see for themselves how bad things looked. The legislators came through with five thousand dollars (a hundred thousand in today's dollars), and Dolley spent it so fast it made heads swim.

No one complained, because within three months of taking charge, Dolley had the lawmakers and half of Washington to her first reception in three resplendent rooms that ran along the south front of the house—the present Blue Room, Red Room, and State Dining Room. She had given the job of decorating them to Benjamin Latrobe, one of the best architects of the day, and he ransacked New York and Philadelphia for furniture and fabric for curtains and drapes. The results were spectacular, particularly the room known as Mrs. Madison's Parlor (now the Red Room), which was done in sunflower yellow, with high-backed sofas and chairs in the same lush color and a yellow damask fireboard in front of the mantel.

Even more splendid was the Elliptical Saloon (the current Blue Room). It had a long mirror above the mantel, the walls were papered in rich cream, and the woodwork shadowed in blue and gray. Red silk velvet draperies and red cushioned furniture, including thirty-six "Grecian" chairs, plus a Brussels carpet and bronze lamps completed the brilliant effect. During receptions the buffet table in the State Dining Room was heaped with the equivalent of a "harvest home supper." Dessert featured one of Mr. Jefferson's most inspired imports, ice cream in pastry shells.

It was a setting that would have made a professional misanthrope cheerful. Dolley's bonhomie further guaranteed an absence of gloom. It might be worth pausing here to recall that her marvelous merriment was achieved only after a painful break with her stern Quaker past. It took courage for her to defy the religion that she later said "used to control me entirely" and marry James Madison.

Dolley did not entirely abandon her Quaker past. She may have rejected the Plain People's ban on stylish clothes and balls and parties, but she retained the virtues of honesty and charity. I am convinced that generosity of spirit was the secret of Dolley's charisma. It was rooted in the Quaker belief in the goodness of most people, even when they were quarreling politicians.

She was particularly kind to young people. William Campbell Preston was presented to Dolley by a relative shortly after he graduated from college. She introduced him to a swarm of pretty young women and announced he would be her guest in the White House as long as he stayed in Washington. Two decades later, when he became a senator from South Carolina, he was still talking about the good time he had.

Dolley's triumph as First Lady is all the more remarkable in the light of her background. Her father was a small businessman who had gone bankrupt when she was young. Her mother supported the family by running a boardinghouse. There is nothing in her past to account for her combination of good taste and impeccable hospitality.

Dolley herself was no beauty. She was forty by the time she became First Lady and was definitely into middle-age spread. She applied rouge and other cosmetics of the day with a heavy hand. But her radiance overcame any and all physical deficiencies. One White House guest left a pen portrait of her in her hostessing prime. She was dressed "in a robe of pink satin, trimmed elaborately with ermine, a white velvet and satin turban with nodding ostrich plumes and a crescent in front, gold chains and clasps around the waist and wrists." The entranced visitor insisted it was "the woman who adorns the dress and not the dress that beautifies the woman."

Dolley had a genius for making every guest feel special. She never forgot a name or a connection. Moreover, she hired the best chef in Washington, and she mingled writers and artists with the usual guest list of politicians and diplomats. But it was Dolley's totally unassuming style that set the tone of the White House. She was nothing if not down-to-earth. Once, chatting with the soon-to-be famous congressman Henry Clay, Dolley offered him some snuff. She was addicted to this form of nicotine and never went anywhere without her snuffbox. While Clay inhaled and sneezed, Dolley whipped out a red-checked handkerchief. "This is for rough work," she said, and snorted into it. Next came a fine lace handkerchief. "And this," she went on, "is my polisher." She applied this to her nose in more dainty fashion.

With marvelous astuteness, Dolley managed to work both sides of the aristocracy versus democracy debate. At her receptions, some people liked the way she insisted that each lady guest curtsy to the President before taking a seat. Others admired the way she mingled "the Minister from Russia and the under clerks of the post office."

"Politics," Dolley once told her sister, "is the business of men. I don't care what offices they hold, or who supports them. I care only about *people*." Few lines are a better summary of one of the fundamental parameters of the First Lady's role. Every First Lady who has

Without Dolley Madison,
James Madison would
probably have been a
one-term president. Here
is a portrait of her in her
hostessing prime.
(American Heritage Library)

lost touch with this principle—or was perceived to have lost touch
with it—has gotten into trouble. I should add, however, that Dolley
was intensely interested in politics, and she frequently asked her husband for the latest developments on the international and national
scenes.

There is another dimension to Dolley which in turn leads us to a
wider view of First Ladies. The uncommon courage she displayed in
the White House rescued Madison's presidency—and even the country—from the debacle of an unpopular war. In 1811, westerners and
southerners in Congress coalesced into something called "the War
Hawks," who breathed sulfur and flame on the English for their high-
handed insistence on boarding and sometimes seizing American ships
to enforce their blockade against Napoleon's France. Dolley, a shrewd
observer of human nature, undoubtedly warned Madison that the
War Hawks' real motive was the hope of getting rich from captured
real estate in British-owned Canada. But the President reluctantly

signed a declaration of war on June 19, 1812, even though it passed the Senate by only seven votes.

The country, already divided, turned savagely on Madison and his First Lady when the American attempt to invade Canada ended in a rout and an invading British army captured Detroit. The President was called "the little man in the palace." Others spelled *white house* in lowercase letters to indicate their contempt for its occupant. Dolley was assailed with accusations of supposed infidelity.

Although Dolley valiantly tried to fill the White House with her usual good cheer, the political situation turned even gloomier when Napoleon collapsed, leaving the United States all alone versus Great Britain, the most powerful country on the globe. The Federalist Party, still potent in New England, talked secession and surrender. The British thought they had a chance to regain their lost thirteen colonies—or a hefty chunk of them. They dispatched a fleet under a big-talking admiral named Cockburn, who cruised off the East Coast, declaring he planned to "make his bow" in Mrs. Madison's drawing room.

Washington seethed with unrest and anxiety. There were rumors of an assassination plot, supposedly to get rid of Madison and put in his place a pro-British puppet. Some friends urged Dolley to flee the city. "I am *determined* to stay with my husband," she replied and began sleeping with a saber beside her bed. She heartily approved when the President stationed one hundred soldiers on the White House grounds to demonstrate his determination to stand his ground.

Deciding their war of nerves had failed, the British landed 4,500 veteran troops in Maryland, less than a day's march from the capital. Dolley could only watch and pray as Madison rode off with 6,000 hastily assembled American militia to stop them. The First Lady mounted to the White House roof and swept the horizon with a spyglass, hoping to see her husband returning in triumph. All she saw were some dispirited militiamen and crowds of Washingtonians fleeing into Virginia. The troops assigned to protect the White House panicked and joined the exodus. Dolley soon learned that the pickup American army had stampeded for safety at the first British volley.

Still she refused to budge. She ordered the servants to prepare dinner and set the table for the President and his staff. She was determined to show the citizens there was no panic or cowardice in the White House. Dinner was almost ready to serve when two dust-covered horsemen pounded up to the door. They shouted orders from the President to abandon the house immediately and flee into the country. Dolley was infuriated. She vowed that if she were a man, she would have found soldiers, posted a cannon in every window, and fought the British to the bitter end. But she realized it was time to be sensible and depart.

She still declined to panic. She had sent Madison's papers into the country the previous day. Now she ordered the red silk velvet draperies in the Elliptical Saloon taken down. She also packed the silver service and the blue and gold Lowestoft china she had purchased for the State Dining Room. Then she saw Gilbert Stuart's portrait of George Washington on the wall of the dining room, in an elaborate gold frame. She could not allow the Father of the Country to be captured by the British. "Take it down," she said.

Sweating and cursing, the steward and his assistants tried, but the frame was bolted to the wall. Dolley ordered them to break the frame and cut the canvas out of it. Finally, as she headed out the door with the painting under her arm, she scooped up a precious copy of Jefferson's Declaration of Independence. At this point, one of Madison's black servants, Jim Smith, rode up, shouting: "Clear out! Clear out!" The British were only a few miles away. Dolley climbed coolly into her carriage and rode off to Rokeby, Virginia, to stay in a friend's house.

The British, as even the most casual students of American history know, marched into deserted Washington and gleefully torched the White House, the Capitol, and other public buildings. The Americans, I regret to say, had it coming to them. They had started the pyromania by burning several public buildings in Toronto during their abortive invasion of Canada. Admiral Cockburn no doubt made a drunken bow in Dolley's parlor before striking the match.

Dolley returned to Washington the day after the British marched back to their ships. She shed tears over the blackened shell of the

White House and took up residence nearby in an elegant brick mansion, Octagon House. The story of her White House heroics, particularly her rescue of Washington's portrait, swept the country, inspiring an outburst of patriotic fervor.

In Maryland a local orator proclaimed: "The spirit of the nation is aroused." Men rushed to volunteer for the Army, and when the British fleet tried to capture Baltimore, a furious nightlong cannonade from Fort McHenry beat them off. The battle inspired a vociferous antiwar critic of the Madisons, Francis Scott Key, to write a song called "The Star-Spangled Banner." Labeled appeasers, the Federalist Party virtually went out of business.

Three months later, a shattering victory over another British invasion fleet on Lake Champlain convinced the King's men to talk peace. Wearing her trademarks, the feathered satin turban and the gold chains, Dolley presided over a reunited nation. Even the new British minister, invited to one of her Octagon House galas, was forced to admit: "She looked every inch a queen."

The sheer dimensions of Dolley's mastery introduced a new problem into the First Ladies' story—how to follow such a performance. Her successor, Elizabeth Kortright Monroe, made a mistake which we will see repeated in our own time: she reacted *against* Dolley's democratic style and became the first example of a First Lady who set the wrong tone for her husband's administration.

A New York beauty, the daughter of a wealthy merchant, Elizabeth and her presidential husband were in charge of rebuilding and refurbishing the incinerated White House. As a result of her years spent in Paris when James Monroe was American ambassador there, she loved things French. (The French had reciprocated, worshipfully calling her *La belle Américaine*.) In private, she often spoke French to her husband and daughters. She and the President filled the mansion with French furniture, some of it their own, in the restrained style of the 1780s and 1790s, the rest in the more flamboyant Empire style of Napoleon's era.

Although the Monroes began their administration with a magnificent and popular reception in the restored White House on New

Year's Day, 1818, their entertaining slid swiftly downhill. Elizabeth found Washington dismally provincial—which it almost certainly was in 1818 and to some extent still is. Here is a glimpse of what she had to contend with at a typical White House reception, as seen by a contemporary newspaperman: "The secretaries, senators, foreign ministers, consuls, auditors, accountants, officers of the army and navy of every grade, farmers, merchants, parsons, priests, lawyers, judges, auctioneers and nothingarians crowd to the President's house every Wednesday evening, some in shoes, most in boots and many in spurs...some with powdered heads, some frizzled and oiled; some whose heads a comb has never touched, half hid by dirty collars, reaching far above their ears, stiff as pasteboard."

Elizabeth found this assortment hard to take and entertained as little as possible. She spent months away from the White House, visiting her married daughters—which meant no women could come to the Executive Mansion while it lacked a lady chaperone. Fuming congressional wives and daughters never had a chance to unpack much less display their party dresses. When and if they finally received an invitation from the First Lady, they were intimidated by her fifteen-hundred-dollar Paris ensembles. All her clothes came from France.

The dark-haired, queenly Elizabeth was forty-eight when she became First Lady but looked thirty-something. One woman visitor became positively indignant when she was introduced to the First Lady's twelve-year-old granddaughter (who looked, she said, eighteen or nineteen). There was only one explanation, the already outraged ladies of Washington concluded: the First Lady was using "paint"—a shocking accusation in 1818, when cosmetics had an aura of immorality. Although no one had said a word when Dolley Madison applied rouge with abandon, this supposed transgression became more fuel for the whispering campaign against her successor.

In another display of her sense of superiority to the locals, Elizabeth absolutely refused to call on congressmen and their wives. This inspired many of them—and their friends—to boycott the White House. In 1819 a Monroe reception was peopled by a "beggarly row of empty chairs," according to one eyewitness.

How did Elizabeth Monroe get away with this behavior? The answer would seem to be what historians call "the era of good feelings"—a sort of bipartisan Bermuda triangle in which party politics temporarily disappeared from the American scene, leaving President Monroe with virtually no opposition for a second term in 1820 and no great sense of urgency to use the White House as a vehicle for wooing Congress and public opinion.

Although they had functioned wonderfully as partners in Paris, in the White House the Monroes operated with only the barest interest in the political side of the First Lady's role. More than once in the rest of this book, we shall see the importance of partnership in shaping a First Lady's career. Without this motivating force, Elizabeth Monroe's upper-class inclinations turned her White House years into a kind of historical vacuum. In spite of Mrs. Monroe's beauty and exquisite taste in clothes and furniture, the most memorable First Lady of this era is the berouged, buxom daughter of a Philadelphia boardinghouse keeper, Dolley Madison.

Chapter 3

—

WOMAN OF

MYSTERY

THERE IS ONLY ONE FIRST LADY WHO HAS SUCCESSFULLY NEGOTIATED the perilous passage between democracy and upper-class style. We all know her name: Jacqueline Bouvier Kennedy. Entering the White House under the flag of the Democratic Party, the supposed voice of the poor and downtrodden, Jackie established a reign of genteel taste which managed to mesmerize Americans without alienating them.

At first, Jackie viewed the First Lady's job with dread. Veteran White House reporter Helen Thomas was amazed to discover that this "polished American aristocrat" hated crowds, abhorred the political handshake, and avoided official White House functions as often as possible. Jackie said she felt like a moth on a windowpane; she hated her title—she claimed it made her sound like a saddle horse. She shuddered at becoming public property and feared for her children's equilibrium.

How did Jackie transform these liabilities into immense popularity? The onrush of the television era played a part—complemented by Jackie's beauty. But there is much more to it than the ubiquitous camera eye. The shyness Jackie projected was part of an aura of mystery, of elusiveness, that her father, John Bouvier, a profound student of women, had taught her to create. It was a public personality, one of many roles she played in the White House. "Jackie wore so many masks, she was impossible to decipher," said a former schoolmate, the journalist Charlotte Curtis. "With her elevation to First Lady she became even more elusive, more secretive, more dramatic."

Among her few close friends Jackie was never shy; on the contrary, she had always been talkative, witty, and, with men, more than a little flirtatious. She did wicked impersonations of everyone from the Queen of England to her own husband, whose Massachusetts accent and chopping hand motions she parodied perfectly. Given the chance, she could also be more than a little sarcastic. In an interview with Nan Robertson of *The New York Times* early in the 1960 campaign, Jackie mocked Pat Nixon's "Republican cloth coat"—a phrase Richard Nixon had enshrined in his famous 1952 speech, defending himself and his wife against accusations that they lived lavishly off a secret slush fund. Jackie noted that Pat bought her clothes at Elizabeth Arden, where you could not get a cloth coat for under $250. She also assailed John Fairchild, owner and publisher of *Women's Wear Daily*, for saying she spent $45,000 a year on clothes. "I couldn't do that without wearing sable underwear!" she said.

When Jack Kennedy saw this remark on the front page of *The New York Times*, he reportedly exclaimed: "That's the last thing Jackie's going to say in this campaign." His reaction underscores the curious, not to say precarious relationship between Jackie and her husband. New York and Washington had abounded with rumors that before Jack Kennedy ran for President, she had seriously considered divorcing him for his compulsive womanizing. Nancy Dickerson, a TV reporter who knew her well, noted that in her pre–White House days, wifely devotion was not one of Jackie's outstanding traits—and you could hardly blame her.

In short, this was not a political partnership at work, in spite of some campaign rhetoric from both Jack and Jackie that strove to give that impression. The Kennedys, male chauvinists all, made no attempt to tout Jackie's intelligence, mostly because they did not believe it existed. In their eyes, she was, like all the other women in their lives, strictly for relaxation. Bobby Kennedy, utterly unaware of his condescension, told one reporter Jackie never bothered her husband with questions like "What's new in Laos?" JFK said the same thing in a slightly more flattering way: "I don't have to fight the day's political battles over again at night."

Note the assumptions underlying those two statements. RFK obviously thought Jackie lacked the brainpower to be interested in Laos. His brother the President seems to have assumed that if he discussed politics with his uncomprehending wife, the result would be warfare.

None of the New Frontiersmen had the slightest inkling that Jackie would size up the situation and cope with it her way. First, she chose an old friend, Oleg Cassini, to advise her on her White House wardrobe. From the start, she and the Paris-born designer seemed to have an almost mystic communion. The first sketch he showed her, while she was still in the hospital in December 1960, recovering from the birth of her son, John, was a white full-length evening dress for the inaugural ball. The fabric was an opulent Swiss double satin. The lines were unusually modest; overall the dress was a unique combination of the simple and the regal. "Absolutely right!" Jackie said.

Next Cassini showed her a fawn-beige wool coat, with a small sable collar and muff and a matching pillbox hat. Cassini urged her to wear this outfit to the inauguration. "All the other women will be wearing [full-length] furs. This coat will set you apart, emphasize your youth. It will set the tone for the whole administration."

"I'm convinced," Jackie said. "You're the one."

From that moment Cassini became her official designer. He was a wise choice. The inaugural outfit created a fashion revolution—the "Jackie look." Within days of the ceremony, pillbox hats filled the shelves of the nation's stores and knockoffs of the coat sprouted on a thousand racks. One magazine assured its readers they could get "the look" for $68.68. None of this bothered Jackie in the least. She had worn it first.

Jackie's conversations and correspondence with Cassini reveal how quickly she grasped the essence of the challenge she faced. She told him she wanted to avoid any taint of sensationalism in her clothes. She had no intention of becoming another Marie Antoinette. At the same time she did not want to look stuffy—"there is a dignity to the office [of First Lady] which suddenly hits you." Trying to sum up the style she was aiming for, she told Cassini she required dresses "I would wear if Jack were President of FRANCE." She also insisted on exclusivity. She wanted only original creations—there was no way she would tolerate "any fat little woman hopping around in the same dress."

With her fashion persona under decisive control, Jackie found a cause in the White House itself—redecorating it, not only to suit her own good taste but to make it a museum, even a historical pageant of American taste. The mansion was far from that estate in 1961. Soon after she moved in, Jackie remarked that the place looked as if it had been decorated by B. Altman, New York's prim and proper department store. She told Oleg Cassini most of the rooms reminded her of another now defunct prototype of conventional taste—a Statler Hotel.

As I mentioned in the opening chapter, Jack Kennedy disapproved of overhauling the White House almost as violently as he disliked Jackie's campaign remarks about sable underwear. Later Jackie would acidly recall she had been "warned, begged and practically threatened" not to go anywhere near the project. JFK asked an old Truman hand, my father's White House counsel, Clark Clifford, to talk her out of it. Clark arrived with terrifying tales of the flak my father had encountered when he decided to add what is now known as the "Truman Balcony" to the South Portico. Jackie's ears had already been filled with horror stories of other Presidents, going all the way back to Martin Van Buren, who had wound up losing votes and even elections for trying to refurbish the White House. Along with political sharpshooters in Congress who were always ready to scream about presidential extravagance (perfect camouflage for their own perks and privileges), there were numerous architects and other self-appointed watchdogs ready to pounce on any supposed desecration of a national shrine.

In his memoirs, Clark Clifford maintains he thought Jackie's idea was wonderful from the start—which strikes me as just a bit dubious when the man who called him into the fray, the President, was furiously trying to talk Jackie out of it. Whether Clark became an instant convert or an eventual one, he soon found himself working as Jackie's right-hand man. Not only was he a good choice because of his insider's knowledge of Washington's pitfalls but he also brought with him memories of our experience in Dad's second term, when the White House was gutted and rebuilt just in time to save the Trumans from being buried in its rubble.

In 1948 we discovered the mansion, after decades of halfhearted, often half-baked repairs, was close to literal collapse. Among other things, a leg of the piano in my sitting room broke through the ceiling above the Family Dining Room, and the architects informed Dad that the ceiling of the State Dining Room was staying up only from force of habit. We had to move to nearby Blair House, the historic town house normally used for VIP guests, for almost three years, while the entire building was reconstructed using twentieth-century steel and concrete.

The cost of that operation ignited Congress's traditional parsimony toward the White House, and the lawmakers declined to put up any serious money to decorate the place. Dad left Washington grumbling that the exterior had been improved but the interior looked worse than ever. Like the historian that he was in his spare time, Dad had wanted to do exactly what Jackie did—make the inside of the house as historic as the outside. Unfortunately he was distracted by a few pressing problems such as Senator Joe McCarthy's Communist witch-hunts and a war in Korea.

This harking back to the Truman White House gave Jackie the key idea that enabled her to overhaul the mansion with an amazing minimum of fuss. Instead of using the scare word *redecorate*, which was certain to arouse penny-pinching congressmen and other assorted busybodies, Jackie chose the golden word *restoration* to describe her efforts. The term cast an aura of irreproachable disinterested authenticity on the project, rendering it almost immune to criticism. No matter that it was a misnomer which could not be applied in any literal sense. There was no previous perfect White House in the past which diligence and research could restore. For most of its long career, the place had been an unnerving mixture of the elegant and the shabby. No President ever had the time—or could persuade Congress to cough up the money—to create the kind of splendor that its spacious public rooms and lofty corridors demanded.

Jackie hurled herself into her task with a passion that swept away obstacles and enlisted enthusiasts everywhere. With Clark Clifford's help, she formed the Fine Arts Committee for the White House, to seek out furniture, paintings, and other historic objects. She did not a little of the seeking herself. Clad in jodhpurs and riding boots, she plunged into the cavernous Fort Washington warehouse on the Maryland side of the Potomac, where White House castoffs were stored, rummaging through hundreds of dust-covered crates to rescue long-discarded chairs and tables and lamps for restoration. She also pursued historic paintings, rugs, and furniture with pleading phone calls to their startled owners, frequently persuading them to surrender valuable family heirlooms on the spot.

Next Jackie formed the White House Historical Association to raise funds for the overall renovation. When a knowledgeable friend predicted she would need a minimum of two million dollars, JFK was ready to abandon the project all over again. He could almost hear the uproar the figure would cause. But Jackie rescued the situation by coming up with the idea for a full-color guidebook, describing the White House through its architecture, furnishings, and history. The book has since become a small publishing industry unto itself. Over eight million copies have been sold, making it the equivalent of an oil well or a gold mine in the basement, pumping funds into ongoing acquisitions of art and antiques, rugs and curtains.

Jackie's French taste coincided in a remarkable, almost spooky way with that of previous upper-class First Lady, Elizabeth Monroe. In fact, she made the Monroe White House the focus of her renovation. Jackie loved France so much, she inserted a French decorator, Stéphane Boudin, into the process, making him more or less coequal with the man who thought he was in charge, Henry Francis du Pont, of the famed Winterthur Museum. Du Pont was the acknowledged greatest living expert on American antiques. Boudin knew nothing about them and cared even less. How could they be any good? They weren't French. The result was some spectacular behind-the-scenes fireworks.

Not only was Boudin arrogant but he was rude—and he listened to nobody. He stunned du Pont and his staff by painting the Blue Room white and the Green Room chartreuse. Jackie backed him, ignoring frantic protests from du Pont and a pointed comment from her husband that he preferred the traditional colors. Redecorating the White House was not a joint venture, as far as Jackie was concerned. It was her thing, and she brooked no interference and very little criticism from anyone, including the President.

Any staffer who talked loosely to the press about the project got into deep trouble, if Jackie did not like the resulting story. Maxine Cheshire of *The Washington Post* wrote a seven-part series that was anything but complimentary, pointing out that several of the newly acquired—and in some cases very costly—antiques were fakes. An outraged Jackie forced Jack to call the publisher of the paper to protest and ruthlessly banned those who had talked to Cheshire from further association with the White House.

Friends and staff alike were amazed by both the energy and the willpower Jackie displayed in her drive for a perfect White House. No detail escaped her often furious attention. She fired off enraged memos to staffers about antique dealers who tried to overcharge them. She badgered old friends in Newport who were reluctant to part with favorite antiques. Only once did anyone recall her being recalcitrant about any aspect of the operation: that was when her passion for privacy clashed with her passion for artistic perfection. The National Geographic editors, who were to produce the White House guide, wanted to include a picture of John Jr.'s second-floor bedroom. Jackie refused, and the picture was removed from the layout.

The climax of Jackie's efforts was her 1962 Valentine's Day television tour of the completed public rooms, which attracted forty-eight million viewers and catapulted 1600 Pennsylvania Avenue into Washington's number-one tourist attraction. It also zoomed Jackie herself into supercelebrity. Historically speaking, she was not a new kind of First Lady, although the media never stopped babbling such clichés. There had been younger—and even prettier—First Ladies. But the public memory is not the same as historical memory. For people used to Eleanor Roosevelt, Bess Truman, and Mamie Eisenhower, Jackie was new in capital letters.

While she was refurbishing the White House, Jackie launched a crusade to make the place a showcase for the best in American culture. She invited the cream of American writers, dancers, actors, musicians to entertain and be entertained. Pablo Casals, the world's greatest cellist and number-one prima donna, was charmed into performing. (It was not, as we shall see, his first visit to the White House.) Jerome Robbins contributed a ballet. Frederic March read excerpts from Ernest Hemingway. Again, the press, with no historical memory worth mentioning, marveled, as if no First Lady had ever done anything like this before.

They were really comparing Jackie's taste with her immediate predecessors'. It was, of course, much more sophisticated. Jackie had been raised to admire and enjoy the best in art and culture, and she wanted more Americans to share her pleasure. She wanted to change the prevailing notion that we were a nation of corporate clunkheads who seldom read anything more challenging than a stock market ticker or hung anything on our walls besides family pictures. If she had planned a way to rocket herself into hyperpopularity, she could not have chosen better tactics. Granted, her main appeal was to the American intelligentsia. But by 1962, a new generation of college-educated reporters and editors were part of that influential group, and they rushed to embrace Jackie and her crusade.

Almost as important was Jackie's success abroad, which seemed to ratify the American intelligentsia's approval. People still talk about her sensational reception in Paris, where her beauty and chic and French heritage and command of the language reduced the entire nation, including their austere maximum leader, General Charles de

Gaulle, to the Gallic equivalent of Jell-O. (Crème caramel?) Less well known is the way she also enchanted the English, who have a tradition of looking down their noses at American Presidents and their wives. "Jacqueline Kennedy," intoned the *Evening Standard*, "has given the American people...one thing they had always lacked—majesty."

Even more astonishing, though not as well remembered, was Jackie's goodwill trip to India. One New Delhi newspaper called her "Durga, Goddess of Power." Screaming millions lined the streets to cheer her. Plain folk walked ninety miles from their modest farms to the cities to get a glimpse of the "Queen of America."

This tidal wave of approval enabled Jackie to escape the consequences of some very undemocratic behavior behind the scenes—and occasionally out front. One of her best-kept secrets was how much money she spent on clothes and other private expenses—$121,000 in 1962 alone. She was totally reckless in the expenditures she ran up renovating the White House's private quarters on the second floor. Working with Sister Parish, one of the nation's highest-priced decorators, she ordered the same room repainted two or three times when the results did not suit her. There was nothing new about Jackie's fondness for endless redecorating. She had done the same thing in every house she and Jack had owned. Once, returning from a trip to their pre-presidential Georgetown mansion, he had cried: "Dammit, Jackie, why can't I come home and find the same house I left?"

Clothes were a major item. Mary Gallagher, her secretary, said one of Jackie's closets "was like...a little private shoe store." Dresses and accessories filled the storage closets on the third floor of the White House. Jackie kept friends busy scouting Europe for the latest and best from Paris and Rome. She even sent Oleg Cassini to Paris to check out his competition. He bought her two dresses from Balenciaga, which she hated. "You picked the two worst," she told him, which was quite possibly true.

Soon Cassini—and Jackie—were prepared to try out some decidedly unstuffy outfits. The first was a one-shouldered evening gown that Jackie loved. She told Cassini the President would not tolerate it: "It's too advanced." Cassini tackled the problem by invading the Oval

Office and giving a lecture on the role of queens as style setters. JFK approved the dress—and later allowed Jackie to appear with both shoulders bare in a pink and white lace dress that she wore to the Elysée Palace when they visited Paris.

Washington Post Executive Editor Ben Bradlee once described the President as "boiling" over his wife's dress and decorating bills. But JFK soon realized he was in a losing war. Jackie used wit as well as willpower to joust with her putative lord and master over who had control of the money. One day she sent a framed painting which consisted of daubs and streaks in a half dozen colors to the Oval Office with a note saying it was the best work of a brilliant new modern painter and she wanted to buy it for a mere nine thousand dollars. JFK exploded—until Jackie informed him it was one of John Jr.'s first experiments in finger painting.

As readers may have gathered from her remark about fat little ladies, Jackie more than equaled Elizabeth Monroe in her dislike for the hoi polloi of American politics. She specialized in what she called the "PBO"—the polite brush-off—for numerous semiofficial visitors to the White House. "I can't stand those silly women," she said, refusing to attend a Congressional Wives Prayer Breakfast. As for the Girl Scouts, the March of Dimes, the American Heart Association—the myriad organizations a First Lady is expected to greet when they convene in or near Washington—Jackie had a standard, all-inclusive phrase: "Give them to Lady Bird." Always agreeable and a hardworking political partner in a way Jackie could scarcely envision, Lady Bird Johnson, the vice president's wife, filled in for the First Lady again and again and again.

Jackie once boasted to Mary Gallagher that "they" had told her ninety-nine things she had to do as First Lady and she had not done one of them. She even boycotted a Distinguished Ladies Reception held in her honor. "Jackie! You can't do this!" her husband roared. In the end the fuming President went in her place and made polite excuses for her. Jackie justified many of these withdrawals by saying she was too busy restoring the White House or wanted more time with her children. But a lot of her PBOs were rooted in a visceral repugnance for average Americans and their inclination to treat her as public property. She escaped with only a few public bruises thanks to the overwhelming success of her ability to project a personality that combined mystery and allure and sincerity while saying hardly a political word.

Not that Jackie lacked good political instincts. In Vienna, when she lunched with Nina Khrushchev at the Palais Pallavicini while her husband, Nikita, the Soviet leader, was talking tough to a flabbergasted President at the Soviet embassy, a crowd gathered outside the palais and began chanting "Jac-kie! Jac-kie." Gradually, Mrs. Khrushchev and her party grew visibly uncomfortable. No one was yelling Nina's name. The uproar also made conversation almost impossible. Finally, Jackie strolled to an open window and waved to the crowd, then persuaded Mrs. Khrushchev to join her. Soon the crowd was chanting "Jac-kie! Ni-na!" and the crisis had passed.

Jackie Kennedy's children often took precedence over her duties as First Lady. Here she introduces Caroline and John to horseback riding at their Virginia retreat, Glen Ora. *(Kennedy Library)*

Behind the facade of public success were glimpses of personal unhappiness. Jackie was essentially estranged from the rest of the Kennedy family, except for JFK's father, Joe. Most of the others regarded her as a political liability and fiercely resented the publicity she got. JFK's mother, Rose, especially disapproved of Jackie's free-spending ways and wrote numerous letters to the President's aides and even to White House staffers, such as Head Usher J. B. West, criticizing Jackie for everything from misuse of Air Force One to sloppy housekeeping.

There were also signs of estrangement from her husband—or deep discontent with life in the White House, or both. We will probably never learn how much Jackie knew about the other women Jack Kennedy enjoyed in the White House and outside it. Some of them included her close friends, such as the painter Mary Pinchot Meyer. But it would be hard to believe she did not pick up the ugly rumors that swirled through Washington. There were flashes of cynicism, even bitterness in some of her remarks. Once she was said to have introduced her press secretary, Pamela Turnure, to a visitor as "the woman my husband is supposedly sleeping with."

Unquestionably significant is how often Jackie escaped the White House, in small and large ways. One friend was invited to tea and arrived to find Jackie's mother, Janet Auchincloss, serving. Jackie had gone for a walk. Then there were the three- and four-day weekends she spent at Glen Ora, the getaway house in Virginia, and more weekends in New York and Palm Beach and Hyannis Port. More publicly noticeable were the long vacations she took without her husband—a 1962 trip to Italy, which included jet set–style partying aboard Italian billionaire Gianni Agnelli's yacht, and her summer of 1963 cruise with Greek billionaire Aristotle Onassis aboard his ultimate yacht, *Christina*. JFK strongly disapproved of both these expeditions, which had lurid over- and undertones of scandal. But he was hardly in a position to do more than feebly protest and insist on Jackie taking her sister, Lee Radziwill, and her husband and some family friends along as window dressing.

There was, I strongly suspect, a hidden drama being played out here, one that future biographers will explore at greater depth. Jackie was challenging Jack's attempts to control her—perhaps warning him that two could play the extramarital sex game. Yet she simultaneously wrote him ten-page letters from the *Christina,* opening with "Dearest dearest Jack." This might not have meant quite as much as it would from an ordinary woman. As we shall soon see in another upper-class presidential marriage, endearing expressions in the mail can go hand in hand with profound alienation.

Betty Beale, one of Washington's more astute journalists, has flatly called the Kennedy union a marriage of convenience. I think it was more complex than that, although there were times when it veered perilously close to such a loveless arrangement. I think Jackie was capable of accepting—or attempting to accept—Jack's unfaithfulness without abandoning her love for him. Her father had not been a paragon of marital fidelity. It was one of the chief reasons why her mother divorced him. Jackie was hardly naive about the male tendency to wander.

What Jackie wanted in the White House—and to a surprising degree she began to get it—was her husband's respect for her intelligence and judgment. This, as much as love of art and beauty, was the motive behind the ferocious energy she flung into renewing the Executive Mansion. The sensational success of that venture stunned JFK and his New Frontiersmen in the West Wing. The President was equally surprised by other demonstrations of his wife's political astuteness. When Prime Minister Nehru came to visit, JFK had a horrible time with this aloof, pompous, humorless man. Jackie charmed him. Similarly, the President was never able to get on a relaxed footing with his U.N. Ambassador, Adlai Stevenson, the two-time loser in presidential runs against Dwight Eisenhower. Jackie took charge, and Adlai became one of her most devoted followers, inviting her to lunch at the United Nations, exchanging witty letters and drawings with her.

"Jack developed enormous respect for his wife's political judgment," says Florida's former senator George Smathers. "His pride in her achievements grew stronger the longer he remained in office." Smathers maintains that even on her nonofficial trips to Italy and Greece, as well as her overtly goodwill tours of India and South

America, her letters were full of shrewd political observations that the President found useful. By their third year in the White House, Jackie was reportedly playing a role in public policy. She consistently took a more liberal (versus hard-line) view of steps toward easing tensions with the Soviet Union, such as the Nuclear Test Ban Treaty and the controversial sales of American grain to bail out the collapsing Soviet collective farm program. Oleg Cassini may have put it a little too strongly, considering what we now know about Mary Pinchot Meyer and other women whom Jack continued to see, but there is probably some truth in his contention that "JFK ... fell in love with his wife a second time when they reached the White House and she was able to demonstrate her gifts and abilities."

What I get from all this is a profile of a courageous First Lady fighting for a place in her husband's presidential life, as a wife, a woman, a person in her own right. This hidden drama of Jackie's life as First Lady reached a sort of climax when she gave birth prematurely to Patrick Bouvier Kennedy in August 1963, while she was vacationing in Massachusetts. The little boy lived only three days, and this harsh reminder that no one is master of the universe seems to have chastened and sobered the President to a remarkable degree. Jackie reached out to him for solace. Suddenly they were united, not by the conventions of marriage and power and fame but by humbling sorrow.

A number of the Kennedys' close friends, such as Bill Walton, noticed that in the weeks after Patrick's death, Jack and Jackie were perceptibly closer. They embraced in public—something they had never done—they went sailing together, and JFK was more deferential, more considerate. He no longer barged through doors, leaving Jackie trailing ten feet behind him, as he did repeatedly in the early White House years.

In September, on their tenth wedding anniversary, JFK gave Jackie a catalog from one of New York's most expensive jewelers and told her to select anything she wanted. She chose a simple bracelet. Jackie gave him a gold St. Christopher's medal to replace the silver one he had put in little Patrick's coffin. A wedding present from her, it had been attached to a money clip.

In the light of these gestures of affection, Jackie's decision to vacation with Aristotle Onassis a few weeks later may have been a last testing of her husband's readiness to trust her to go her own way but to return to him, genuinely committed now, an equal partner in the pursuit of a second term. That would seem to be a reasonable interpretation of her response to Jack's wary request for her to join him on a trip to the politically troubled state of Texas in November: "Sure I will. I'll campaign with you wherever you want."

We all know what happened in Texas on November 22, 1963. No one will ever forget those gunshots in Dallas, a frantic Jackie reaching out to the Secret Service man over the rear of the presidential limousine, her terrible cry: "My God, they've killed Jack. They've killed my husband!"

In the next few unforgettable days, Jacqueline Bouvier Kennedy taught the nation the deeper meaning of aristocracy. An aristocrat may have some wayward, willful patches in his or her character. But by and large aristocrats also have a sense of their own stature, as well as life's depths. They have been trained to speak and behave in a style that befits the occasion, no matter what their private feelings may be. Jackie's previous three years, in which, behind her various masks, she had forged her own unique identity as First Lady, became a resource on which she drew to sustain not only herself but the American people in this tragic ordeal.

Imagine, for a moment, what might have happened if Jackie had simply collapsed, like wives of other assassinated Presidents. Mary Lincoln became hysterical and stayed that way for the rest of her life. Epileptic Ida McKinley was the least visible First Lady in our history and remained an absent blank when her husband was gunned down in 1901. Fortunately, there were strong men ready to take charge of the nation, without their help. But America *needed* Jackie Kennedy's help in 1963.

Jackie's dignity, her sense of history, enabled the nation to focus on its grief. The riderless horse with the reversed boots preceding the casket on its solemn cavalcade to the Capitol, the grace with which she greeted Charles de Gaulle and other heads of state, the serenity with which she presided over the entire funeral with her children beside her, became a kind of catharsis, an antidote to thoughts of violence and revenge. The woman in the black veil became as much a part of Jackie's mystery, her complex public persona, as the smiling, joyous advocate of beauty and art in the resplendent, festive White House.

If I am right, Jacqueline Kennedy's struggle to become her own woman in the White House is one of the most important hidden dramas in American history. Her success was not only a personal triumph, it is a legacy that continues to live in the American soul.

Chapter 4

—

PIONEER

CRUSADERS

MOST FIRST LADIES HAVE HAD NO TROUBLE EVADING THE PITFALLS OF an aristocratic style, even though they often were several notches above their husbands in social standing (a little-known fact which suggests—but does not prove—that Presidents start aiming for the top at an early age). Until recently it was a basic part of a woman's role to be agreeable and charming. Also, Presidents soon recognized the folly of offending the sensibilities of Mr. and Mrs. John Q. Citizen with anything that smacked of highfalutin ways. A number of First Ladies have thus felt free to use the symbolic power of their office to do some quiet—and sometimes not so quiet—crusading to solve national problems or correct injustices in the American scheme of things.

The pioneer in this department is a First Lady I had smugly dismissed until I started writing this book: Lucy Webb Hayes. She was the wife of Rutherford B. Hayes, elected in 1876 thanks to the only stolen presidential election in American history. It was a contest shadowed by the million dead of the Civil War. The Democrats won the

White House by a hefty half million popular votes, but the Republicans, appalled at seeing the party of rebellion and secession returning to power, self-righteously purchased the electoral votes of several southern states which were still under military occupation, putting Hayes in the White House by a whisker—one electoral vote. For a while it looked as if we were going to have another civil war.

Although President Hayes himself seems to have had nothing to do with the moneybags that were highballed south in the night, he entered the White House as a President violently disliked by more than half the voters. That made First Lady Lucy Hayes loom large in the administration—and she seemed equipped for the challenge. Lucy was the first First Lady to have a college degree (from Cincinnati Wesleyan)—and according to some historians the first to be called the First Lady.

Today she is primarily remembered as the First Lady who banned liquor from the White House. Although the decision was as much her husband's as her own, it has earned her the nickname Lemonade Lucy in the history books. That makes her sound like a puckered puritan without an iota of grace or charm. The real woman was the exact opposite of this libel—witty, intelligent, with sparkling hazel eyes and glistening dark hair. She was also a wonderful mother to her five children. The liquor ban was not a decision the Hayeses made casually, or on impulse. They knew it was going to cause them trouble. They made it because they feared America of 1877 was in danger of drowning in booze.

These days we laugh at the thought of Carry Nation and the other women who took axes to saloons and fought the lobbying power of the liquor interests. But in nineteenth-century America the number of homes and marriages destroyed by alcohol was astronomical. As governor of Ohio, Hayes told a columnist he had seen too many "noble minds rendered unfit to be trusted with public office because of drink."

Washington, D.C., probably had more heavy drinkers per capita than any other city in the union in those days. (According to some reports it still holds that dubious title.) It took courage for Lucy Hayes to support her husband's decision—and take most of the heat for it, as

White House hostess. But the President and his wife wanted to send a message to the nation about their opposition to alcohol—a message 1877 America needed as badly as it needed a strong stand against drugs in the nineteen eighties.

As an old White House hand, I was not surprised to discover that some of the staff managed to circumvent the ban for the topers who came through with a backstairs tip. About midway through the three-hour state dinners of the era, the stewards served a sherbet inside the frozen skin of an orange. A Massachusetts senator recalled that for those who needed it, "as much rum was crowded [into the sherbet] as it could contain without being altogether liquid."

Officially designated Roman Punch, the course was known to the insiders as "the Life Saving Station." The staff told the President the rum taste was only flavoring—and served him and Lucy and other temperance supporters a version so mild they apparently believed it. I suspect the Hayeses knew exactly what was going on, but being good politicians, they pretended to ignore it.

Although Lucy herself did not drink alcohol, she never objected to Rutherford downing a few steins with his fellow Civil War veterans. She often sent gifts of good vintages to friends who had wine cellars. These facts make it clearer than ever that the White House ban was a symbolic gesture for the sake of the nation's mental and physical health.

As First Lady, Lucy Hayes stirred a great upheaval of hope in the minds and hearts of many women, who were beginning to resent their separate but not quite equal status in American life. They saw college-educated Lucy as the embodiment of the New Woman, who wanted the vote, equal pay for equal work, and the right to enter the professions and politics. Lucy had displayed some New Woman tendencies in her youth. Not long after they married, she had told her husband she favored "violent measures" to win better wages and other reforms for women.

At Hayes's inauguration, Mary Clemmer Ames, one of Washington's first women reporters, rhapsodized over Lucy's "gentle and winning face," her "bands of smooth dark hair with that tender light in the eyes we have come to associate with the Madonna." For some women, this First Lady was a creature with divine powers.

To the consternation of these true believers, in her four years in the White House (to survive the scandal of the stolen election, Hayes had to promise to serve only a single term) Lucy did not say a single word on behalf of women reformers. When Susan B. Anthony, the founder of the woman suffrage movement, and her colleague, Elizabeth Cady Stanton, visited the White House, President Hayes met with them and promised "sincere consideration" of their call for a constitutional amendment giving women the vote. Only after the meeting did he introduce them to Lucy, who showed them around the White House but carefully avoided saying a word in their favor.

Why? Because woman's rights was an extremely unpopular issue in the late eighteen seventies, and Lucy Hayes was first, last, and always a politician's wife. Only a tiny percentage of American women, and an invisible percentage of American men, supported Anthony's lonely crusade. When the National Woman Suffrage Association met in the capital, *The Washington Post* felt free to refer to them as "unwomenly women who wished to change their condition" and their program as a "horrible reform." Lucy never even became a member of the Women's Christian Temperance Union, an organization whose militancy also won it numerous enemies. Politicians' wives live in the present, not some theoretical future, and Lucy Hayes was acutely aware that her husband was in no position to tolerate a controversial wife.

Instead of joining the woman's rights movement or the WCTU, Lucy became the honorary president of the Woman's Home Missionary Society, an organization that campaigned to better the lives of the poor in the appalling slums of nineteenth-century America's cities. This was a cause that was beyond criticism from all points of the political spectrum.

Proof of Lucy's political astuteness was her tremendous popularity. Although President Hayes continued to receive brickbats from reporters, who referred to him as "Rutherfraud" and "His Fraudulence," almost no one except the booze hounds of Washington, D.C., had a bad a word to say against Lucy. Advertisers printed her picture on their household products. The big-name poets of the day, Henry Wadsworth Longfellow, John Greenleaf Whittier, and Oliver Wendell Holmes, praised her in verse. Old Washington press hand Ben Perley Moore declared Lucy was the most influential First Lady since Dolley Madison.

In 1880 the Republicans cruised to another four years in the White House, easily electing James Garfield in spite of the stench of the stolen election of 1876. Unquestionably, Lucy Hayes had done more than her share to dispel the odor.

At the time, some women faulted Lucy for her silence on woman's rights, attributing it to lack of courage. A few historians have made similar remarks. But I have long thought this was an unrealistic view

Reporters called Lucy Hayes "Lemonade Lucy" because she refused to serve liquor in the White House. She is one of our most underrated and misunderstood First Ladies. *(Hayes Presidential Center)*

of a First Lady. Politics is a way of life. A politician's career is crowded with decisions about issues to support, issues to oppose, issues to avoid. I do not see how anyone can expect the woman who has shared his political journey—in Hayes's case from Congress to the governorship of Ohio to the White House—to take political positions which he regards as wrong and possibly ruinous.

Politics, we should always remember, is the art of the possible. Every time a politician—and many First Ladies have been politicians—backs an issue, he or she makes a judgment call. Is it worth backing? Can anything be achieved by backing it? Is there any support out there if I back it—or am I being asked to commit political suicide? Can other equally important issues and causes be derailed or damaged if I back this one?

Lucy Hayes demonstrated her political shrewdness by limiting her crusading to temperance and bettering the lives of the poor. She never wavered in her decision to ban liquor from the White House. The Women's Christian Temperance Union was able to use her as a symbol, even though she never joined its ranks. At the end of this First Lady's career, the WCTU paid Daniel Huntington, one of the best artists in the country, to paint her portrait. Even here Lucy managed to defuse potential reproaches from critics of the Union's headstrong tactics. Journalist Mary Clemmer Ames, who sometimes functioned as Lucy's covert spokesperson, urged that the portrait be considered "a tribute to Mrs. Hayes—to the grace and graciousness of her womanhood . . . not to any one thing she has done, but to herself, for all she is."

The portrait, which shows Lucy in a wine-colored dress with simple lace collar and cuffs, includes in the background a female figure leaning on a vase from which flows a stream of water. This was the First Lady's only concession to the WCTU's desire to use the portrait to send a message. It is Lucy Hayes the gracious woman who dominates the foreground, with proud eyes and a mouth that emanates generosity and strength.

———

NEARLY FORTY YEARS LATER, ANOTHER PIONEERING FIRST LADY launched a crusade that sent a message to her President, as well as to the people. Ellen Axson Wilson, Woodrow Wilson's first wife, managed this feat in the brief eighteen months fate allotted her in the White House. In some ways she is our most forgotten First Lady. Not only is she often grouped with invalid spouses such as Letitia Tyler, Caroline Harrison and Ida McKinley but she has been overshadowed by the woman Woodrow Wilson married fourteen months after her death.

I have always been fond of Ellen Wilson, not only for the cause she backed but because she had a daughter named Margaret, who had an excellent singing voice. Ellen herself was a gifted painter who had given up her career to marry Woodrow Wilson. She staunchly encouraged Margaret's desire for a musical career, in spite of the fact that her father was President. Who says lightning can't strike twice in the same place?

Born in Savannah, raised, like Woodrow Wilson, in a segregated South, Ellen Wilson never saw herself as a crusader for radical reform. But she was a woman who believed all our citizens deserved the basic rights that America seemed to guarantee everyone in the pursuit of happiness. While few Presidents have equaled Woodrow Wilson in broadcasting this message to the entire world, his administration, dominated by conservative southerners, was curiously blind to racial injustice at home.

Many progressive whites and blacks had hoped Wilson would play a leading part in breaking down the Jim Crow practices that prevailed in the federal government. Instead, by the summer of 1913, six months after Wilson was inaugurated, there was more, not less segregation in all departments of the government. Over twenty thousand angry black Americans from thirty-four states signed a protest to the President, urging him to change this policy.

Around this time, Ellen Wilson had tea with Charlotte Wise Hopkins at the White House. Mrs. Hopkins was one of those early women "doers," as Lady Bird Johnson calls them. She was a force in the District of Columbia branch of the National Civic Federation, which was committed to better living conditions for the poor, regardless of race, creed, or color. The First Lady listened with dismay to Mrs. Hopkins's account of the way thousands of Washington's blacks were living in shacks in fetid alleys, some of them only a short walk from the Capitol.

Mrs. Hopkins blamed segregation, which made it impossible for blacks to buy homes in many parts of Washington. Not only did she have a diagnosis but she had a cure: model homes which could be built inexpensively, with plumbing, electricity, and running water—amenities most of the alley shacks lacked.

Within a week Ellen Wilson was visiting the alleys with Mrs. Hopkins. They had picturesque names—Logan's Court, Goat Alley, Willow Tree. She also visited 109 model homes which the Civic Federation had built and talked with the residents, without letting them know that she was the First Lady. The next day she became a stockholder in the company that was building these homes, the Sanitary Housing Company—and soon agreed to become the honorary chairman of the woman's department of the National Civic Federation.

These gestures swiftly became public knowledge. Suddenly concerned congressmen were touring the alleys, and everyone in Washington society was discussing how to improve them. A committee of fifty prominent Washingtonians gathered to draft an "Alley Bill" that would clear the slums of the shacks and erect model homes in their place. Ellen Wilson invited the committee to the White House for tea. At another meeting, held in a private mansion, Secretary of State William Jennings Bryan, considered the greatest orator of the era, addressed the group. "The most eloquent speech here tonight," Bryan said, pointing to Ellen, "is the one that has not been made at all, for actions speak louder than words.... As crowded as my days are, I feel that if the wife of the president can find time out of her busy days to be here and to work for this cause, I can too."

After the Alley Bill was introduced in Congress, Ellen went to work on the conditions in which women and blacks labored in government offices. She visited the Post Office Department and was appalled by the lack of light and air and the deplorable rest room facilities. She went to Postmaster General Albert Burleson, an ultraconservative Texan, who gave her the standard Washington runaround. At a White House luncheon, an angry Ellen Wilson brought up the problem in a very determined way with Colonel Edward House, one of her husband's top aides. Soon the whole table was listening to the agitated House assure the First Lady he would do something about it.

Ellen made similar inspections of the Government Printing Office, where conditions were equally deplorable. Soon in the black ghetto of Washington, D.C., praise was being showered on Ellen Wilson. She was described as a "noble woman" who had set an example that black Americans hoped other white women would follow.

Ellen Wilson sent this message while maintaining a full-time pace as First Lady, with the usual White House round of entertaining politicians and visiting diplomats. She also functioned as her husband's adviser and partner, going over his speeches with him, discussing his legislative program, doing research on problem countries, such as Mexico, with whom Wilson almost went to war in 1914.

Suddenly, on the advice of her doctor, Ellen sharply curtailed her activities. She retreated to a summer cottage in New Hampshire, where she painted and communed with nature and exchanged longing letters with her equally lonely husband in the White House. When she returned to Washington, the doctor still urged her to rest. He did not have the heart to tell the President or the First Lady that she was suffering from Bright's disease, a fatal kidney disorder for which we still have not found a cure.

Ellen took only part of his advice. She summoned the energy to superintend the weddings of her daughters Jessie and Eleanor and presided at state dinners and receptions. But she noticed how easily she became exhausted. On March 1, 1914, she slipped and fell on the polished floor of her bedroom. She never recovered from this accident. In a letter to a relative, she described the fall as "sort of an all around crash." Gradually, Ellen read the truth in her doctor's mournful eyes. She was a dying woman.

One spring day she visited the rose garden on her nurse's arm. The gardener was working on a design that Ellen and he had created. "It will be so lovely, Charlie," she said. "But I'll never live to see it finished."

Throughout this slow, sad decline, the First Lady continued to take a strong interest in her slum clearance program. But the Alley Bill was stalled in Congress by segregationists and obstructionists. Inevitably, in the summer of 1914, Ellen Wilson slipped away. Her husband, frantic with anxiety and grief, barely left her bedside, in spite of the ominous war clouds that were gathering in Europe.

On the morning of August 6, it was apparent that Ellen would live only a few more days, perhaps only a few hours. She reached out for Woodrow's hand and whispered: "I would go away more peacefully if my Alley Bill was passed by Congress." Wilson's secretary, Joseph Tumulty, rushed to the Capitol with this request, and the Senate passed the bill on the spot. The House of Representatives made a solemn promise to pass it the next day. Tumulty dashed back to the White House with the news. Less than an hour later, Ellen Wilson smiled at her husband and daughters and died.

I would be exaggerating if I said Ellen Wilson started a mass movement. But one woman watched and remembered that a First Lady could back causes that subtly—and perhaps not so subtly—opposed the policies of her husband's administration. The shy, plain wife of Wilson's assistant secretary of the Navy, she was much too busy raising five children and playing adoring second fiddle to her handsome husband to imagine herself presiding at the White House. But Eleanor Roosevelt was a very perceptive woman. She undoubtedly grasped the inner meaning of Ellen Wilson's quiet crusade.

Chapter 5

—

THE LOST

COMPANION

THE WHITE HOUSE HAS SEEN ITS SHARE OF COMPLEX MARRIAGES, BUT none has been quite as complicated as Eleanor Roosevelt's union with Franklin D. Roosevelt. On one level they loved—or at least esteemed—each other. Their letters are addressed to "Dearest Babs" and "Dearest Franklin." Uninitiated readers would assume they were exchanged between deeply affectionate spouses—and to some extent they would be right. But initiates knew that beneath this veneer of affection was a gulf of simmering anger which frequently boiled up as exasperation throughout their White House years and more often manifested itself in Eleanor's prolonged absences.

Mrs. Roosevelt had the same mildly panicked reaction as other First Ladies when her husband was elected President of a Depression-racked America in 1932. In her case, she feared she would be reduced to a ceremonial figure—a podium person—by the hoary weight of tradition. One story has her weeping bitter tears on election night and exclaiming: "Now I'll have no identity."

She swiftly shook off the podium tradition and proceeded to reinvent the job on her own terms. Claiming that her wheelchair-bound husband, crippled by polio, needed her as his eyes and ears, hands and feet, she became the most ubiquitous First Lady in history. She hurtled around the country, inspecting everything from prisons to coal mines, speaking in Boston one night and Des Moines the next and Denver the next, often taking stands on the issues of the day that left the President's spokesmen red faced and floundering.

I am sometimes amazed by how many otherwise reliable historians accept FDR's crippled state as the explanation for Eleanor Roosevelt's hyperactivity. Every President, not merely FDR, stayed pretty close to the White House until the airplane brought almost instant mobility. The White House is, after all, the President's office *and* his home. The claim also suggests that, because he was confined to a wheelchair, FDR was *unable* to leave the White House, when we know he was one of the great campaigners of the twentieth century. Some of his most famous speeches were delivered in Boston, Detroit, Chicago, and other bastions of the Democratic Party.

No, Eleanor Roosevelt left the White House repeatedly because she was not happy there. She was not happy in any house with her husband. Moreover, she felt free to differ with her husband's positions on a wide range of issues because she saw herself as something other than a wife or partner.

Two years before she entered the White House, when FDR was Governor of New York, Eleanor Roosevelt had been profiled in a magazine as the ideal modern wife. She gave the journalist a thoughtful, penetrating analysis of contemporary marriage. Ideally, for a woman, it consisted of three things: motherhood, partnership, and companionship. In the past motherhood had taken first place, almost obliterating the other two ideals. Now, thanks to labor-saving devices and the rising expectations of modern women, the other two goals had become paramount.

Eleanor Roosevelt made no attempt to apply this analysis to her own life. No one expected such candor from a politician's wife in 1930. It was just as well, because the companionship side of the Roosevelt marriage had collapsed in 1918, when Eleanor discovered FDR was having an affair with Lucy Page Mercer, a Maryland beauty who had been her social secretary for the previous four years. Seldom has a wife been as humiliated by both parties in an infidelity. Lucy and Franklin made a fool of Eleanor, deceiving her literally under her nose in her own house. The marriage teetered on collapse. But in straitlaced 1918 that would have meant the end of the assistant secretary of the Navy's promising political career, something he found difficult to contemplate. Lucy, a devout Catholic, was ready to sin for love but hesitated to marry a divorced man and cut herself off from her church.

With the help of Sara Roosevelt, FDR's strong-willed mother, a truce was arranged, mostly on Eleanor's terms. FDR was banned from her bedroom forever. The shy, primly correct society matron who had marveled over attracting the handsome Hudson River scion also vanished forever, to be replaced by a disillusioned woman determined whenever possible to go her own way.

This determination only redoubled when FDR contracted polio in 1921 and emerged from the ordeal a crippled man, bound to a wheelchair except for public appearances, when he donned leg braces heavier than anything worn by Georgia chain gangs. Most betrayed wives would have accepted this cruel fate as more than enough retribution for their pain and grief. But Eleanor Roosevelt was not your average betrayed wife. Her husband's infidelity had triggered an upheaval in her soul which exhumed the deepest trauma of her childhood—her love for her forlorn father.

Eleanor was the daughter of Theodore Roosevelt's brother, Elliott, who despaired of competing with his aggressive older brother at an early age and slowly sank into alcoholism and failure. He married a cold, wealthy New York beauty, Anna Hall, who seems to have disliked her daughter almost as much as she hated her husband. She called Eleanor "Granny" and described her before visitors as a "funny" [strange] child—"so old fashioned." Only her absent father loved Eleanor without qualifications, and she returned his love with absolute adoration—even when he took her on an outing to his club, parked her in the cloakroom, and adjourned to the bar, where he got so drunk he went home without her.

Elliott died when Eleanor was ten. Two years earlier her mother had died, leaving her to be raised by her stern, puritanical Hall grandmother, who did not have the word *love* in her vocabulary. In her heart, Eleanor clung to a vision of her father that approached the saintly. She treasured stories of how he once gave away his overcoat to a shivering boy on a New York corner. "With him the heart always dominated," she said. She carried his letters with her and read and reread them with rapturous intensity.

This was the young woman Franklin D. Roosevelt married—a person who willed herself into absolute love and refused to see human blemishes. A few days after FDR proposed, Eleanor wrote him a prophetic poem:

> *Unless you can swear "For life, for death!"*
> *Oh, fear to call it loving!*

At the time, she had added: "I wondered if it meant 'for life, for death' for you at first." Franklin's infidelity with Lucy Mercer confirmed this primary doubt, and—in the opinion of more than one biographer—triggered all the anger Eleanor felt but could never express about her charming, dissolute father.

Henceforth Eleanor Roosevelt vowed to seek love and consolation elsewhere. She distinguished sharply between the "personage" who was the public wife of Franklin Roosevelt and the "personal" woman, who lived a very different life. For a long time these were almost two separate people. "I think the personage is an accident and I only like the part of life in which I am a person," she told one friend.

When she became First Lady, this habit of mind intensified. "It was almost as though I had erected someone a little outside myself who was the President's wife. I was lost somewhere deep down inside myself. That is the way I lived and worked until I left the White House," she told another friend.

She summed up her psychological technique in a letter to still another friend: "I have the power of disassociating myself from things, because I've had to do it so often, and I'm not unhappy that way, you should cultivate it, you won't be happy but you won't be unhappy."

All this does not add up to a parable of forgiveness. There must have been times when Eleanor yearned to achieve that spiritual ideal. But it remained tragically beyond her reach. The marital wound never really healed, the resentment never ceased to fester. Their son Jimmy described his parents' relationship as an "armed truce which endured to the day [FDR] died." Jimmy added that several times he saw his father "in one way or another hold out his arms to Mother and she flatly refused to enter his embrace."

This was the context in which Eleanor Roosevelt launched her epochal career as First Lady. It deserves that imposing adjective. The mere catalog of her activities would fatigue a squadron of Olympic athletes. She held 348 press conferences in her twelve years in the White House. She received and tried to answer as many as three hundred thousand letters a year. She wrote books, a monthly magazine column, a daily newspaper column, and she worked tirelessly to win access to the President for people and groups she supported.

At first she seemed to do everything right. When departing First Lady Lou Hoover offered to send a car for her first visit to the White House, Mrs. Roosevelt replied she would walk—neatly recapitulating the decision of the founder of the Democratic Party, Thomas Jefferson, to walk to his inaugural rather than ride in a coach and four. At her press conferences she allowed only women reporters—a neat riposte to the male chauvinists of that era of newspapering, who relegated females to the women's page, when and if they put them on the payroll.

These self-satisfied males were soon an envious green—or furious purple—over the press coverage Eleanor Roosevelt generated. One scholar has taken the trouble to count the number of stories on her in *The New York Times* during her first year in the White House—320. Only Jacqueline Kennedy won more ink in a comparable period. Barbara Bush, for example, while a popular First Lady, did not even come close to such a figure. Another interesting statistic, which I freely admit astonished me, shows how Eleanor Roosevelt increased the coverage of her successors: Bess Truman had 118 articles in *The Times* in her first White House year.

The newspapers were only the first of Eleanor's targets in her campaign to expand job opportunities for women. Even before she got to Washington, she had established a network of activist women inside the Democratic Party. In 1928 she had served as head of the national women's campaign for Democratic candidates, one of whom was her husband, who was running for governor of New York. One of the people Eleanor recruited for this endeavor, which included the doomed attempt to make Al Smith the first Roman Catholic President, was a dynamic social worker named Molly Dewson.

When Eleanor went to Washington as First Lady, Molly Dewson went with her as head of the Women's Division of the Democratic Party. Even before she acquired that title, Party Chairman Jim Farley was calling Molly "The General." On April 27, 1933, six weeks after FDR was inaugurated, Molly sent Eleanor a seven-page letter listing the names and qualifications of ten women who "absolutely" had to be recognized with good jobs and another thirteen who were next in line. In FDR's first term, they put over a hundred women into jobs that ranged from employees of the National Aeronautics Board to the secretary of labor, Frances Perkins, the first woman to hold a cabinet post.

Eleanor Roosevelt backed Madame Perkins, as my father sometimes called her, from start to finish. A shy New Englander, Ms. Perkins was appalled by the way the Washington, D.C., press corps wanted to know every imaginable detail of her private life. (She was married to an economist and had one daughter.) Her reticence eventually gave her a poor public image, which her mostly male enemies did not hesitate to use against her. She constantly sought the First Lady's advice and support. Often that took the form of telling her to become resigned to the fact that "men hate a woman in a position of real power."

Laws and social programs we now take for granted were born under Frances Perkins's leadership, with Eleanor Roosevelt's vigorous endorsement: unemployment insurance, social security, the Wagner Act, which made trade unions viable. The reserved Yankee became a devoted admirer of the First Lady. "She was a very easy woman to know," Ms. Perkins said.

Meanwhile, another Eleanor Roosevelt surrogate, Ellen Woodward of Mississippi, became head of the women's division of the Works Progress Administration, better known as the WPA. Woodward was there to make sure women got a fair share of the jobs being funneled to the state directors of this gigantic effort to put America back to work. (For a brief while Missouri's director was Harry S Truman— until he decided to run for the U.S. Senate.) The First Lady forwarded to Ms. Woodward over four hundred letters a month from desperate women seeking help.

Eleanor Roosevelt also recognized the importance of access to the President. "When I needed help on some definite point," Molly Dewson later recalled, "Mrs. Roosevelt gave me the opportunity to sit by the President at dinner and the matter was settled before we finished our soup." The First Lady also used the White House to strengthen friendships within her women's network. She compiled a list of women in executive positions in the government and regularly invited them to receptions and dinners. So many of them shared their problems with her, she launched a series of spring garden parties exclusively for them—where they could really communicate with one another.

During these same dramatic years of FDR's first term, Eleanor Roosevelt led the fight against the Depression notion that women should be fired from as many jobs as possible to aid men with families to support. She also played a key part in opening up lesser jobs for women in various federal departments. In the Post Office alone, one historian credits her for the hiring of four thousand women.

Eleanor Roosevelt's visibility soon began to attract criticism. She regularly issued disclaimers to possessing any political power. "I [have] never tried to influence Franklin on anything he did," she declared at one of her press conferences, "and I certainly have never known him to try to influence me." The latter part of that statement is probably true. FDR remarked more than once that it was impossible for him to win an argument with his wife. The first part, though, is a country mile from the truth.

Virtually every insider in the Roosevelt White House testified to Eleanor's often relentless attempts to influence her husband. She sometimes shocked friends by talking of "getting my time with him"—as if she were simply one of several members of the inner circle—and was determined to use her access to the fullest.

Many Presidents' wives have wielded political influence, back to the second First Lady, Abigail Adams, whose enemies called her "the presidentress." What was unique about Eleanor Roosevelt was the incredible scope and variety of the causes and issues she embraced— and the tenacity with which she pursued them, not only with her husband but with other members of the administration. Seldom if ever did she invite a cabinet officer or other official to the White House without having an agenda of what she called "ideas I think we should work on."

More than one cabinet officer expressed irritation at her intrusions into his department. When she pestered Interior Secretary Harold Ickes to spend budget-busting amounts of money on a housing project in West Virginia, Ickes, who shared many of the First Lady's liberal views, confided to his diary: "She is not doing the president any good. She is becoming altogether too active in public affairs and I think she is harmful rather than helpful."

As early as 1934 Willard Kiplinger, author of a powerful Washington newsletter, warned Treasury Secretary Henry Morgenthau, Jr., that he was going to attack Mrs. Roosevelt. "She is throwing monkey wrenches into the government departments and they are all afraid to say something because she is the wife of the President," Kiplinger said.

These were comments from Eleanor's *friends*. From her legions of conservative enemies came a barrage of invective and denunciation that portrayed her as a walking, talking menace to the American way of life.

Eleanor brushed aside these criticisms. Early in her husband's presidency, she appointed herself its conscience. She was determined to extend the range of the reforms that the New Deal promised, often in vague terms, as it struggled to renew the American economy. As one of her biographers put it grandiloquently, "That conscience of hers was like a steady Gulf Stream of goodness radiating out from the White House through all the ambits of New Deal power and along its coasts of ambition, gentling them to beneficent purposes."

The First Lady was an early proponent of civil rights and did everything in her power to support that cause in the teeth of ferocious hostility from conservative southerners. In Birmingham, Alabama, when she attended a meeting of the Southern Conference on Human Welfare, she found the auditorium segregated. She calmly moved her chair into the center aisle, symbolically bridging the racist gap. She entertained blacks in the White House. She pushed again and again for blacks to be appointed to government jobs—usually with little success. FDR, always a political realist, feared the wrath of the southern Democrats, who chaired many powerful committees in Congress.

In 1939, when the Daughters of the American Revolution barred the great opera star Marian Anderson from singing in Constitution Hall, Mrs. Roosevelt resigned from the DAR and denounced the ban as a disgrace. Her protest, in which thousands joined, led to a triumphant concert on the mall in front of the Lincoln Memorial. Although the DAR remained unrepentant, the episode was a major step forward in American race relations.

Perhaps the most important cause in Eleanor Roosevelt's activist panoply, after equal rights for women, was American youth. She maintained they were the hardest hit by the Depression—unable to marry or start careers, the last to be hired, the first to be fired. It was not an idea for which FDR had much enthusiasm. In his memoirs, the magazine editor and author Fulton Oursler told of attending a White House dinner during Roosevelt's first term at which Eleanor urged her husband to set up youth programs. He curtly told her the young were no different from the millions of other Americans looking for jobs. As the dismayed guests watched, the president and his wife were soon redfaced and snarling at each other. She persisted until he wearily agreed to consider the matter.

Eventually, Eleanor persuaded FDR to launch the National Youth Administration, whose goal was to propose and execute measures to help young Americans. In pursuit of this, Mrs. Roosevelt developed close links with two private organizations, the American Youth Congress and the American Student Union. Unfortunately, both of these groups were heavily infiltrated by Communists, who devoted a great deal of their time and energy in the thirties to wooing idealistic young people. Until 1939 the AYC backed most New Deal legislation, asking only for larger and more forceful programs, such as a five-hundred-million-dollar government loan fund to enable young people to establish homes and families. Internationally, both organizations agreed wholeheartedly with the President's growing hostility to the fascist dictatorships of Germany, Italy, and Japan. But when Russia's dictator, Joseph Stalin, signed his infamous nonaggression pact with Hitler in 1939, the two organizations did a 360-degree turn and launched an all-out attack on a flabbergasted FDR, calling him a militarist and a warmonger for trying to rearm the country.

Seldom if ever has a President been more politically embarrassed—and it got worse. The following year the AYC met to pass still more anti-Roosevelt resolutions, including a condemnation of the President for his criticism of the Russian invasion of Finland. Nevertheless, when AYCers made a February 1940 "pilgrimage" to Washington to publicize their views, Mrs. Roosevelt urged FDR to address them. She persuaded friends up to the level of cabinet wives to provide beds, and squeezed some of the AYC leaders into the third floor of the White House. The U.S. Army was requisitioned to provide additional beds and meals.

In a cold drizzle, several thousand AYC members gathered on the lawn of the White House. While the First Lady sat in mortified silence, FDR gave them the tongue-lashing of their lives. He told them their ideas were "twaddle." The future of freedom in the world was at stake, and they were trying to sabotage American attempts to defend it. Never before or since has a President so totally repudiated his wife's politics in public. Several months later Eleanor severed her connections with the AYC and the American Student Union.

The failure of her youth outreach wounded Eleanor Roosevelt deeply. Even before this disappointment, there were signs that she was wearying of her role as the conscience of the New Deal. She told several friends she did not want FDR to run for a third term, unless a world crisis made it necessary. She felt he had nothing more to give the country. These comments need to be viewed against the background of the drift and irresolution that engulfed the Roosevelt administration in its second term. FDR's attempt to increase the number of justices so he could pack the Supreme Court with New Deal supporters triggered a tremendous revolt in Congress, ending in a humiliating defeat for the President. In 1937 a recession almost as bad as the first Depression left the New Deal's social engineers looking feckless and dismayed.

As the emphasis of the Roosevelt presidency shifted to foreign affairs, Eleanor felt herself more and more excluded from the inner circle around FDR. She was sometimes driven to desperate expedients to keep in touch with what was happening inside his administration. One of the saddest stories I came across while researching this book was told by Betsy Cushing, Jimmy Roosevelt's wife, who happened to be in the Oval Office when Cordell Hull, the secretary of state, called. FDR greeted him, then paused and said: "Mamma, will you please get off the line—Mamma I can hear you breathing, will you *please* get off the line?"

Another reason why Eleanor opposed a third term may have been her awareness of FDR's deteriorating physical condition. As early as 1938 he had suffered a fainting spell at Hyde Park but quickly recovered and joined his guests for dinner. However, Eleanor eventually concurred with his decision to shatter the two-term precedent in 1940 because she shared his fear that the southern conservatives under Vice President Jack Garner or British-hating Irish Catholics under London Ambassador Joe Kennedy would seize the presidency and capitalize on the widespread American loathing for another European war to make a deal with Hitler. The President himself was aware that his fragile health made another four years in office a risky gamble. At a 1940 meeting with Jim Farley, the Democratic Party chairman, he said he would run, even if it meant he would only live a month into a third term.

After Pearl Harbor propelled America into World War II, FDR's physical decline accelerated. Electrocardiogram readings revealed a worrisome lack of oxygen to the heart, caused by hypertension and worsening arteriosclerosis. When cardiac specialist Dr. Howard Bruenn examined him in March of 1944, he was appalled by the President's condition. His heart was alarmingly enlarged, a prime symptom of congestive heart failure. His lips and fingernails had a bluish tinge. Bruenn told the White House physician, Dr. Ross McIntire, Roosevelt could die at any moment.

Although a regimen of ten hours sleep each night and a reduction of his workday to four hours produced some slight improvement, the President's condition was visible to anyone who saw him up close. When my father conferred with him after he had been nominated for the vice presidency in the summer of 1944, he came home and told my mother FDR was a dying man.

No President more desperately needed the zone of peace within the White House that other First Ladies have felt it was their primary duty to create. But Eleanor Roosevelt was unable to provide it for her husband. Instead, she continued to play FDR's political conscience. Again and again she pressured him to do something about segregated rest room facilities in southern post offices or the conservative policies of a federal housing administrator when the President was grappling with the complexities of global coalition warfare and a recalcitrant, ever more hostile Congress.

By this time the Roosevelts' daughter, Anna, was old enough to pass judgment on her mother—and it was harsh. She felt Eleanor constantly miscalculated people's moods and insisted on bringing up issues and problems when they wanted to relax. Anna described her parents as living virtually separate lives during the war years, when she spent a lot of time in the White House as her father's companion.

Even loyalists like Frances Perkins noticed the alienation and the frequency of Eleanor's absences from the White House. "I really think you ought to be here in the White House more often," Ms. Perkins told her. "I think it would be better for the President."

"Oh no, Frances, he doesn't need me anymore," Eleanor said. "He has Harry Hopkins.... Harry tells him everything he needs to know." The former head of the WPA, Hopkins had emerged as FDR's foremost wartime adviser.

Those words confess the tragic diminishment of the Roosevelts' marriage as they neared the end of their lives together. For me this sad fact makes the First Lady's struggle to uphold her ideals immensely—heartbreakingly—touching. After Pearl Harbor, when a hysterical Congress stampeded the President into rounding up Japanese Americans and confining them in camps far from the West Coast, the First Lady went out of her way to pose for a picture with four young Nisei. Afterward she visited these unhappy people in their desolate camps to express her regret for the government's action.

In spite of what she described as "an almost violent argument with FDR and Elliott," Eleanor decided to become assistant director of the Office of Civilian Defense. She wanted to help bring more women and local volunteers into this vital home-front program. FDR predicted she would make herself a political target, and he was soon proved right. The Hearst papers raked the First Lady's liberal appointments as "pinkos and commies," and other papers savaged her choice of an old friend, dancer Mayris Chaney, as an assistant in the physical fitness program, calling her unqualified for the post. After several months of this sort of abuse, Eleanor resigned.

Another major effort that added to Mrs. Roosevelt's sense of wartime displacement and failure was her losing struggle to persuade Congress to admit generous numbers of refugees—Jewish fugitives from the Nazis as well as war-orphaned children of other creeds and nationalities—into the United States. But Congress was adamantly hostile to the idea, and FDR, always the politician, hesitated to antagonize them. One Republican congressman, perhaps heady from the success in driving the First Lady from her OCD job, sneered he was not going to let the President's wife tell him what to do. Eleanor's proposals died in committee.

More successful were her visits to GIs on all the fighting fronts. She wore out military aides as she plodded through miles of wards full of wounded. Invariably she returned to the White House with notebooks bulging with names and addresses and telephone numbers of wounded men and spent hours calling or writing their parents or wives.

On Guadalcanal, she reportedly told one of the few jokes I have seen attributed to her—a story that got a huge laugh and reveals she was well aware of the violent antipathy many people felt for her and FDR. She said she had heard one of the Marine cooks had persuaded his commanding officer to let him go to the front with a rifle because he yearned to shoot at least one enemy before the war ended. The next day the man came back very discouraged. He said he had met an enemy and could not kill him. "He yelled, 'To hell with Roosevelt,'" the cook said. "I couldn't shoot a fellow Republican."

Wonderful as she was in the wartime White House as a spokesperson for a caring government, Eleanor Roosevelt continued to see her husband largely as a personage, a man to prod and lecture. FDR grew more and more disenchanted with his First Lady's style. Once a White House visitor remarked that Eleanor would be very tired when she returned from a trip to the South Pacific. "No," FDR snapped. "But she will tire everybody else."

Not only was Eleanor unable to recognize her husband's need for a zone of peace within the White House but she inflicted on him the worst imaginable housekeeper, a New Yorker named Henrietta Nesbitt. Later, for a few awful months, the Trumans inherited this creature. From the start Mrs. Nesbitt made her regime synonymous with atrocious cuisine. Once she served mutton and boiled carrots at a cabinet dinner, washed down by a New York State champagne which FDR pronounced the worst he had ever tasted.

During the wartime years, with state dinners and almost all other official functions canceled in the name of national austerity, Mrs. Nesbitt's menus became even more abominable. She almost gloried in their badness—as if indigestion were her contribution to the war effort. If the President criticized a dish, he got it again and again. At one point FDR said he was eating chicken six times a week, and when he complained Mrs. Nesbitt gave him sweetbreads six times a week. She repeatedly served him broccoli, even though he said he detested it. For months she served him oatmeal for breakfast, until he was reduced to sending her advertisements for cornflakes and Wheaties.

Some books on the Roosevelt White House have tried to make Mrs. Nesbitt seem amusing. Having dealt with this dragon in skirts, I disagree. This sort of aggravation was the last thing a very sick President needed.

Even in the final year, with the war roaring to a climax on a dozen fronts and FDR's health so precarious—at least six times he toppled to the floor of his study and had to be lifted back into his wheelchair by one of his Secret Service men—the First Lady persisted in playing his social conscience. She would invade his cocktail hour with sheaves of memos pushing her various causes, insisting on immediate decisions. Once, Anna Roosevelt recalled, "Father blew his top. He took every single speck of that whole pile of papers, threw them across the desk at me and said, 'Sis,' you handle these tomorrow morning.' " A humbled Eleanor apologized—but several weeks later, when she asked to accompany FDR to the last summit meeting of the war at Yalta, he coldly refused—and took Anna instead.

Inevitably, FDR sought love from other women—notably his beautiful secretary, Marguerite (Missy) LeHand, until she collapsed from the strain of trying to combine overwork and adoration. In the last two years of his life the still beautiful, still devoted Lucy Mercer, now the widowed Mrs. Winthrop Rutherfurd, returned—with the tacit collaboration of Anna Roosevelt.

A few of Lucy's visits were in the White House. Most were at Warm Springs, the Georgia rehabilitation center which FDR had found when he was struggling to recover from polio. Mrs. Rutherfurd had an estate in nearby Aiken, South Carolina. During a particularly felicitous stay in late 1944, Lucy told Anna of a marvelous hour she had just spent with FDR, sitting in his car on a nearby mountaintop, listening to him talk about the problems of the world, interspersing global concerns with lively anecdotes about his years as a visitor to that part of Georgia. Anna realized, "Mother was not capable of giving him this—just listening."

Anna's brother Elliott agreed: "What he [FDR] missed more and more was a woman's warm inspiriting companionship, which Mother by her very nature could not provide.... She was no kind of company when he wanted to relax without listening to her voice of conscience."

When Eleanor Roosevelt learned that Lucy Mercer Rutherfurd had been sitting with FDR, watching him having his portrait painted, at the moment of his death on April 12, 1945, the deep-buried pain of the primary wound erupted in terrible rage at her daughter. In Washington, D.C., she demanded an explanation of how she could have let "that woman" above all others return to her father's inner circle. Anna told her mother that she was only trying to comfort a very sick, very lonely man.

Eleanor Roosevelt was unquestionably a great First Lady. Her pioneering in behalf of woman's rights, African-American rights, and a dozen other causes is beyond comparison with any other woman of her time. But her achievements as a symbolic personage have to be assessed against her tragic limitations in the private role of loving counselor, companion, protector—in a word, wife.

PARTNERS

IN PRIVATE

I HAVE ALWAYS SYMPATHIZED WITH ANNA ROOSEVELT'S ATTEMPT TO help her father. I saw at first hand how the White House can tear apart a couple. Yes, it almost happened to that seemingly perfect White House marriage of Bess and Harry Truman—and for a while I, like Anna, was a daughter trapped in the middle. There was, thank goodness, a happier ending, but the experience still left a few scars.

My mother did not want my father to become President—especially through "the back door," as he himself called it—moving up from vice president. She had read her history books, and knew that almost every one of these accidental Presidents had a miserable time in the White House. Lincoln's successor, Andrew Johnson, almost got impeached. John Tyler, William Henry Harrison's successor, was a President without a party. Chester Arthur, James Garfield's successor, was considered a joke.

Bess Truman also loved being a senator's wife. For her it was a perfect combination of being near the center of the political stage while remaining more or less anonymous to everyone but a circle of chosen friends. Harry Truman, after his tremendous achievements as head of the Truman Committee, which saved billions of dollars by uncovering waste, mismanagement, and corruption on the home front during World War II, was guaranteed his Senate seat for life. Why give it up for something as clouded with portents as vice president to a dying President?

There was another, deeper reason why my mother did not want to become First Lady. She saw the ferocious press scrutiny Eleanor Roosevelt received and dreaded that similar treatment would exhume a family tragedy which would cause her and her brothers and above all her mother a great deal of pain. When Bess was eighteen, her handsome father shot himself in the bathroom of their Independence home. Unable to support his wife in the style she had acquired as the daughter of the wealthiest man in town, David Willock Wallace had sunk into depression and finally into suicide.

Bess's mother never recovered from that trauma. Madge Wallace became a recluse for the rest of her long life—and mostly her daughter's responsibility. The thought of some Hearst papers "sob sister" spreading this story across the pages of their seven-million-copy Sunday supplement, *The American Weekly,* forerunner of today's supermarket tabloids, or the front pages of all the papers in their huge chain, horrified my mother. But she found herself outflanked and overruled in her struggle to persuade my father to reject the vice presidency. Too many major voices in the Democratic Party practically ordered him to run to avoid the disaster of the incumbent vice president, Henry Wallace, becoming President.

Piling irony on irony, Henry Wallace was Mrs. Roosevelt's ardently supported choice to succeed her husband. I wonder what she would have thought, had she known that Bess Truman was her secret ally in this subterranean struggle.

Henry Wallace represented Eleanor Roosevelt's boldest venture into the politics of the presidency—what you might call politics with a capital *P.* The secretary of agriculture in FDR's cabinet, Wallace was not close to the First Lady at first. Like many other cabinet officers, he resented her intrusions into his bailiwick. Their alliance did not take shape until FDR proposed him as his vice president in 1940.

Most of the delegates to the Democratic National convention did not want Wallace. They thought another liberal added nothing to the ticket. They wanted a moderate or a conservative like the outgoing vice president, "Cactus Jack" Garner of Texas. For a while it looked as if Wallace was beaten. Fearful of being labeled dictatorial, FDR hesitated to insist on him as his one and only choice. Instead, he sent the First Lady to give an unprecedented speech to the delegates, which persuaded them to swallow Henry, though little more than half voted for him.

In her newspaper column, "My Day," a pleased Eleanor Roosevelt wrote: "Secretary Wallace is a very fine man and I am sure will strengthen the ticket. I have always felt in him a certain shyness that has kept him aloof from some Democrats. But now that he will be in close touch with many of them, I am sure they will soon find in him much to admire and love."

Alas, to know Henry Wallace was not to love him. He was, quite simply, an inept politician. He did not know how to schmooze, unbend, fraternize. His idea of communication was a press release. The notion that he was FDR's chosen successor went to his head. He picked turf fights with prominent Democrats in and out of Congress and infuriated the secretary of state, Cordell Hull, by speaking out on foreign policy in semimystical terms, calling on Americans to export the New Deal to the entire world to achieve "the century of the common man." In her column and among her friends, Mrs. Roosevelt continued to back Wallace enthusiastically. But the harder she pushed him with FDR, the more antagonistic the President became.

There are some historians and biographers who suggest that FDR's alienation from Eleanor in the last years of his presidency changed the course of history. Unquestionably, her attempt to make Henry Wallace President of the United States backfired disastrously and, by ironic coincidence, helped make Senator Truman his replacement. After telling Wallace he was his "personal choice," FDR, warned that large sections of the party would revolt rather than nominate him again, told Harry Truman he had to take the job or risk breaking up the Democratic Party in the middle of a war.

Both the incumbent First Lady and her soon-to-be successor watched with dismay as the Democratic Convention beat off an attempt by Wallace supporters to stampede the delegates and nominated Harry S Truman. When a rhapsodic crowd engulfed us as we left the Chicago convention center at the end of that sweltering July night, my mother exclaimed: "Are we going to have to put up with this for the rest of our lives?" That negative reaction acquired ominous momentum nine months later, when FDR's death catapulted us into the White House.

Bess Truman underwent a terrific inner struggle to overcome her deep aversion to becoming First Lady. She was still worried about the Wallace family secret and as my father's longtime political partner, she was deeply concerned about how he could cope with the enormous responsibility that had descended on him. "This is going to put a terrific load on Harry," she said to one of their close friends. "Roosevelt has told him nothing."

Never has any President in American history had to learn more about the problems facing him—and make world-shaping decisions about them faster—than Harry S Truman. Between that fateful April 12 when he took the oath of office in the Cabinet Room of the White House and September 2, he presided over the close of the war against Germany, supervised the opening of the United Nations, and ended the war with Japan by ordering atomic bombs dropped on Hiroshima and Nagasaki. In this avalanche of decisions and events, Bess Truman played little part. More and more, she began to feel that the presidency had virtually dissolved the political partnership that had been at the heart of her relationship with her husband for so many years.

For the rest of that tumultuous year 1945, my father worked at the same frantic pace, trying to stabilize a war-ravaged world, deal with a steadily more hostile Russia, and solve a dozen domestic crises. My mother struggled to give some shape and coherence to her role as First Lady in the shadow of her famous predecessor. At first she announced she would hold a press conference, but the closer she got to it, the more the idea horrified her. She canceled it at the last moment and said she would only answer written questions, submitted in advance. That left the White House press corps underwhelmed, to put it mildly.

Their sniping comments about her inaccessibility only deepened Bess's resistance. When a reporter called to inquire what Mother was wearing to a reception, she was blunt: "Tell her it's none of her business." Her secretary managed to stutter out something about the First Lady being undecided for the moment.

Bess's letters to friends in Independence became a lament about how homesick she was. This from a woman who had spent most of the previous eleven years in Washington. Bess was suffering from the White House blues. She told someone that her favorite First Lady was Elizabeth Monroe—primarily, I suspect, because of her success at virtually disappearing from the White House for most of her husband's two terms. She may also have been identifying with a First Lady who succeeded the media icon of her era, Dolley Madison—as Mother had succeeded Eleanor Roosevelt.

It got worse—as things tend to do in the White House. Bess was invited to a DAR tea in her honor at Constitution Hall. The moment she accepted, New York Congressman Adam Clayton Powell went for her jugular. He claimed his wife, the gifted jazz pianist Hazel Scott, had been banned from playing at Constitution Hall because of her race. He wired Bess that "if you believe in 100 percent Americanism, you will publicly denounce the DAR's action" and refuse to attend the tea.

Congressman Powell aroused Bess Truman's stubborn streak. She had accepted the invitation, hundreds of DARs were coming to the tea, and she had no power to change their policy of banning blacks from performing in the hall. She wired a response along these lines to Congressman Powell, who promptly released it to the press with another denunciation. When Bess went to the tea anyway, he called her "the last lady" and reminded everyone of Eleanor Roosevelt's stand on Marian Anderson's right to sing in the hall.

Bess's White House mood went from blue to black. She had been compared with her famous predecessor, and even her friends had to admit the result was not in her favor. But she refused to back down or apologize. She also refused to resign from the DAR, as several friends urged, and stuck to her argument that Bess Truman had no power to change their policies. Mother was still trying to deny that she was public property. She was also still very angry at her political partner, the overworked President, who had gotten her into this mess.

True to her instincts for privacy, Bess waited until she got back to Independence to explode. She and I went home to our wonderful old house on North Delaware Street on December 18, 1945. My father, embroiled in negotiations with the Russians, did not leave Washington aboard his plane, *The Sacred Cow,* until Christmas Day. He flew through weather that had grounded every commercial airliner in the nation and arrived to be confronted by a glowering wife. "So you've finally arrived," Bess said. "As far as I'm concerned you might as well have stayed in Washington."

I was having too much fun with old Independence friends to detect the chill in the air. But I noticed a certain lack of warmth when Mother said good-bye to Dad on December 27 as he rushed back to Washington to deal with yet another crisis, this one with a runaway secretary of state.

Back in the Big White Jail, Dad wrote Mother the most scorching letter of his life and mailed it special delivery. He then spent the night worrying about it rather than sleeping. The next day he called me in Independence and told me to collect the letter at the post office before it was delivered and burn it. "It's a very angry letter," he said. "I don't want your mother to see it."

I headed for the post office, wondering why the President of the United States could not get some unoccupied Secret Service agent to handle this job. I had no trouble extracting the letter from the grasp of the U.S. Postal Service. They joked about how nice it was of me to help deliver the mail. I took it home, wandered casually (I hoped) into the backyard, and dropped it into the metal basket where we burned trash in those pre–air pollution days.

I felt bewildered, appalled, and guilty. I had never before in my life concealed anything important from my mother. I could not imagine why Dad had sent her an angry letter. Not until I wrote Bess Truman's biography, forty years later, did I figure it out.

Back in the White House, Dad wrote Bess one of the most important letters of both their lives. He said he felt like "last year's birds nest...on its second year." It was not very often, he added, that "I admit I am not in shape. I think maybe that exasperates you...as a lot of other things I do exasperate you."

Then he got to the heart of the matter: "You can never appreciate what it means to come home as I did the other evening after doing at least one hundred things I didn't want to do and have the only person in the world whose approval and good opinion I value look at me like I'm something the cat dragged in."

Time and *Life* were saying he was the "No. 1 man in the world." But he somehow lacked "a large bump of ego" that would enable him to believe such nonsense. On the contrary, he knew he needed help from "you, Margie [that's me], and everyone else who may have any influence on my actions." If he could get that help, "the job [would] be done." If he could not get it, William Randolph Hearst and his fellow Republican critics, who were saying Harry Truman lacked presidential stature, would turn out to be right.

Mother came back to the White House in a much improved mood. She was still unreconciled to the job in many ways, but the air had been cleared of her smoldering resentment. The President had made it plain that he was ready and eager to resume their partnership whenever she was so inclined. The world outside the White House cooperated with this spirit of marital détente, subsiding from the global-size crises of 1945 to the ordinary upheavals we have come to regard as politics as usual.

One of the first things Bess tackled was a problem left behind by Mrs. Roosevelt—the housekeeper, Henrietta Nesbitt. A few months after we moved into the White House, I met Elliott Roosevelt, who cheerfully inquired: "Has Mrs. Nesbitt begun starving you yet?" When I politely shook my head—the food was bad but starvation seemed an extreme term—Elliott replied: "Don't worry, she will."

At one point during our first troubled months in the White House, I was serving as substitute First Lady (I had just turned twenty-two) while my mother was in Denver trying to decide what to do with her mother, who was living unhappily with her son, my uncle, Fred Wallace. Mrs. Nesbitt served my father brussels sprouts, a vegetable he detested. I offhandedly told her not to serve brussels sprouts again. Little did I know I had issued a declaration of hostilities. Brussels sprouts were on the table the next night. I again told Mrs. Nesbitt not to serve them—and there they were the following night. I called Mother in Denver and warned her that the next time I saw brussels sprouts, Mrs. Nesbitt was going to get them between the eyes.

Bess brought my grandmother back from Denver to take up permanent residence in the White House. She soon had a talk with Mrs. Nesbitt. The brussels sprouts vanished, but the food did not otherwise improve. Mrs. Nesbitt was determined to show the new First Lady who was boss. Whenever Mother suggested the slightest change in routine, she was told, "Mrs. Roosevelt did not do it that way," apparently presuming the new First Lady would be cowed by the mere mention of her predecessor's name.

Bess bided her time. She knew firing top personnel in the White House was always a delicate matter. They can go straight to the nearest reporter with outrageous lies about you. One day Mother stopped by the White House kitchen to pick up some butter to take to a potluck luncheon with her Senate wives' bridge club. "Oh no!" Mrs. Nesbitt said, acting as if Mother had never heard of wartime food shortages and government rationing. "We can't let any of our butter leave this kitchen. We've used up almost all this month's ration stamps already."

Mrs. Nesbitt did not have to add, "Mrs. Roosevelt would not do it this way." By now that was implied. Not content with bullying the new First Lady in private, she was now intent on humiliating her before the entire White House kitchen staff.

Bess kept her temper—and her head. She consulted the boss of White House bosses, the chief usher, Howell Crim. "Mrs. Nesbitt tells me I can't take a speck of butter out of the kitchen," Mother said.

"Of course you can!" gasped the flabbergasted Crim. "She is entirely out of line."

"Maybe it's time to find a new housekeeper," Mother said.

That was the beginning of the end of Mrs. Nesbitt, with the chief usher, not the First Lady, wielding the ax.

Meanwhile, a much more important change was taking place in the Truman White House routine. Each night after dinner, Bess began meeting with my father in his upstairs study to discuss the problems before him and the people he was choosing to help him solve them.

People, personalities, were Bess's forte. She was a listener, and she had a deadly eye for character. In his first days in the Oval Office, my father asked his old friend, insurance executive Eddie McKim, to be his chief of staff. Eddie was a wonderful man, but being propelled from Omaha to Washington, D.C., did terrible things to his judgment.

One day he rushed into the social secretary's office in the East Wing and demanded to know who was doing what. He was told that two secretaries were typing answers to the thousands of letters Mrs. Roosevelt had received from sympathetic admirers when FDR died. "Mrs. Roosevelt is no longer riding the gravy train!" Eddie said and fired both women on the spot.

The social secretary, an old pro named Edith Helm, informed Mother of this decision. She was appalled. Within twenty-four hours the women were rehired, Mrs. Roosevelt's letters continued to be answered, and Eddie McKim was on his way back to Omaha.

Bess also repelled an invasion by Jake Vardaman, an old Missouri friend of Dad who had become his naval aide. Looking for work, Captain Vardaman decided he would "organize" the First Lady's correspondence and introduce efficiency into the East Wing. Bess told the President that Vardaman spelled T-R-O-U-B-L-E, and he was soon kicked upstairs to the Federal Reserve Board, where he proved her a prophet by voting against any and all Truman policies and proposals.

Mother did a lot more than spot would-be power grabbers. She also made some very valuable positive suggestions. Probably the most important was her urgent recommendation that Harry Truman ask their old Independence schoolmate Charlie Ross to become his press secretary. Head of the *St. Louis Post-Dispatch*'s Washington bureau, Charlie was one of the most respected newsmen in the capital. It is hard to think of any single appointment that did more to stabilize the Truman presidency.

Bess's judgment of character came into play on a national level when she started warning my father about the danger of keeping Henry Wallace in his cabinet. Here I have discovered another invisible encounter with Eleanor Roosevelt. This time, however, the two First Ladies were in collision.

Almost everyone above the age of reason when FDR died recalls my father's exchange with Mrs. Roosevelt when he rushed to the White House on April 12, 1945, and discovered the President was dead. "Is there anything I can do for you?" he asked the First Lady.

"Is there anything *we* can do for *you?*" Eleanor replied. "You are the one in trouble now."

Several days later Mrs. Roosevelt wrote a letter to Henry Wallace: "Though I hope to see you today and perhaps to talk with you more about my hopes for America and the future, I want you to know that you are peculiarly fitted to carry on the ideals which were close to my husband's heart and which I know you understood."

Here, instead of doing something for Harry S Truman, Mrs. Roosevelt did something *to* him. That letter gave Wallace the idea that he was still FDR's anointed successor, no matter what the Democratic Convention in Chicago had decided in July and the American people had ratified with their votes in November 1944. In defense of the former First Lady, one can say she probably did not realize what Henry Wallace would do with this endorsement.

Harry Truman had inherited Henry as secretary of commerce from the Roosevelt cabinet. Emboldened by Mrs. Roosevelt's backing, Wallace proceeded to make the new President's life miserable. He went public with repeated denunciations of Dad's get-tough approach to the Soviet Union, which was busily clamping a one-party straitjacket on Poland and the other countries of Eastern Europe. The newspapers heaped scorn on the Truman administration's "two-headed foreign policy."

Against Mother's advice, Dad tried to reach an understanding with Mr. Wallace. His response was a series of double crosses. Henry per-

My mother chats with Eleanor Roosevelt and Edith Wilson at a reception. She was a warm friend of both and exchanged many letters with them. *(Bettmann Archive)*

suaded Dad to "approve" a speech he was giving—then used a completely different version. He promised to stop speaking about foreign policy—then gave a speech to reporters on his way out of the White House. Some of this happened while Bess was taking a summer break in Independence, and Dad's letters reveal what she was telling him in sulfurous terms. "It was nice to talk with you [last night]," he wrote on September 16, 1946, "even if you did give me hell about making mistakes."

Finally, Dad wrote a letter that his First Lady had been urging on him for months. He asked Henry Wallace to resign from his administration. Henry departed and for the next two years grew loonier and loonier, at one point comparing the Soviet Communist Party with the early Christians. When Henry ran for President on the Progressive Party ticket in 1948, Eleanor Roosevelt endorsed Harry Truman.

Neither she nor anyone else knew that she had lost a covert struggle with her quiet successor, Bess Truman.

Meanwhile, Mother was going her own way as First Lady. Generous hearted as always, Mrs. Roosevelt staunchly supported her determination to shun publicity and keep the press at arm's length. She reiterated what almost every First Lady has said about the job: each woman must find a fit with her own personality and inclinations. I suspect Mrs. Roosevelt also saw that the Truman marriage was a productive working partnership with the right to lay down its own White House ground rules.

There was nothing furtive about Mother's decision to opt for minimum visibility; her role was never completely invisible. Dad often referred to her as his helper. As senator he said he never made a report or a speech without her editing it. In her early interviews Bess did not try to conceal her contributions. When Harry Truman ran for vice president, she told a reporter she would help him write his speeches "because we've done that so long, it's a habit." The following year another reporter asked her if she had ever held a job: "I've been in politics for more than twenty-five years," she said.

A major principle of the partnership was no nagging. Bess would state her opinion on an issue. If Dad differed with it, and went in another direction, that was the end of the matter. She did not waylay him and try to change his mind. Only when he hesitated between two agonizing choices, as in the case of Henry Wallace, would she prod him to act one way or the other.

A good example of how the partnership worked was the decision to run for the presidency in 1948. Harry Truman wanted to do it, even if his poll ratings had sunk so low you needed a wet suit and a few tanks of oxygen to find them. He was determined to become President in his own right, with the full endorsement of the American people. Bess did not think he could win. She was almost always the pessimist (she called it realist) in the duo. If she had had her way, they would have let some other qualified Democrat take to the campaign trail in 1948 and gone home to Independence, satisfied that they had done their best and kept their dignity.

Once Dad decided to run, Mother never said another negative word. She climbed aboard the Ferdinand Magellan, the armor-plated railroad car General Motors had designed for presidential train travel, and gamely whistle-stopped through most of the forty-eight states.

Though she sometimes denied it, Mother loved every minute of that campaign. Bess too had a few scores to settle with Republicans. Congresswoman Clare Boothe Luce had called her an ersatz First Lady. The day after our victory, Bess came across a copy of *Time* magazine, owned by Mrs. Luce's husband, Henry. There was the Republican candidate, Thomas E. Dewey, on the cover, described as the next President of the United States. "I wonder if Mrs. Luce thinks I'm real now?" Mother asked.

Another partnership role Mother played was censor. Harry Truman's greatest (I am tempted to say only) flaw was his quick temper. Bess did not think the President of the United States should tell people to go to hell or inform someone he was an SOB. Dad did not use profanity in his everyday speech. But when he got angry, his language could be purple. George Washington, Andrew Jackson, Dwight Eisenhower, and several other Presidents who spent some time in the U.S. Army had a similar predilection. In the White House, it became a running joke among the staff, who would inquire whether the President "was in the doghouse again" for sounding off.

Another partnership role, which Bess shared with many other First Ladies, was protector. My father had an enormous appetite for work. He is probably the only modern President who read every line of the immense national budget—and understood it—before it went up to Congress. When a crisis was raging in the White House—and Dad liked to say we had one a week—he would work until 3:00 and 4:00 A.M., driving himself and his staff to the brink of exhaustion.

That was when Partner Bess stepped in and said, "Harry, it's time for a vacation." He rarely demurred. Often in his letters to me, he confessed how badly he had needed the break. In 1947, after frantic weeks of work to rescue Greece from a Communist takeover, when he retreated to his favorite hideaway, the submarine base in Key West, he wrote: "I had no idea I was so tired. I have been asleep most of the time [since he arrived]. No one, not even me (your mother would say) knew how worn to a frazzle the chief executive had become."

I hope I have not given the impression that while the President was working his head off, his wife was hiding out on the second floor, doing little but avoiding the press. Even before she became reconciled to the job, Mother worked at "First Ladying," as I called it, eight and ten hours a day.

In 1946 the White House returned to peacetime status. That meant a full social schedule, and then some. With the United States now a superpower, the official guest lists, which included ambassadors, members of Congress, heads of federal agencies, generals, admirals, and the like, had grown to two thousand. The public rooms could only handle one thousand at a reception, so this meant the President and First Lady had to hold two of almost every event. Between November 26, 1946, and February 18, 1947, Mother had to superintend eleven "official" gatherings, ranging from two state dinners for the diplomatic corps—they had grown so large they could no longer fit into the State Dining Room—to a congressional reception, with a thousand plus hands to shake. On top of this schedule were piled innumerable teas, luncheons, and personal appearances with groups who thought they could benefit from a photo with the First Lady.

Not only did Bess Truman work hard at these events but she was extremely good at being a hostess. Lady Bird Johnson told me a charming story when I interviewed her for this book. She went to one of the congressional receptions in 1946 or 1947. "I was only a congressman's wife," Lady Bird said. "I was awed to find myself visiting the White House. When I finally got to Mrs. Truman, she was so warm and outgoing, as I passed off the line I turned to Lyndon and said: 'I think she knew me!' "

As the social season wound down, Mother wrote me a letter in which you could almost hear her sigh: "These two weeks are really going to be a handshaking two weeks—conservative estimate forty one hundred." After a reception for the Governor-General of Canada and his wife, she wrote to tell me how much she liked them, and added almost matter-of-factly: "The reception of course was horrible—1341 & my arm is a wreck this A.M."

Though her arm ached, Mother's hand survived this ordeal, thanks to some tutoring from a master of the political handshake, Harry S Truman. He taught Mother—and me—that the essence of the art was to seize the other person's hand before he or she grabbed yours—and to slide your thumb between the other person's thumb and index finger, so that you, not he or she, did the squeezing.

Even with this expert advice, by the time Mother left the White House, the glove size of her right hand had gone from 6 to 6½. My hand too had gone up a half size. I cannot claim to have shaken nearly as many hands as she did, but I shook enough to produce the damage.

Dad's miracle victory in 1948 worked a transformation in Mother's attitude toward First Ladying. She no longer saw it as something inflicted on her by one of fate's crueler blows. Instead it became a job she had chosen to do, in concert with her presidential partner. One of the first signs of this more positive attitude was the intense interest she took in choosing her inauguration dresses and evening gowns.

She had been buying most of her clothes from Agasta, a well-known Washington couturier. They were tasteful but not very exciting. Moreover, Agasta did not make evening gowns. So Mother chose Madame Pola of New York to supply these. Meanwhile, she put pressure on Agasta to come up with some more creative day wear. Twelve days before the inauguration, they still had not agreed on a fabric for her inauguration outfit.

Agasta was getting palpitations when she found a piece of silk that was an intriguing mixture of iridescent black and gray. Mother gave her an emphatic go-ahead, and Agasta created the outfit Bess wore to the ceremony. It had a straight skirt and a peplum jacket, which went beautifully with her blackish gray hat, trimmed with a single, massive mauve-pink rose.

The fashion triumph of those triumphant days, however, was Mother's ball gown. It was made of black panne velvet cut on slender lines, the skirt draped to one side. The circular collar was covered with layers of white Alençon lace and fell gracefully over her shoulder, forming a lovely oval neckline.

Both these dresses signaled Mother's new enthusiasm for her job—a mood which continued to build throughout 1949, the happiest of our White House years. That summer she undertook a diet that shed more than twenty middle-age pounds and returned to the White House more ready than ever to wear stylish clothes. One of my favorite pictures is of the two of us at the opening night of the Metropolitan Opera a year or so later. Mother is wearing a high-necked dark blue satin coat, embroidered with flowers, over a long, full gown. Her hair is stylishly curled. On her face is a happy smile. She looks several years younger than the frowning woman who stood beside Dad when he took the oath of office in 1945.

Then the Korean War erupted in June of 1950, and Mother's euphoria began to evaporate. Dad's second term became an even more severe test of the Truman partnership. Dad had to rally the free world against this naked Communist aggression and simultaneously cope with the constant insubordination of his Far East commander, General Douglas MacArthur. In this confrontation, his First Lady unwaveringly supported his decision to fire the general, even though some people—including numerous members of Congress—acted as if the world were coming to an end.

On the home front, anarchic Senator Joseph McCarthy tempted Republicans into smearing Democrats—including the President—as Communists. Living in the White House became a little like inhabiting a fortress under siege. Several aides crumpled under the pressure. The most heartbreaking loss was Charlie Ross, who died of a heart attack at his desk during one particularly horrendous crisis in late 1950. By the time the presidential election year of 1952 appeared on the horizon, President Harry S Truman was very tired—and so was his First Lady.

Yet Dad seriously considered running for another term. Although Congress had passed a constitutional amendment limiting the presidency to two terms, they had exempted Harry Truman. This time the President's partner gave him something stronger than advice. She told him she could not survive another four years in the White House pressure cooker and neither could he.

Dad took it under advisement, but he still retained the freedom to decide otherwise, if the Democratic Party could not find a decent candidate to oppose the man who was beginning to emerge as the Republican nominee, General Dwight D. Eisenhower. Dad's first two choices, Chief Justice Fred Vinson and Governor Adlai Stevenson of Illinois, had proved elusive. President Truman called a meeting of his White House staff to discuss the problem. They agreed, almost unanimously, that he should not run again. They were almost as tired as the Chief Executive.

Still Dad put off the decision. Finally, one night in the spring of 1952, his appointments secretary, Matt Connelly, a genial Irishman who had become Dad's closest confidant since Charlie Ross's death, brought up the subject while they were working late, as usual. Matt had been designated by a group of prominent Democrats to tell the President he had to accept another nomination.

Dad listened, visibly upset, and asked Matt if he thought this pressure was serious enough to make "the old man run again." Matt dropped his role as messenger and gestured toward the portrait of Mother on Dad's desk, next to that famous sign, THE BUCK STOPS HERE. "Would you do that to her?" he asked.

"All right," Dad said. "That settles it."

The Truman partnership had made its final White House decision. In later years, Dad was fond of saying that most people in Washington leave in only two ways: by getting kicked out or carried out. Thanks to his First Lady and his own common sense, he and Bess walked out, smiling.

Chapter 7

—

THE PERILS OF
PARTNERSHIP

BESS TRUMAN WAS BY NO MEANS THE ONLY FIRST LADY TO OPERATE as her husband's political partner. The tradition began with the second First Lady, Abigail Smith Adams. She and her husband, President John Adams, spent most of their single term in Philadelphia, the interim capital of the United States. Not until 1800 did Abigail and John move into the unfinished White House, where she had the dolorous privilege of watching her husband become the first incumbent President to lose his bid for reelection.

Abigail has another, happier distinction. She is the only First Lady who became the mother of a President. Her oldest and favorite son, John Quincy Adams, succeeded James Monroe in 1825. Unfortunately, for reasons which seem inherent in the Adamses' genes, John Quincy too was a one-term President.

Like almost every other First Lady, Abigail wondered if she could do the job—though there was scarcely a woman in America who was more qualified. Abigail Adams had been a political wife for twenty years before John won the highest office in the new republic in 1796. She had unwaveringly supported her husband as he and Thomas Jefferson and George Washington led the American people into independence and revolutionary war.

In 1776 Abigail, in a now famous letter, had urged John to include woman's rights in the new American order. "Remember the ladies and be more generous to them than your ancestors! Do not put such unlimited power in the hands of the husbands. Remember that all men would be tyrants if they could," she wrote. John declined to repeal "our masculine systems," which he maintained were "little more than theory." That last remark is, I suspect, a tribute to the power of Abigail's personality.

During John's diplomatic assignments in Paris, London, and Amsterdam, Abigail had dealt deftly with royalty and the sometimes shocking mores of the Old World. She had been a superb vice president's wife for two terms. But as First Lady, she feared she lacked the "patience, prudence, and discretion" of her predecessor, Martha Washington.

Politics did not particularly interest Martha. She kept her few opinions to herself or shared them with one or two close relatives. Abigail lived and breathed the hugger-mugger of issues and arguments day and night. Her letters are full of astute comments on the crises of the day and even more incisive pen portraits of the major players.

Listen to her description of Timothy Pickering, the Massachusetts-born secretary of state in John Adams's cabinet. "There is a man in the cabinet whose manners are forbidding, whose temper is sour and whose resentments are implacable, who nevertheless would like to dictate every measure." Take a look at a portrait of Pickering sometime; I guarantee his pickled puss will persuade you that Abigail was on target. Five months after she wrote this, the President fired Pickering—something Abigail thought John should have done the minute he became President.

Just as Abigail felt intimidated by Martha Washington, John Adams felt overshadowed by George. He hesitated to remove any of Washington's appointees until it was too late to stop them from getting the Philadelphia equivalent of Potomac fever. Pickering in particular regarded Adams as an idiot and regularly leaked vicious stories about his incompetence and instability.

Abigail's propensity for politics kept her in hot water in the over-heated ideological atmosphere of the late 1790s, when the French Revolution and the emergence of Napoleon had the whole world boiling with extremism. The Antifeds, now formally organized as the Democratic-Republicans, used her as a handy weapon to bludgeon the President. Swiss-born Congressman Albert Gallatin, a supporter of John Adams's rival, Thomas Jefferson, claimed to be outraged when he heard "Her Majesty" going down the list of congressmen and nam-ing those who were "our people." Gallatin thought this was "not right." He wanted women to stay on the sidelines of life, demure and submissive.

Abigail returned the favor by calling Gallatin "sly, artfull...insidi-ous," and little more than a double agent for French attempts to manipulate the United States into backing France in its war with England. However, she reserved her most ferocious adjectives for a member of her own Federalist Party, Alexander Hamilton, not only because he was a notorious ladies' man but because he attempted to dump John Adams as the party's presidential candidate in 1800. Abi-gail insisted she could see "the very devil" in Hamilton's eyes.

Abigail Adams was the first First Lady to leak stories to the press. It was part of an attempt to defend her husband's foreign policy, which aimed at neutrality in the war between the era's superpowers, England and France. Abigail had a "channel" in Europe, her son John Quincy, who was the American minister to Berlin. He sent her inside information on Europe's seething politics, which she forwarded to friendly newspaper editors, carefully underlining the paragraphs she wanted to see in print.

As a sometime actress, I was fascinated to discover how Abigail and her friends once used the theater to score a propaganda triumph for her husband. Traveling "perfectly in cogg" (incognito), she told her sister, the First Lady slipped into Philadelphia's New Theater in the spring of 1798 and joined some congressional friends and their wives to hear a political song that had been inserted between the acts of a double bill. Titled "Hail Columbia," the song had new lyrics to the tune of "The President's March," the music that had regularly greeted George Washington. The added lines reaffirmed America's political independence.

> Firm, united let us be
> Rallying round our liberty
> As a band of brothers joined
> Peace and safety we shall find.

The audience loved it. Recent news of French arrogance and aggression had dampened enthusiasm for Paris's revolutionary notions. The idea of taking neither side in this ugly war suddenly seemed brilliantly original. Abigail rejoiced as the audience almost clapped their hands off in the final chorus and leaped to their feet to shout cheers for President John Adams.

Criticism of Abigail as First Lady was mostly whispered in drawing rooms by politicians like Albert Gallatin. Far more unnerving was the public beating her husband took in the frenetic newspapers of the day. In one letter to her sister, the First Lady complained that reporters had recently called the President "Old querulous bald, blind crippled toothless Adams." Goaded by such abuse, Abigail became a fierce advocate of censorship. She furiously supported the Alien and Sedition Acts, which the Federalist Congress passed in 1798, giving the courts the right to jail anyone who "shall write, print, utter or publish ... scandalous or malicious writings against the government of the United States, either house of Congress ... or the President."

Abigail applauded when Congressman Matthew Lyon of Vermont got four months behind bars for denouncing President Adams's "unbounded thirst for ridiculous pomp." She took even more pleasure in seeing James Thomson Callender, a newspaperman who had written a slanderous book about President Adams, sentenced to six months in another jail.

Abigail's enthusiasm for the Alien and Sedition Acts was the first—but not, alas, the last—example of bad advice from a First Lady political partner. The backlash against these tyrannical laws helped sweep John Adams out of the presidency in 1800. Even Abigail's son John Quincy, the future President, mournfully admitted in later years that the acts "operated like oil upon the flames." The attempt to muzzle the press was savagely attacked by Thomas Jefferson, James Madison, and other opposition leaders. The newspapers added *tyrant* to the list of insulting adjectives they regularly applied to old John Yankee, as Adams liked to call himself.

The Adams experience underscores a seldom recognized danger when First Ladies become political partners. In many ways John and Abigail Adams were too much alike; they rarely if ever disagreed on the issues of the day. This can be a wonderful reinforcement—but if the partners make a blunder as serious as the Alien and Sedition Acts and then sit around telling each other they are right and the rest of the

Abigail Adams was our first intensely political First Lady. Doesn't she look it? Note those shrewd eyes. This portrait by Gilbert Stuart was begun while she was in the White House. *(AP/Wide World Photos)*

world is wrong, the mistake can swiftly become a political disaster that engulfs the presidency.

Still another danger of intense political partnerships was glimpsed in Abigail Adams's experience in 1798. After nearly two years as First Lady, the savage name-calling and reckless accusations against her husband had taken a fearful toll on Abigail's nerves. That summer, as she journeyed to the Adamses' farm in Massachusetts, she began hearing voices, warning her that "this Life's a dream, an empty show." She felt "ligaments" in her body giving way one by one. At home Abigail took to her bed and plunged into a four-month-long mental and physical collapse. She was racked by diarrhea and disabled by insomnia, which left her sleepless five nights out of six.

In the fall, the President returned to Philadelphia without her, and Abigail tormented herself for deserting her "post." John filled the mails with letters urging her to banish such gloomy thoughts and forget politics for a while. But Abigail stubbornly upheld her side of the partnership, making sure the President's secretary sent her all the Philadelphia papers plus a stream of confidential reports on the administration's ongoing crises.

There were some nonpolitical factors in Abigail Adams's collapse, which brings up another side of the First Lady's job. Most presidential partners have been mothers as well as wives. Abigail worked at her maternal role as intensely as she tried to be a super First Lady. A stream of letters poured out to her four adult children, full of advice, concern, and more advice.

A heritage of mental instability haunted the Adams family. Abigail's brother had died of alcoholism, and her husband was as subject to bouts of depression as she was. Their second son, Charles, after a brilliant start as a lawyer in New York, developed a fondness for alcohol which rapidly destroyed his marriage and his career.

Abigail's youngest son, Thomas, was another headache, though a less serious one. Twenty-four when his father became President, he set up as a lawyer in Philadelphia and in his first case defended the owners of a local brothel. Thomas scorned the hairstyles of the establishment, which called for wigs or powdered hair. Any parent who has lived through the hair wars of the nineteen sixties and seventies can only groan, "The more things change the more they remain the same."

As seriously troubling as Charles was Abigail's son-in-law, William Smith, who had married her beloved only daughter and namesake. A courageous soldier in the Revolution, Smith was a disaster as a peacetime husband, spending himself into bankruptcy with high living and feckless speculations. When the President, with partner Abigail's full support, proposed to make Smith adjutant general of the American army, they had the humiliation of seeing him rejected by the Senate, in spite of being endorsed by none other than George Washington. This occurred in the summer of 1798 and undoubtedly contributed to Abigail's prostration.

In the spring of 1799, a recovered Abigail returned to First Ladying. She heartily backed her husband's decision to defy Secretary of State Pickering and the rest of the inherited cabinet and send to France an envoy who defused the undeclared war Americans were already fighting at sea against French raiders. She also supported one of the President's most controversial decisions, pardoning John Fries, an eccentric Pennsylvanian who had been sentenced to death for leading a ragtag revolt against federal taxes that the government crushed in about ten minutes.

This humane act outraged conservative Federalists such as Pickering and Alexander Hamilton, and they resolved to jettison Mr. and Mrs. President Adams. Their machinations only succeeded in splitting the Federalist Party and handing the presidential election of 1800 to the father of all Democrats, Thomas Jefferson.

Thanks to Abigail's busy pen—she left behind over two thousand letters—we have interesting descriptions of her first days in the White House, which everyone called the President's Palace. Abigail arrived in the middle of November 1800, with the presidential election roaring to a climax. The White House was still unfinished; wet plaster oozed from the walls; the entire place was pervaded by a chill which twelve fireplaces could not banish. Gazing at the sea of mud surrounding the mansion, she described Washington as "a city only in name." But Abigail, ever the politician, was careful to confide her opinions only to family members. "When asked how I like it," she advised her daughter, "say that I wrote you the situation is beautiful."

On December 4, the first election returns arrived, putting Jefferson narrowly ahead of Adams. Abigail was not surprised; unlike her husband, who had persisted in hoping against hope, she had been pessimistic about his chances. On the same day, a letter from New York told Abigail news she had dreaded far more than a lost election: her son Charles had died of alcoholism. She had visited him en route to Washington and realized there was little or no hope for his recovery. Eight days later, in the middle of a blizzard, a post rider from South Carolina arrived with the news that the Palmetto State had gone for Jefferson, making him the certified winner.

Abigail accepted political defeat far more graciously than her husband. John Adams met his former friend Thomas Jefferson at the door of the White House with a roar: "You have put me out! You have put me out!" Four years as a presidential partner had left Abigail feeling old at fifty-six. No doubt the death of her son Charles contributed to this feeling. She claimed to have only one regret about relinquishing political power: the loss of "one of the principle pleasures of my life"—to "do good according to my ability."

That was a touching tribute to the reality and nobility of a political partnership that had helped to create the United States of America. It was also, I suspect, an attempt to solace the pain of defeat. But this first presidential partner deserves credit for helping her husband set an example of a peaceful transfer of power between political parties who thoroughly detested each other. She also set another example which succeeding generations have followed. For the rest of her long life, Abigail referred to John Adams in letters and conversation as "the President."

———

FORTY-FIVE YEARS LATER, ANOTHER PRESIDENTIAL PARTNER, IN SOME ways more formidable than Abigail Adams, strode the halls of the White House. Sarah Childress Polk also has the distinction of being the only First Lady who was selected by a preceding President. James

Polk was an almost thirty-year-old bachelor, going nowhere in politics, when he sought advice from his mentor and fellow Tennessean, Andrew Jackson. What was he doing wrong?

"Stop your philandering!" Jackson roared in his usual blunt style. The handsome Polk was known as an incorrigible lothario. "You must settle down as a sober married man!"

"Which lady shall I choose?" asked the startled Polk, no doubt thinking the question would confound the white-haired old warrior, who was U.S. senator from Tennessee at the time of this exchange.

"The one who will never give you any trouble!" Jackson growled. "Her wealth, family, education, and health are all superior. You know her well."

"You mean Sarah Childress?" Polk asked. He thought it over for a moment and decided he had just gotten some good advice. "I shall go at once and ask her," he said.

That conversation bears witness to nineteen-year-old Sarah Childress's remarkable gifts. Tall and dark, with features that usually won the adjective *handsome* rather than *beautiful,* she was the daughter of a wealthy Tennessee planter who believed in educating his daughters as well as his sons. She was attracted to Polk, but not to the point of instant capitulation. She told him she would accept his offer of marriage if he ran for a seat in the state legislature—and won.

With the office and Sarah safely in hand, Polk was ready for his next political move. Within a year of their marriage on January 1, 1824, he had run for Congress and won. Unlike most congressional wives of the era, Sarah abandoned their Tennessee homestead and went to Washington with him. Among several reasons why I have always felt an affinity with Sarah Polk was her frank dislike of housework and cooking. My father used to say, "If you can't stand the heat, stay out of the kitchen." (He was talking about politics, of course.) My Grandmother Truman taught me an even more useful lesson about kitchens: "If you can't cook, no one will ever ask you to."

In Washington, Sarah Polk became famous for having the boldest political opinions of any woman in the capital. She was a frequent visitor to the House gallery, where she listened more intently to the ora-tory than ninety percent of the congressmen. A skillful hostess, even if she did not go near the kitchen, Sarah played a major role in Polk's rise from legislative nobody to Speaker of the House of Representatives in just ten years.

Andrew Jackson's backing did not hurt, of course. Sarah charmed not only the General-turned-President (in 1828) but a host of other important politicos as well. Congressman (and future President) Franklin Pierce of New Hampshire said he liked to discuss politics with her more than with most men. Another conquest was Supreme Court Justice Joseph Story, the most famous jurist of his time after the legendary John Marshall. A lover of good books and intelligent women (his favorite author was Jane Austen), Justice Story wrote a poem in praise of Sarah when the Polks left Washington to run for the next step in their political game plan, the governorship of Tennessee:

> For I have listened to thy voice and watched
>   thy playful mind
> Truth in its noblest sense thy choice, yet gentle,
>   graceful, kind.

While Polk hit the campaign trail in Tennessee, Sarah stayed home and played political boss, organizing support for him among influential politicians in the state capital. In one of her letters she speaks of "operating" on a group of prospective allies. She used the same technique to marshal support for his 1844 presidential candidacy, when Polk came out of nowhere, comparatively speaking, to win the Democratic nomination at a divided convention.

During the campaign Sarah made political history, of sorts, by becoming the first First Lady to take on the wife of her husband's opponent, Henry Clay. Mrs. Clay was portrayed as a model wife who knew how to make good butter and keep a spotless house. Sarah tartly replied that if she got to the White House and had the President's salary of twenty-five thousand dollars a year (a huge sum in those days, when state governors were paid two thousand dollars) she would "neither keep house nor make butter." And people gave Hillary Rodham Clinton a hard time for scoffing at the idea of staying home to bake cookies!

The Polks arrived in the White House with a four-year plan that was breathtaking in its ambition. They were going to push the border of recently annexed Texas to the Rio Grande, even if it meant war with Mexico, settle the disputed border with Canada in the Oregon Territory, even if that meant war with England, and acquire New Mexico and California, extending the United States to the shore of the Pacific. They accomplished all three of these large goals, settling the Oregon question through astute diplomacy and the other two by fighting and winning the Mexican War.

The war made James Polk an unpopular President in some parts of the country, notably New England, where it was seen as a covert attempt to expand slavery. But Sarah Polk remained popular with all parties. During a White House reception, a southern visitor said, "Madame, I have long wished to look upon a lady upon whom the Bible pronounces a woe!"

Everyone waited for an explanation, which was forthcoming. "Does not the Bible say, 'Woe unto you when all men speak well of you?' "

Sarah retained her popularity in spite of the way she let her religious beliefs intrude on the management of the White House. A devout Presbyterian, she forbade liquor at receptions and dinners and also banned music and dancing. This was not an attempt to make a statement against alcohol, as in the case of Lucy Hayes. The President went along with her, explaining to his thirsty Tennessee friends that "Sarah directs all domestic affairs."

Polk's acquiescence made more than a few politicians think his wife was the real boss in their partnership. His own vice president, George Dallas, told his friends: "She is certainly mistress of herself and I suspect of somebody else also." Yet a search of Polk's detailed diary of his White House days uncovers little evidence of a henpecked man. Rather, it offers admiring examples of his wife's political astuteness.

When Senator Henry Clay visited the White House, he told Sarah he might be a critic of her husband but he was an admirer of "her administration." Sarah gallantly replied that of all the politicians in

Sarah Polk combined
brains and a somewhat
austere beauty. With her
at his side, President
James Polk barely needed
a cabinet. *(White House
Historical Society)*

America, he was the man she hoped would succeed her husband. Their powerful rival departed, Polk noted in his diary, "in an excellent humor."

Sarah was far less agreeable toward another critic, Congressman John Van Buren, the son of former President Martin Van Buren. Flamboyant Prince John, as he was known, was an antislavery Democrat who denounced the annexation of Texas and almost everything else the Polks supported. Sarah banned him from the White House. The President, perhaps hoping to conciliate him, decided to invite the young firebrand to a reception. When Sarah came across the invitation, she destroyed it. In his diary, Polk merely found this "amusing"—and let his partner have her way.

In only one role did Sarah falter as a presidential partner-wife—protector. It was not for want of trying, at least in the early years of her marriage. Polk's health was always fragile. Sarah's letters to him are full of cautionary advice about getting some rest on the campaign trail, avoiding overexcitement. But in the White House, where work was only a step away, both Polks seemed to have succumbed to their mutual appetite for politics, and the President literally worked himself to death.

Only on Sunday did the Polks pause for church services. The rest of the time they labored on affairs of state, Sarah toiling beside her husband as secretary and political counselor, frequently redrafting his speeches and letters. She also devoured stacks of newspapers and marked the stories she thought he should read. Polk freely admitted he almost never consulted his cabinet, and he had no circle of unofficial inside advisers, like Andrew Jackson's kitchen cabinet. He and Sarah ran the government virtually alone.

Even Sarah's White House entertaining had a political focus. At dinners, politics often dominated the First Lady's conversation to the point of letting her food grow cold upon the plate. After dinner, when the ladies retired to a sitting room for coffee in the custom of the day, she frequently stayed behind at the table to hobnob with the men.

Sarah's tactical skills had not a little to do with reducing congressional criticism of the Mexican War to an occasional speech from opposition congressmen such as Abraham Lincoln. This was no small feat. The South disliked the peace terms almost as much as New England disliked the war. Many southerners thought the United States should make Mexico a colony or state. But President Polk and his artful First Lady outmaneuvered both factions and kept control of a comfortable majority in Congress.

On July 4, 1848, James Polk signed the treaty of peace with Mexico in the White House, with a proud First Lady watching. Sarah later said she regarded the addition of 800,000 square miles of territory, making the United States a truly continental power, as "one of the most important events in the history of this country." It would be hard to argue with her.

This immense political effort took a fearful toll on President Polk. He left the White House a victorious but exhausted man and died three months later. Like everything else in life, White House partnerships can get out of hand. Few have blended triumph with tragedy more poignantly than James and Sarah Polk's bold alliance.

Chapter 8

—

THE FIRST LADY
WHO WANTED
THE JOB

Several other First Ladies have functioned as political partners, one by accident, the rest by design. It is ironic that the accidental one, Edith Bolling Galt Wilson, achieved more political power than any presidential wife, from Sarah Polk to Hillary Rodham Clinton, has ever dreamt of wielding. Edith's reign must have been particularly galling to her predecessor, Helen Herron Taft, who had an unusual appetite for power—especially when it came wrapped in the presidency.

Helen Taft is one of the few First Ladies who wanted the job. In fact, she wanted it far more than her husband, William Howard Taft, wanted to be President. Will Taft is one of my favorite historic characters, even though his son Senator Robert Taft was one of my father's chief Republican tormentors during the Truman years in the White House. A big (six foot two), easygoing man who frequently joked about his enormous girth, Will had only one ambition, to become a Supreme Court justice.

Unfortunately, this desire, which perfectly suited his laid-back temperament, clashed with Nellie Taft's determination to become a First Lady. She had acquired a passion for politics from her father and grandfather, both of whom served in Congress. Her father had been Rutherford B. Hayes's law partner, and at the age of seventeen Nellie visited the Hayeses' White House. Some say her ambition to become First Lady was born the moment she set foot in the place. Fiercely intelligent and hypercharged with nervous energy, Nellie was a latter-day Abigail Adams, with a lot more willpower. She ran her amiable husband's life, down to selecting his friends and his jobs.

Nellie also seems to have been driven by a burning determination to get out of Cincinnati. When Will Taft was offered the job of governing the newly acquired Philippine Islands, she started packing on the spot, ignoring the trepidations of relatives who fretted over tropical diseases and the real possibility of a native uprising.

From 1900 to 1904, Nellie was a well-publicized success as a minor-league First Lady in Manila. In her memoirs, she pronounced her Philippine years among the happiest of her life. She enjoyed presiding over dozens of servants in a palace where she entertained a stream of visiting congressmen, generals, and assorted other VIPs. She especially enjoyed a costume ball at which she and Will received guests dressed as the doge of Venice and his consort.

Once, when a typhoon hit the Philippines, toppling trees and smashing windows, Nellie was up all night, checking on damage to the governor's residence and supervising mop squads. Taft slept through the howling wind and breaking glass. In the morning Nellie was understandably cross with her somnolent spouse. "How could you sleep?" she demanded.

"Now Nellie," Taft said. "I knew you could handle it."

Nellie could handle almost anything—but there were signs of trouble to come. A perfectionist, she fretted over minute details of housekeeping and protocol. She held herself to impossibly high standards of conduct; her diary is full of self-reproaches for minor social gaffes or for failing to produce witty comebacks. In spite of wall-to-wall servants in Manila, she collapsed for several weeks with what was described as "nervous prostration."

When President Theodore Roosevelt brought William Howard Taft back from Manila in 1904 and made him secretary of war, Nellie and her husband began dining regularly at the White House. Roosevelt grew fond of Taft; it was almost impossible to dislike him; he told funny stories and loved a good laugh. Someone described his smile as "a huge pan of sweet milk poured over [you]."

One night during dinner, Roosevelt pretended he was a swami having a vision. "I am the seventh son of a seventh daughter and I have clairvoyant powers. I see a man weighing 350 pounds. There is something hanging over his head. I cannot make out what it is.... At one point it looks like the presidency, then again it looks like the chief justiceship."

"Make it the chief justiceship," Taft said.

"Make it the presidency," Nellie said.

She had an uphill fight converting Will into a candidate. As early as 1903, when he was still in the Philippines, he was telling friends: "Don't sit up nights thinking about making me President. I have no ambition in that direction. Any party which would nominate me would make a great mistake."

That last line would prove to be prophetic. But Nellie pressed on, fighting off another Roosevelt attempt to put Taft on the highest court by demanding a private meeting with the President at which she vehemently turned down the offer. "A half hour talk with your dear wife," Roosevelt told Taft, convinced him it was not a good idea.

Although Taft remarked to friends that he could not believe he was "foolish enough to run for the presidency," he was elected handily in 1908 with Roosevelt's backing. Even before Nellie got to 1600 Pennsylvania Avenue, she began paying a price for her ambition. When Ellen Maury Slayden, wife of a prominent Texas congressman, saw her at a White House dinner, she noted that Nellie "looked dreadful and spoke of not being well." She confessed to Mrs. Slayden that she had been tormented throughout the campaign by a fear that someone would kill her husband with a gun or a bomb. Only seven years before, an anarchist had assassinated William McKinley.

The Roosevelts invited the Tafts to spend the night before the inauguration at the White House. In another presage of trouble, Nellie lay awake until dawn, wondering "if this had been done, if that had been attended to"—petty details, she admitted in her memoirs, "with which I had no reason to be concerned."

Nellie was jolted from two hours of restless predawn sleep by "cracking reports" just outside her window. In the gray light she saw that she had plenty to worry about. The sounds were caused by tree limbs snapping all around the White House. Washington was frozen solid in one of the worst snow and ice storms in its history. Downstairs she found Roosevelt and Taft joking about the foul weather. "I always said it would be a cold day [in hell] when I got to be President of the United States," Will said.

Nellie was not amused. The inauguration parade had to be delayed, and the swearing-in ceremony was moved indoors to the U.S. Senate chamber. The First Lady's white satin inaugural ball gown was sitting on a stalled train somewhere between Washington and New York. Nellie did not realize it, of course, but she and her husband had had a curse laid on them by Theodore Roosevelt's rambunctious older daughter, Alice. She had taken a hate to Nellie almost on sight, perhaps because they were similar types. It would be a toss-up to decide who had more barbed wire in her temperament. Shortly before leaving the White House, Alice buried a voodoo doll on the lawn and called on the gods to visit woe on the new occupants.

I don't actually believe in such things, but the series of disasters that soon struck Helen Taft is enough to make me wonder. At a reception the day before the inauguration, Nellie wore a small hat trimmed with a long white egret feather. As she chatted with well-wishers, the feather came in contact with a gas jet, and the hat and Nellie almost went up in flames. Undeterred, she wore the hat to the inauguration, with the feather "trimmed down some."

After the ceremony, Nellie signaled her intention of being the new Chief Executive's highly visible partner by riding back to the White

House with him in his limousine. Previously, the outgoing President had accompanied the new occupant to the Executive Mansion. Theodore Roosevelt, afraid that he would steal the spotlight from his friend, had left Washington as soon as the inaugural ended—and Nellie preempted his seat, all but trampling several dignitaries in the process.

"For me," Nellie wrote in her memoirs, "the drive [to the White House] was the proudest and happiest event of Inauguration Day." She confessed to "a little secret elation" because she was doing something no First Lady had done before. Some people criticized her for this conspicuous gesture, but Nellie brushed them off. She had never made a secret of her role as Will Taft's political alter ego. A month before they entered the White House, an article in the *Ladies' Home Journal* credited her with having the final say on every move Taft had ever made.

Like Eleanor Roosevelt and other political partners, Nellie issued disclaimers about her influence, but her actions spoke much louder than her words. At their first White House reception, Nellie ignored the protocol that the President enters the East Room first. She charged ahead of Will and had greeted a half dozen guests while he was still working on his first couple. Hostile White House watchers of the Alice Roosevelt camp wondered if Nellie thought she, not her husband, was the President. The First Lady attributed this gaffe to being "nervous and upset." Again, no one suspected that this glimpse of her inner tension was another portent of coming grief.

In the White House, Nellie tried to take charge of everything in sight. But she soon discovered she and Will had tackled a very big job. Their intense involvement with each other and Nellie's jealousy of potential rivals for the presidency had left them with few close friends from whom to seek advice. Instead of charming powerful congressmen and other Washington insiders in the style of shrewd Sarah Polk, Nellie had kept them at arm's length. People were soon murmuring about the President's indecision, as he took months to name a cabinet.

Nellie insisted on joining conferences in the President's office on any and every subject. She claimed, believe it or not, that she was needed to make sure her husband did not fall asleep! Eyewitnesses recall her berating Taft's aides with a ferocity that made their teeth chatter. At receptions the sight of a politician in a private tête-à-tête with her husband brought the First Lady rushing over to make sure Will was not being inveigled into a policy she disapproved.

I am sorry to say Nellie also used her power in petty ways. Some twenty years before, on her honeymoon in Europe, she had asked Henry White, at the time a minor diplomat in the American Embassy in London, for tickets to Parliament. Instead, she and Will had gotten tickets to the Royal Mews—a tourist attraction, to be sure, but not quite on the level of Parliament. She had never forgiven the man. When Nellie became First Lady, firing White became a top priority for the Taft administration. The President hated to do it but finally let Nellie have her way. Ex-President Roosevelt was shocked and outraged. White was a personal friend, currently serving as ambassador to France, and Teddy considered him the finest diplomat in the State Department's ranks.

The incident marked the beginning of a split between Taft and Roosevelt that would eventually wreck the Republican Party. Nellie added fuel to the soon-to-be conflagration by vetoing the appointment of Alice Roosevelt's husband, Nicholas Longworth, a distinguished congressman from Ohio, as ambassador to China. Maybe she had heard about Alice's wicked imitation of her stiff posture and what Alice called her "Cin-cin-nasty" accent. Or perhaps Nellie had found out about that voodoo doll buried on the White House lawn. In any case, shooting down Nick Longworth was a mistake. Backing the nomination would have been a perfect way to get Alice and her savage tongue far away from Washington, D.C.

While Nellie turned alienation into an art, Taft was writing letters to Roosevelt, assuring him he did "nothing in the executive office without considering what you would do under the same circumstances and without having in a sense a mental talk with you over the pros and cons of the situation." The poor man did not seem to realize that he was trapped between two irresistible forces—and he was not an immovable object.

Simultaneously, Nellie was trying to turn her time in the White House into a replay of her reign as queen of the governor's palace in Manila. She fired the traditional ushers virtually en masse and replaced them with an all African-American staff wearing blue livery. For a while she even considered putting the rest of the staff into gaudy uniforms, but she backed off when people began murmuring that her changes were far too regal for a democracy.

Nellie also bounced the steward, who had been responsible for meals and general housekeeping, and hired the first of the housekeepers, a tyrant named Elizabeth Jaffray, who reportedly was a forerunner of Henrietta Nesbitt in terror tactics. Nellie wanted everything "spotless," and Mrs. Jaffray made sure the White House lived up to its name, inside and out. Behind her back the staff murmured that apparently neither the First Lady nor Mrs. Jaffray had heard of the Emancipation Proclamation.

Nellie also embarked on a laudable campaign to get the First Family out of the horse and buggy era. She extracted a twelve-thousand-dollar appropriation from Congress for motorcars, which were already becoming ubiquitous. When she found the prices of the best cars too high, she struck a deal with their manufacturers for a handsome discount, giving them the privilege of advertising their brand as the choice of the White House. I can almost hear what Harry Truman would have to say about such a commercialization of the presidency. Nellie was acting more like a Queen than a First Lady.

Making the car deal even more unpalatable was the fact that the Tafts could easily have afforded to pay a little extra for the models Nellie wanted. Congress, in a fit of uncharacteristic generosity, had just raised the Chief Executive's salary to $75,000, plus a $25,000 travel allowance. According to economist Michael Ahearn, who is good at historical statistics, in those days of low pay and even lower inflation, $100,000 was equivalent to $1.5 million in 1993 dollars, making William Howard Taft the highest-paid President in real dollar terms in our history.

Instead of loosening her purse strings a little, Nellie resolved to save $25,000 a year ($350,000 in today's dollars) from this bonanza.

Mrs. Jaffray was ordered to comparison shop for everything from let-tuce to lamb chops. The First Lady succeeded in departing with $100,000 (again, $1.5 million of our funny money) in the bank at the end of her husband's term.

While Nellie fretted over money and housekeeping minutiae, things drifted politically. President Taft moaned that he felt like a "fish out of water" and confessed he was glad that "my wife is the politician" in the family. The unhappy Chief Executive consoled him-self with his favorite indoor sport: eating. Soon his weight had bal-looned, and the White House plumbers had to install a special bathtub, seven feet long and forty-one inches wide, weighing a ton, to accommodate him.

Recognizing the need for some good publicity, Nellie embarked on a project to beautify Washington. During her Manila days she had been impressed by the throngs that gathered each evening in the city's beautiful waterside park, the Luneta. With some help from the Army officer in charge of public grounds, Nellie chose a road along the Potomac River, renamed it Potomac Drive, and had a bandstand built nearby. On April 17, 1909, she and the President drove down to the site in one of the new White House cars. A crowd of ten thousand gathered around them to enjoy a concert by the U.S. Army band.

The swampy, mosquito-infested landscape along Potomac Drive left a lot to be desired, and Nellie solved that problem with another inspiration from her years in the Far East—the beautiful pink-blossomed cherry trees of Tokyo. She sent out a rush order to all the nurseries in America to ship their Japanese cherry trees to Washing-ton. When only a hundred showed up, the mayor of Tokyo offered another two thousand trees. The first shipment died, but subsequent deliveries created the beautiful cherry blossoms that are one of Wash-ington, D.C.'s spring joys. They would prove to be Nellie Taft's chief accomplishment as First Lady.

Meanwhile, former President Roosevelt and his wife had embarked on a trip around the world. As newspaper stories about their warm reception in various capitals multiplied, Nellie's jealousy of Teddy tended toward paranoia. One report from Naples quoted the ex-

President as saying that if Taft did not carry out his progressive policies, he would return and run him out of the White House. Major Archie Butt, the White House military aide who had also served Roosevelt, told Taft he was sure the story was a fabrication. "Oh I don't know," Nellie said. "It sounded just like him."

By now I think it is all too clear that Nellie was a First Lady under terrific stress. In May 1909, two months after her husband's inauguration, the Tafts and a party of friends, including several cabinet officers, boarded the presidential yacht, *Sylph*, for some much needed relaxation. The First Lady was pale and drawn from an ordeal that had nothing to do with money or politics. Her son Charles had had his adenoids removed that morning. In those days surgery of any kind was life threatening, and Nellie's tense nerves and vivid imagination had redoubled her anxiety. As the *Sylph* plowed toward Mount Vernon, the attorney general sat in a deck chair beside Nellie, making polite conversation. Suddenly he noticed the First Lady's eyes were glazed, her face wooden. She was unconscious.

Nellie was rushed back to the White House, unable to speak, her right side paralyzed by a devastating stroke. The distraught President spent hours each day in her bedroom, helping her regain her speech. He barred all mention of politics from the second floor of the White House, fearing it would trigger another, possibly fatal episode.

On his own as President, Taft soon became the captive of the conservative Republicans in Congress. These retrograde politicos were determined to destroy Theodore Roosevelt's progressive reforms and the easygoing Taft, a conservative by instinct, became their half-hearted collaborator. As one disgusted progressive senator put it, "Yes, Taft carried out Roosevelt's policies. [He] carried them out on a shutter."

As critical letters from progressives reached him abroad, Teddy grew dismayed by Taft's performance. When the Roosevelts returned from their world tour, Edith Roosevelt received an almost incoherent letter from Nellie Taft. She addressed Edith as "Mrs. Roosevelt," as if she were a stranger, and referred to Teddy as "President Roosevelt." Nellie invited them to the White House "soon" but said she was about to retreat to the Taft summer home in Beverly, Massachusetts, to "recuperate" from the White House season.

This mishmash shows how much Nellie's stroke had unraveled her, as well as the Tafts' partnership. They were still concealing her illness from the press, referring to it only in the vague terms used at the time to explain ladies' indispositions. (Taft confessed how serious it was in a letter to Roosevelt, however.) She had recovered the ability to walk, but her speech was slurred and she had to grope for every other word. The letter suggests that she was also not thinking very clearly.

When the Roosevelts visited the Tafts in Beverly later that summer, Nellie insisted on joining the meeting. At first, she scarcely spoke a word because of her speech impediment. Roosevelt told Taft that during his tour of Europe he had encouraged the major powers to convene an international peace conference. With all the industrial nations armed as never before and threatening one another with annihilation, it was an eminently worthwhile proposal. Teddy suggested Andrew Carnegie as a natural choice to lead the American delegation to this conclave. The Pittsburgh industrialist had donated millions to various peace movements. "I don't think Mr. Carnegie would do at all!" Nellie blurted out. She was reacting to press criticism of Taft's tendency to hobnob with millionaires. She did not seem to realize—or care—that she was inflicting yet another wound on the Taft-Roosevelt friendship.

Nellie's speech gradually improved, but her health remained fragile. As late as January 1911, nineteen months after her stroke, Ellen Slayden noted in her journal, "Poor Mrs. Taft is still too ill to take part in anything." Almost certainly the stroke affected the First Lady's political judgment. Her paranoia about Roosevelt made her an easy target for the schemes of Taft's secretary, Charles Norton, a Chicagoan who saw himself as a Machiavelli destined to reshape the Republican Party. Together, he and Nellie relentlessly poisoned Taft's mind against Roosevelt, persuading him to fire still more of TR's appointees, notably Gifford Pinchot, the man who had helped found the conservation movement in America.

Further evidence of deteriorated judgment was Nellie's decision to invite four thousand people to a twenty-fifth wedding anniversary party at the White House. She all but solicited expensive presents from every prince, potentate, politician, and tycoon in the world. The result was a mountain of silver whose total value had to exceed a million dollars. Virtual strangers such as the head of U.S. Steel sent a silver tureen worth eight thousand dollars. John D. Rockefeller came through with an entire cabinet of silver tea caddies. The guests wandered the White House grounds asking each other sotto voce how much they had "put up" to get in. Ellen Slayden, who liked Nellie, was sorry that presents had been permitted. "Many of the Tafts' friends regret it and feel it was a mistake," she said.

By this time Roosevelt had given up on Taft and was openly advertising himself as a candidate for the presidency in 1912. Rather than split their Grand Old Party, Taft was inclined to let him have the Republican nomination. He told Nellie that he was ready to retire "with the consciousness that I have done the best I could." Nellie promptly informed him that he would do no such thing. By this time she was so consumed with hatred of Theodore Roosevelt, she was determined to deny him the presidency, even if the Democrats nominated the Akhond of Swat.

As the incumbent President, Taft controlled enough party machinery to win the Republican nomination. But he had long since lost the confidence of the people. The 1912 campaign was one long humiliation for him. After a particularly abusive assault by Roosevelt, running on the impromptu Progressive Party ticket, Taft broke down. "He's my best friend," he sobbed.

Poor Will carried only two states, one of the worst beatings ever inflicted on a sitting President. But he won enough votes to keep Teddy out of the White House. The winner was the Democratic candidate, Woodrow Wilson, who polled 1,413,728 votes less than the combined Roosevelt-Taft total.

Although I admire Helen Taft's determination to make her woman's voice heard in an era when this was anything but fashionable, objectivity forces me to conclude she was a disaster as a political partner, by almost any standard. Part of this failure must be attributed to bad luck. She had more than her share of strength and courage, two of the three gifts Grace Coolidge said all First Ladies need. But Nellie fatally lacked the third, health.

In spite of all Nellie put him through in the White House, Will Taft, the good-natured old slug, went right on worshiping her. Maybe that proves love really is the mystery of life Victor Herbert said it was in that song.

Chapter 9

—

PARTNERS

IN LOVE

THAT MAGICAL WORD, LOVE, IS A PERFECT TRANSITION TO THE REIGN
of an accidental political partner—one could even call her an accidental First Lady—Edith Bolling Galt Wilson. She was very much
alive when the Trumans came to 1600 Pennsylvania Avenue in 1945,
and I met her several times. My mother maintained a warm correspondence with her.

Formidable is a word that comes readily to mind when I think of
Edith Wilson—large and formidable—and extremely charming
when she wanted to be. My mother often invited her to dinners and
receptions, where she was invariably a Presence. In 1961 John F.
Kennedy invited her to ride in his inaugural parade. By that time she
was in her late eighties, and no one recognized the woman who had
virtually run the country for almost two years in 1919–21.

Ellen Axson Wilson, Woodrow Wilson's first wife, died, readers
will recall, in August 1914. Her grief-stricken husband buried himself
in work, of which there was plenty. In that same month the nations of

Europe had plunged into fratricidal war on a hitherto unimaginable scale, and Americans began arguing violently about which side to support. The President struggled, mostly in vain, to be a mediator between the combatants.

Wilson's fog of personal grief lifted when a rain shower canceled his golf game one March day in 1915 and he found himself drinking tea with the temporary White House hostess, his cousin Helen Bones, and her friend, forty-two-year-old Edith Galt. A widow, Mrs. Galt's interest in politics seemed close to zero. She claimed she had not even known who had been running for President in 1912—an astonishing statement for a resident of Washington, D.C. An astute woman in other ways, Edith Galt successfully managed her late husband's jewelry store, considered the best in the capital. Independent as well, she traveled abroad, bought her stylish clothes in Paris, and drove her own electric automobile.

The lonely fifty-eight-year-old President was smitten from the moment he saw her. Edith's hair was a dark, sultry red; her figure was not uncharitably described as Junoesque—and her apparent political naïveté only increased his ardor. Wilson was essentially a teacher, and he adored the idea of educating this beautiful woman in the intricacies of the subject that was absorbing his every waking hour. At least as important, they were both southerners by birth and upbringing, with exacting preacher fathers. If you believe in destiny—and after a few years in the White House most people subscribe to some version of that faith—here were two souls that seemed meant for each other.

Wilson saw Edith as often as the demands of his office permitted, taking her for rides in White House cars, inviting her to dinners, teas, and even baseball games. By the last week in April, she was dining at the White House every night, and the President was addressing letters to her as "Dear Friend." He talked to her with total frankness about his desperate attempts to play peacemaker between the belligerents in Europe, and his dread that America would be sucked into the war. She confessed that her first marriage had been unhappy and described her well-to-do widow's life as mostly boring and empty. She hinted that she considered herself no longer capable of experiencing love. In her restlessness, she was thinking of a long trip to the Orient.

After dinner on May 4, 1915, Woodrow Wilson took Edith Galt out on the South Portico, with its view of the Washington Monument soaring into the moonlit sky. He told her that he loved her and asked her to marry him. Edith's instinctive response was resistance. She said they had not known each other long enough—she was not sure how she felt about him. Wilson pleaded that in the White House time had a special dimension; days were mere minutes, weeks, hours. In this fearful condensation a lonely man was threatened with destruction. When she returned to her house on Dupont Circle, Edith wrote the President a letter that revealed to him—and perhaps to herself—how deeply he had stirred her:

E.B.G. to W.W.

1308 Twentieth Street
May 4, 1915

Your dear love fills me with a bliss untold
Perfect, divine,
I did not know the human heart could hold
Such joy as mine.
But it does more for me, it makes
The whole world new
Dreams and desires within my soul
it wakes more high and true
Than aught I have ever known
For I do see, with sad surprise
how far I am beneath your thought of me.
For, lover wise, you've crowned me queen
of grace and truth and light
All pure and good
In utter faith have set me on the height of womanhood.
Since you exalt me thus, I must
not prove your wisdom vain,
Unto those mighty heights, oh help me
wondrous love I must attain!

Edith described "this little poem" as something she had learned "years ago," never dreaming that someday it would perfectly express what was in her heart. She went on to assure Wilson that she wanted to help him. She would consider it an "unspeakable pleasure and privilege to be allowed to share these tense terrible days of responsibility.... I am a woman—and the thought that you have need of me is sweet!" She ended by pledging him "all that is best in me—to help, to sustain, to comfort" and sent her spirit "into the space that separates us to seek yours. Make it a welcome guest."

Scholars now think Edith is the author of the poem. Libraries have been ransacked without finding the original. While she was writing it and the letter that followed, Wilson lay sleepless in the White House in near despair, thinking he had been rejected. In the dawn he wrote her a letter which began with a sonnet from Shakespeare, "When to the sessions of sweet silent thought," and another poem in sonnet form which he may have written himself, about the song of a thrush to his mate at morning, and how it reminded him of her. He told her he would try to bear his grief and dismay—"terrible companions in the still night." He ended by begging her not to go to the Orient. "Don't put every burden on me," he pleaded.

Edith's letter crossed this one and enabled the sleep-starved Wilson to stagger through a day of mounting international tension. The Germans were smashing the British and French on the Western Front and rampaging into Russia. The secretary of state, William Jennings Bryan, impatient with the pro-Allied tilt to Wilson's neutrality, was threatening to embarrass him by resigning. The President responded to Edith that night, in spite of being "infinitely tired—in brain and body and spirit." Her letter, he wrote, was

the most beautiful note I ever read, whose possession makes me rich.

Every glimpse I am permitted to get of the secret depths of you I find them deeper and purer and more beautiful than I knew or had dreamed of. If you cannot give me all *that I want ... it is because I am not worthy. I know instinctively you could* give it if I were—*and if you understood— understood the boy's heart that is in me and the simplicity of my need, which you could fill so that all my days could be radiant.*

He begged her to stop thinking of him as a "public man." He told her she had not yet "looked with full comprehension on your friend and lover, Woodrow Wilson." He described himself as a "longing man, in the midst of the world's affairs, a world that knows nothing of the heart he has shown you and which would as lief break it as not." He could not face this wolfish world with his "full strength" unless she loved him.

Could any woman on earth resist such a proposal? Especially since this response had barely reached Edith Galt's door when the most horrifying news of the war exploded in Wilson's face. A German submarine had torpedoed the thirty-two-thousand-ton British luxury liner *Lusitania* off the Irish coast, drowning over 1,000 men, women, and children, including 124 Americans. More than two thousand telegrams demanding war with Germany poured into the White House. On top of this came shocking British reports of German atrocities in Belgium. After the war, almost all were found to be fabrications, but at the time most Americans believed them.

Secretary of State Bryan whipsawed the President by insisting the drowned Americans should not have been on the *Lusitania* in the first place. He tended to believe the German contention that the liner was carrying weapons as well as passengers. (We now know it was.) The anguished Wilson turned to Edith for advice. She responded with bewilderment: "Why should I be chosen to help you? ... The thought makes me tremble and grow afraid."

Previously Wilson had told her about his problems with Bryan, and she had responded mischievously that he should fire the secretary of state and appoint her in his place, so she could see him every day. But she soon realized the *Lusitania* crisis had carried them to a far more serious point in their political and personal relationship.

Wilson's response was a long letter, at the heart of which was embedded a simple cry: "I *need* you." He begged her not to doubt that "blessed fact." He urged her to think of him as he worked on a speech he was scheduled to make in Philadelphia to four thousand newly naturalized citizens and also on his note to Germany about the *Lusitania*. "Every sentence would have greater force and meaning if I could feel your mind and heart were keeping me company," he wrote.

Edith rushed to the White House and gave Wilson her reply in writing as he was leaving for Philadelphia: "If you with your wonderful love can quicken that which has lain dead so long within me, I promise not to shut it out of my heart but bid it welcome—and come to you with the joy of it in my eyes."

It would be nice to report that Wilson's speech in Philadelphia was a huge success. It was full of soaring rhetoric about the meaning of America and the value of the chance a free society gave immigrants for a new life. But at the close he could not resist a comment on his neutrality policy: "There is such a thing as a man being too proud to fight. There is such a thing as a nation being so right that it does not need to convince others by force that it is right."

Ex-President Theodore Roosevelt led a chorus of denunciations, accusing Wilson of moral double-talk and rank cowardice. But Wilson stuck to his policy. His note to Germany was stern but did not threaten war. Edith was now a presence in this struggle. "Oh, how I have needed you tonight, my sweet Edith," the President wrote. "What a touch of your hand and a look into your eyes would have meant to me of strength and steadfastness as I made the final decision as to what I should say to Germany." Later, when he had finished the note, he told her that he felt "you have been by my side all evening, for a strange sense of peace and love has been on me as I worked."

As spring lengthened into summer, Wilson's passion for Edith intensified. He saw her so often—on the presidential yacht, at the White House, in impromptu visits to her house—tongues began to wag. His closest advisers started to worry about the impact of a hasty marriage on his chances for reelection. Meanwhile, one of his old loves, Mary Hulbert Peck, showed up at the White House demanding a loan of seventy-five hundred dollars to bail her son out of bankruptcy. All his life Wilson had been attracted to pretty, vivacious women. His first wife, Ellen, had been amazingly tolerant of these infatuations, most of which remained platonic. But Mrs. Peck may have been an exception. She had letters from Wilson that would have ruined him politically if she showed them to a newspaperman. He gave her the money—a mistake.

Meanwhile, Edith inspired him to get tough with the Germans. They had answered his *Lusitania* note in a rather obnoxious way. Wilson told Edith that "when I see your eyes alight with the holiest thing in the world and hold you close in my arms and kiss you with pledges as deep as my soul," he was ready to give the Germans the answer they deserved. I hate to criticize a President my father considered one of our greatest, but there are times during his pursuit of Edith when Wilson seems unhinged.

He showed her a draft of his reply to the Germans, and she assailed it with startling severity. "There was nothing of you, yourself, in it and therefore it seemed flat and colorless," she told him.

Wilson went back to work on the note. "I have strengthened it in many ways and hope I have brought it nearer the standard my precious sweetheart, out of her great love, expects of me," he wrote. Has any other woman gone from managing a jewelry shop to influencing the course of world history in four months? Edith Galt's ascent leaves one openmouthed.

The revised note was so tough, Secretary of State Bryan said it would lead straight to war and refused to sign it. Edith told Wilson to let Bryan go. On the day he resigned, shaking the Democratic Party to its foundations—his support had won Wilson the nomination in 1912—the President wrote Edith three letters.

She responded to these and other messages about politics with rapture. "Much as I enjoy your delicious love letters," she wrote, "I believe I enjoy even more the ones in which you tell me what you are working on ... for then I feel I am being taken into partnership as it were." There was the magical word that won Edith's hitherto empty heart.

Escaping Washington's beastly summer, Edith retreated to Cornish, New Hampshire, where Wilson soon joined her. Surrounded by carefully chosen friends and relatives, they managed to keep the press at bay. On June 29 they consummated their love and Edith responded with

A Pledge:
I promise with all my heart absolutely to trust and accept my loved Lord and unite my life with his without doubts or misgivings.

During the rest of that summer of love and into the fall, Woodrow Wilson shared every aspect of his presidency with Edith. He showed her notes from the German Foreign Office, from the Mexican President, from Haiti (a headache then as now), from the American ambassador to England, often laced with critical comments that would have provoked an international upheaval if she had mentioned them to anyone. He was taking with utmost seriousness the task of educating Edith to be his political partner.

Gradually, this heady combination of love and political power made Edith critical of the men around Wilson. She took an especially strong dislike to his secretary, Joseph Tumulty, partly because of what she called his "commonness" and partly because he was emphatic about urging Wilson not to marry Mrs. Galt before the 1916 elections.

Tumulty was a shrewd, affable Irish American from Jersey City. Without him Wilson would never have survived his political baptism as governor of New Jersey. In the White House, he kept Wilson in touch with shifts in public mood and was the President's chief liaison with Congress and the press.

Next Edith went to work on Colonel Edward House, the Texan who had made himself invaluable to Wilson as his personal envoy to the warring powers. From reading his letters, Edith decided he was a "weak vessel." Wilson thought she was "partly right" but defended the colonel, who had played a crucial role in his 1912 campaign, as a "noble and lovely character." Nevertheless, a wound had been inflicted on this relationship too.

In October of 1915, Wilson and Mrs. Galt announced their engagement. This inspired Wilson's secretary of the treasury, William Gibbs McAdoo, to try to scare the President into renouncing or at least delaying marriage. McAdoo, who had married the President's daughter Eleanor in 1914, hoped to succeed Wilson in 1920. He said he had received an anonymous letter from California, warning him that Mary Hulbert Peck was threatening to release Wilson's compromising letters to the press—and reveal his even more compromising seventy-five-hundred-dollar loan.

A distraught Wilson's first thought was not of the damage to his presidency but of Edith. He told her the whole story of his indiscretion with Mrs. Peck and offered to release her from their engagement. That only made her love him more than ever. "I will stand by you—not for duty, not for honor—but for love—trusting protecting, comprehending love," she told him. Negotiators managed to defuse Mrs. Peck.

On December 18, 1915, the President and Mrs. Galt were married at her house on Twentieth Street and took a train to Hot Springs, West Virginia, for a honeymoon at the palatial Homestead Hotel. When Colonel Edmund Starling, the head of the Secret Service detail, entered the presidential car the next morning, he saw Wilson, still in his wedding tailcoat, top hat, and gray morning trousers, whistling a tune. As the startled Starling watched, the President clicked his heels in the air and began singing: "Oh you beautiful doll! You great big beautiful doll!"

Wilson's renewed zest for life may well have had a lot to do with the vigorous campaign he waged for reelection in 1916. He became the first Democrat to win a second consecutive term since Andrew Jackson in 1832. Edith accompanied her husband everywhere. When he introduced her from the platform, she received enormous applause, proving the American people were far less stodgy than Wilson's cautious advisers with their worries about him offending "standards" by marrying too soon after his first wife's death.

On the second floor of the White House, where Ellen Axson Wilson and her husband had maintained separate bedrooms, the huge Lincoln bed was moved into Wilson's room and the new First Couple shared it nightly. They spent almost as much time together during the day. Edith sat beside the President in the Oval Office from eight to ten thirty while he answered mail and signed documents. Usually she spent this time reading important diplomatic messages in "the drawer"—the most secret part of Wilson's desk—often decoding them in the process.

At White House receptions, Wilson taught Edith how to shake hands hundreds of times without winding up in a hospital for special surgery. His formula was to put the middle finger down and cross the index and ring finger above it. That way, people could not get a grip and the welcomer's hand slid through the guest's hand almost

Edith Wilson often worked in the Oval Office beside Woodrow Wilson. She frequently read confidential papers in the diplomatic drawer of his desk. *(AP/Wide World Photos)*

untouched. Edith claimed Wilson's technique worked beautifully. At any rate, she was a great success as a White House hostess.

When Colonel House returned from Europe, he was shocked to discover that Wilson expected him to report his supersecret negotiations with the warring powers not only to the President but to the First Lady. Ever the diplomat, the Texan struck a secret deal with Edith—in return for her support, he would help her get rid of Tumulty, whom he considered a rival as well as a political liability because he was a Catholic. Their unsavory intrigue, which did neither of them any credit, seemed to triumph when Wilson yielded to Edith's repeated urging and fired Tumulty at the beginning of his second term. But the heartbroken New Jerseyan, who worshiped Wilson, begged the President to change his mind and Wilson relented. Tumulty had no illusions about who had tried to cut his throat. The result left Wilson woven in a web of antagonistic advisers, not a good formula for sound politics or presidential peace of mind.

Soon after his reelection, Wilson's renewed attempts to build momentum for a negotiated "peace without victory" collapsed when Germany announced it would resume unrestricted submarine warfare and began sinking American ships. The President asked Congress to declare war in a magnificent speech that converted the decision into a crusade to make the world safe for democracy. How many times I heard my father describe the way that speech transformed Missouri and the rest of the Midwest, where people had voted for Wilson on the basis of the 1916 campaign slogan, "He kept us out of war."

Edith continued to work at the President's side as America plunged into a frantic effort to create an army and ship it to France before Germany won the war. She introduced austerity into White House entertaining, joined the Red Cross, and bought some sheep to trim the White House lawn, releasing men for war work. When Wilson, tormented by the thought of young Americans dying in France, drove himself relentlessly, she turned protector and coaxed him away from his desk to go horseback riding or take a night off at the theater. Dr. Cary Grayson, the White House physician, had warned Edith that Wilson suffered from arteriosclerosis, making overwork especially dangerous for him, because it increased the risk of a stroke or heart attack.

After some harrowing months in the spring of 1918, when it looked as if massive German offensives on the Western Front were unstoppable, the weight of American manpower and the exhaustion of the German army and civilian populace ended the war with startling suddenness on November 11, 1918. The Germans accepted an armistice based on Wilson's proposals for a negotiated peace. But this good news came too late to rescue Wilson and the Democratic Party from a dismaying defeat in the 1918 congressional elections, giving the Republicans control of both houses of Congress.

At least part of the cause of the debacle was the ongoing feud between Edith and Joe Tumulty. He had urged the President to issue a call for a Democratic Congress to support him in the peace negotiations. Edith wanted the President to appear nonpartisan—above politics—in the midst of a war. The Republicans, led by Teddy Roosevelt, denounced Wilson's idea of a negotiated peace and called for Germany's unconditional surrender. They persuaded American voters to all but repudiate the President. A furious Edith became even more hostile to Tumulty's opinions—and more sure of her own.

Wilson had been working on a draft of his idea for a League of Nations to prevent another war. He still wanted a peace without victory (without vengeance and punishment) and wondered if he should go to Europe to make sure it was achieved. All his advisers—Colonel House, Joe Tumulty, his son-in-law McAdoo—urged him to stay home and let his secretary of state do the negotiating. They feared the British and French, bitter over their terrible battlefield losses, were going to insist on peace terms that were far from Wilson's benevolence. Only Edith told Wilson he *must* go.

We have seen—and will see—other occasions when First Ladies changed the course of history. But this advice from Edith Wilson must rank near the top of any conceivable list. Most historians have concluded it was bad advice. Not only was it a mistake for the President to handle difficult negotiations personally—he also abandoned domestic politics at the worst possible time, with his Republican enemies in control of Congress.

With Edith at his side, Woodrow Wilson toured Europe while millions cheered. But this hero worship turned many Americans against the President and his First Lady. They seemed oblivious to soaring inflation and serious labor unrest back home. The year 1919 saw a staggering thirty-six hundred strikes. With its leader three thousand miles away, the Democratic Party drifted, headless and divided. Worse, at Edith's urging, the President jettisoned Colonel House and other advisers he had brought to Paris, making himself largely responsible for the peace conference's results.

Wilson came home with a treaty that was a virtual parody of a peace without victory. It saddled the Germans with huge reparations that wrecked their economy and forced them to accept a clause stating they were guilty of starting the war. Wilson admitted the treaty was imperfect, but he claimed the defects could be corrected in the

League of Nations. He attached the "Covenant" for this great experiment in idealism to the treaty, demanding that the Republican-controlled Senate ratify both in the same vote. The reply to this political brinkmanship was a resounding *no*.

Although the President was exhausted from the strain of months of negotiating in Paris, he decided to take his case to the American people and scheduled a whistle-stop tour across the nation. Edith and Dr. Grayson tried to talk him out of it, but he dismissed their pleas. With passionate idealism that awed and thrilled her, Wilson reminded his wife that he had sent Americans to die in the trenches of the Western Front to achieve this treaty, which he saw as a guarantee of world peace. "I cannot put my personal safety, my health, in the balance against my duty," he said. "I must go."

In blistering September heat, Wilson struggled through the hostile Midwest to California, where he drew huge, cheering crowds. By then he was teetering on the brink of collapse, tortured by insomnia, headaches, and attacks of indigestion and asthma. "Let's stop," Edith begged him. "Let's go somewhere and rest!" Wilson refused. He had become a President even the most loving wife could not protect from himself and the murderous pressures of history.

In Pueblo, Colorado, Wilson's condition became truly alarming. One side of his face collapsed, he could barely talk, and he wept uncontrollably. Edith canceled the rest of the trip. The train raced back to Washington with the President writhing in agony. Alas, the rescue was too late. Three days after he returned to the White House, Wilson suffered a massive stroke that left him paralyzed on one side. For days he lay in a coma. One historian has called it a "wonder and tragedy" that he lived. It is hard not to agree with both sides of that observation.

Even after he emerged from the coma, Woodrow Wilson was incapacitated within the meaning of that word in the Constitution, and he could, perhaps should, have been removed from office. But many of the people around him objected strenuously to abandoning the White House. The First Lady was not one of them. In her memoirs she told of asking the doctors if they thought the President should resign. The neurologist in charge of the case convinced her, she claimed, that doing so would deprive Wilson of his motivation to recover. It would be better if he remained President, providing she could protect him from "every disturbing problem" for several months.

Edith asked him how this tranquillity could be achieved at 1600 Pennsylvania Avenue. The doctor told her it was up to her to screen the problems and select the very few that merited the President's attention. The neurologist insisted that Wilson's mind was unimpaired by the illness—a judgment historians now consider ludicrous. Even in 1918 the doctor should have known that "mind" involves more than abstract thinking. While his mental processes retained their clarity, the President's emotional makeup was profoundly altered. He wept with no warning, grew vastly agitated over trifles, and developed an almost paranoid view of his political opponents. This was not difficult, I should add; the enmity between Wilson and Senator Henry Cabot Lodge, the leader of the Republican opposition, was lethal well before Wilson's collapse.

Edith naturally shared this view of Lodge, who was willing to accept the treaty and the League of Nations only with numerous "reservations" to protect American sovereignty. She and others in the inner circle feared that if Wilson resigned, the vice president, Thomas Marshall, would be willing to compromise with Lodge. The struggle became a clash between idealism and realism. Unquestionably, Woodrow Wilson was a great spokesman for the idealistic side of the American character. But in 1919 his damaged brain was unable to distinguish the limits of idealism in politics.

When he was healthy Wilson had been a genius at making such distinctions. He used to tell a story about a steamboat that bumped into a mudflat on a dark night on the Mississippi. One of the passengers asked the captain why he did not steer by the stars, which glittered brightly above them in a clear sky. "We are not going that way," the captain said. A ship can steer by the stars on the open ocean, but they are useless on a river. Like the captain, the politician has to follow the winding course of the darkened river of national life and occasionally collide with unexpected obstacles.

A great many Democratic senators, Wilson's secretary of state, Robert Lansing, Colonel House, Tumulty, and Lord Grey, the British special ambassador, thought Wilson should compromise with Lodge and the Republicans. But the President remained intransigent, and the First Lady, keeper of the presidential sickroom, declined to let any of them present their arguments. Colonel House's numerous letters were never even opened until the Wilson papers were deposited in the Library of Congress in 1952.

Once, as the struggle roared to a climax, Edith wavered, trying to rescue her husband from his self-imposed ordeal. She urged him to accept Senator Lodge's reservations "and get this awful thing settled."

"Little girl," Wilson said. "Don't you desert me. That I cannot stand. Better a thousand times to go down fighting than to dip your colors in dishonorable compromise."

On November 19, 1919, the Senate voted on the treaty and the league. Wilson needed a two-thirds majority. Instead he was buried in a tidal wave of nays, fifty-three to thirty-eight. Toward midnight the First Lady tiptoed into the sickroom to tell her husband. She was trembling inwardly; she thought the news might kill him. Instead, after a long silence, he said: "All the more reason why I must get well."

For the next six months, Edith continued to be the gatekeeper of his room. In the 1970s her story was dramatized in a TV show entitled *The First Woman President.* Edith Wilson would have objected strongly to such a term. She described her regime as a "stewardship." She said that first, Woodrow Wilson was "my beloved husband" and, second, he was "President of the United States." She insisted she never made a "single decision" on public affairs, she only decided "what was important and what was not."

However, anyone who has ever worked in the White House knows that the power to make such decisions can often be tantamount to running the country—or letting it run itself and hoping for the best. During the early months of his illness, Wilson's cabinet officers, spooked by the rise of Communism in Russia and left-wing agitation elsewhere in Europe, sided with big business in breaking a miners' strike and numerous other union walkouts, alienating millions of workers from the Democratic Party. The attorney general, Mitchell Palmer, expelled thousands of "aliens" with total disregard for their civil rights, dismaying influential liberals. By doing nothing to stop these disastrous policies, Edith gave them the President's tacit approval.

As Wilson's condition improved, Edith almost certainly played an important role in a decision that had a devastating impact on the President's public image. The First Lady regarded Secretary of State Robert Lansing with loathing because he had shown up at the White House soon after Wilson's collapse and insisted the President be replaced immediately. While Wilson lay paralyzed, the secretary had chaired some twenty cabinet meetings over a four-month period to deal with the nation's business; he had not received a word of reproach from the second floor of the White House. Suddenly, in February 1920, a note from the Wilson asked him how he dared to do such a thing without the President's authority—and demanded Lansing's resignation. The newspapers exploded with outrage. One called it "Wilson's Last Mad Act."

Cut off from Tumulty, who sent letter after letter of advice that Edith discarded, Wilson's political judgment grew almost pathetically bad. Although the President was incapable of working for more than a half hour a day, he became a candidate for a third term, hoping to make the election a referendum on the lost treaty and league. The Democratic Party spurned its crippled leader. Undeterred, he issued a statement calling the election of 1920 a referendum, even if he was not running. The American people responded by giving Woodrow Wilson a historic kick in the teeth. With women, supposedly more idealistic, voting for the first time, the Republicans won in a stupendous landslide.

I am not blaming Edith Wilson for this sad close to her political partnership. She was an intelligent woman, and she must have known Wilson was no longer capable of making sound decisions. Her dilemma is summed up in an undated note on a scrap of paper, found among Woodrow Wilson's papers:

My Darling:

Whenever I fail to live up to the great standards your dear love has set for me a passion of sorrow and remorse sweeps over me which my self control cannot always withstand.

Your own
Woodrow

I love you! I love you! I love you!

That says it all. Love was First Lady Edith Wilson's triumph—and her immolation. Maybe—a really unnerving thought—love and politics do not mix very well.

Chapter 10

—

THE
MOST CANDID
PARTNER

I AM NOT SUGGESTING LOVE SHOULD BE BARRED FROM THE WHITE House. On the contrary, it is an inescapable part of the President–First Lady equation. How it operates varies immensely from couple to couple. In the case of Betty and Gerald Ford, love was the secret ingredient in a First Lady's readiness to unleash controversial opinions that made national headlines. She and her husband remained loving political partners even though at one point he told her she had cost him twenty million votes.

Betty Bloomer Ford's vivid performance as our most candid First Lady has made her memorable. To further understand her meteoric trip through the political stratosphere, we need to remember how she reached the White House. Gerald Ford was the first unelected President in American history. He was appointed vice president by Richard Nixon to replace the disgraced Spiro Agnew little more than ten months before President Nixon himself was forced to resign or face the threat of impeachment in the Watergate scandal. No President and First Lady ever entered the White House with a more tenu-ous grasp on their legitimacy. Neither the Fords nor their advisers nor the American people expected them to be there for more than the remaining two and a half years of Richard Nixon's term.

This sense of being temporary played a strong part in encouraging Betty Ford to be herself and to express unorthodox opinions. She did not feel that she was harming her husband's political career—which seemed to be ending with this fillip of honor and prestige. She had already extracted a "blood oath" that he would retire from Congress in 1976. On that hot August day in 1974, as she gripped the Bible on which her husband vowed to uphold the Constitution, Betty thought, "My God, what a job I have to do!"

Note the use of the first person singular. At that point, Betty saw herself as the partner with more freedom to influence events. It was not clear that an unelected President could be more than a caretaker. It took Jerry Ford several months to acquire a sense of himself as Pres-ident and begin thinking that he might be good enough at the job to run for election. By that time Betty had acquired a reputation for can-dor that was unique among First Ladies.

In his inaugural remarks, Jerry Ford testified to his bond with Betty. He declared he came to the presidency "obligated to no man and to only one woman, my dear wife." Unquestionably, Betty Ford returned that love. But when you examine her life, you discover a woman who had trouble loving some aspects of being a political wife. As leader of the Republican minority in the House of Representatives, Jerry Ford was on the road, speaking at fund-raisers and party gatherings over two hundred nights a year, leaving Betty to raise their four children pretty much on her own. Jerry's great ambition was to elect enough Republicans to make him Speaker of the House of Representatives—a job he is not alone in rating the second most powerful post in the federal government.

In 1970, while Jerry continued to pursue this elusive prize, Betty found herself talking to a psychiatrist. Eighteen months with an understanding therapist helped her deal with her anger and loneli-ness and convinced her it was important to express her own thoughts and feelings more often—a conclusion that strongly influenced her performance as First Lady.

Another factor was Americans' low opinion of the prevailing level of honesty in Washington, D.C. in 1974. With Spiro Agnew pleading nolo contendere to charges of bribery and President Nixon engulfed by the labyrinthine cover-ups of Watergate, there was a strongly felt need for some frank talk in our nation's capital. Betty Ford was ready to supply it.

Her decision perfectly fitted her personality and inclinations. But most people forget she was also acting on the principle that her husband, in his inaugural remarks, declared would be the bedrock of his presidency: "I believe truth is the glue that holds government together," he said. "Not only our government but civilization itself.... I expect to follow my instincts of openness and candor with full confidence that honesty is always the best policy in the end."

Although she is another First Lady who seemed to be the antithesis of Bess Truman in many ways, Betty has told me that my mother was one of her inspirations in the White House. She admired her because Bess did not let eight years in the glare of the presidential spotlight change her. She remained "humble." That is not an adjective I would volunteer to describe my mother, who was the granddaughter of one of the richest men in Independence, and in private did not hesitate to tell people exactly what she thought about a lot of things. I think what Betty shared with Bess Truman was a midwestern dislike for any and all kinds of pretentiousness.

While Betty never tried to hide her views—during the few months her husband was vice president she startled reporters by casually admitting she took a Valium a day—she also did not go looking for confrontations. When she was asked if she had a favorite good cause, she shook her head and ran through a veritable laundry list of "interests," from the ballet (she had been a dancer in her youth) to handicapped children to better treatment for senior citizens. As First Lady she gave time to all these things. But she never even mentioned the cause that meant the most to her: woman's rights in general and the Equal Rights Amendment in particular.

On other issues in the early months of the Ford presidency, Betty was often more cautious than her husband. When he decided to pardon President Richard Nixon, putting an end to talk of prosecuting him for his Watergate malfeasances, the First Lady warned him not to do it. She foresaw the political uproar that ensued. But Gerald Ford insisted he was acting in the country's—not Richard Nixon's—best interest. During his first month in the Oval Office, Jerry spent twenty-five percent of his time wrestling with questions surrounding Nixon's fate. He decided it was time to put Watergate and its attendant nightmares behind us. When he issued the pardon, Betty Ford said nothing about their disagreement.

Then Betty had an experience which profoundly strengthened her inclination toward candor. In September, a little more than a month after she and Jerry took over the White House, she was diagnosed as suffering from breast cancer. Living in those "eighteen acres under glass," it was impossible to hide the illness from the press. But it could have been handled in hush-hush fashion. After talking it over with Jerry and her children, Betty decided to be as frank and forthcoming as possible. Members of the press were given all the information they needed to report the course of her surgery and recovery.

As 55,800 cards and letters from women who had survived the disease or feared they might have it flooded into the White House, Betty realized the power of what she likes to call "the office of First Lady." Her forthrightness had apparently encouraged millions of worried women to seek breast examinations. She had also emboldened doctors to talk more frankly about this form of cancer than ever before. Betty admitted to me that she was uncomfortable with this publicity about her surgery at first: "I felt people were asking whenever I appeared in public: 'Which one did she lose?' But I got over it by reminding myself how much good I'd accomplished."

There is a side story to Betty's struggle with cancer which explains why I and so many other people like her so much. It demonstrates her courage and makes it clear that she did not publicize her illness out of any neurotic desire for sympathy. On her schedule, before she learned the bad news, was an engagement with Lady Bird Johnson and her daughters to dedicate the LBJ Memorial Grove, a cluster of white pine trees planted along the Potomac in memory of the Lone Star State's only President. Betty insisted on keeping this date and invited the Johnsons back to the White House for tea and a tour of the private quarters without saying a word about her condition. Only after they parted did she hurry to Bethesda Naval Hospital to prepare for her surgery the next morning.

Not long after the operation, Betty Ford held a press conference at which she announced to 150 reporters that she was going to support the Equal Rights Amendment. It had taken a lot of midnight floor pacing and long talks with her husband to reach this turning point in the history of First Ladies. Forty-two years earlier, when Eleanor Roosevelt had held the first ever press conference by a President's wife, she had promised to avoid serious issues and any and all comment on pending legislation.

A lot had changed since the 1930s. The woman's rights revolution of the 1960s had made it far less shocking for a First Lady to take a

Betty and Jerry Ford share a private moment in the White House. Betty used "pillow talk" to persuade Jerry to appoint numerous women to high posts. *(Ford Library)*

stand. But Betty's declaration was still an act of considerable political courage. When we discussed it, however, she scotched the idea that she was disagreeing with her husband. On the contrary, she stressed the way the Ford partnership had supported her decision. "Jerry had rounded up crucial votes to get the ERA onto the floor of Congress when it was passed in 1972," she told me. "He felt I had a perfect right to speak out on the issue. The Republican Party had included the ERA in its platform at many national conventions."

Early in 1975 President Ford affirmed his support by issuing an executive order establishing a national commission on the observance of International Women's Year. The Fords hoped this would create a positive aura that would reinforce the ERA's chances for ratification.

At the time of Betty's announcement, the ERA was struggling to win approval from three more states to reach the two-thirds required for a constitutional amendment before the ten-year deadline for its adoption expired. Betty Ford became the first First Lady to "work the phones," as the professional pols call it, direct from the White House to state capitals like Jefferson City, Missouri, urging legislators to vote for the ERA.

Betty tried to make her approach as low-keyed as possible. She claimed she just wanted to let wavering legislators know that she and the President were "considerably interested" in ERA. She told recalcitrant antis she admired "the sincerity" of their opposition but hoped they would change their minds. Unfortunately, no matter how hard she tried to avoid it, Betty found herself in the middle of a raging political conflict.

Opposition to the ERA ran deep in many parts of the country, from Phyllis Schlafly's conservative followers to huge swatches of the southern and midwestern Bible Belt, where Protestant clergy—and quite a few Catholic priests—saw the amendment as an attempt to loosen moral standards and ratify abortion rights. Letters to the editor blossomed in papers around the country, accusing Betty of "arm-twisting" tactics. Marchers paraded in front of the White House chanting: "Betty Ford is trying to press a second-rate manhood on

American women." The mail flooding the White House post office was three to one against her.

Betty tried to reef her sails in this political squall. She made it clear that she was not a member of NOW or any other branch of the women's movement. She denied she was a "wild-eyed liberal" and reminded people she had four grown children and had enjoyed being a wife and mother. She was not trying to denigrate women who stayed home and raised their children. She saw the ERA as a fight for equal opportunity, equal freedom of choice, for women in the future.

Straddling was good politics for the First Lady but not for the ERA. The amendment won in Nevada but lost in Missouri and other swing states as the apostles of the status quo carried the day. Betty turned her attention to a better deal for women inside the Ford administration. She played no small part in persuading her husband to appoint Carla Hills his secretary of housing and urban development—and Anne Armstrong the ambassador to Great Britain. She spent a lot of what she called "pillow talk" hours trying to get him to appoint a woman to the Supreme Court.

Betty's ERA exercise in political outspokenness had identified her as a new kind of First Lady. That made an invitation to CBS's top-rated news show, *60 Minutes*, virtually inevitable. She appeared on August 21, 1975, eleven days after her husband had announced he was going to seek the GOP nomination in 1976.

Betty told me she went on the air with no inkling that her host, Morley Safer, had any controversial questions in mind. Suddenly she found herself being asked what she thought of the Supreme Court's ruling on abortion rights. She said it was "the best thing in the world...a great great decision." Safer asked what she thought about smoking marijuana. If it had been available in her youth, Betty replied, she would have tried it. What did she think of premarital sex? She did not "personally favor it," Betty said. But she thought it might lower the divorce rate.

What would she say if her seventeen-year-old daughter Susan told her she was having an affair? Betty said she would not be surprised. "She's a perfectly normal human being." She added that she would counsel Susan on the matter and would want to know a lot about the young man.

At the marijuana remark, Jerry Ford, watching with Betty in Vail, Colorado (the show had been taped earlier), reportedly gasped: "You just cost me ten million votes!" At the premarital sex reply, he groaned: "Twenty million!" When I discussed this episode with Betty, she described these remarks as "facetious." Alas, there was nothing humorous about the public's reaction to the show.

The next morning, newspaper headlines across the country told people what Betty had said, and the White House post office was buried in an avalanche that made the number of letters received on the ERA seem like a light dusting, to use weatherman lingo. Twenty-eight thousand Americans told Betty Ford they were very, very mad at her. A paltry seven thousand supported her frankness.

A Dallas preacher roared that Betty had descended to a "gutter type of mentality." A New Hampshire newspaper editor howled that she had "disgraced the nation." A Texan informed her that she was "not an individual. You are, because of the position your husband has assumed, expected and officially required to be PERFECT!" America's foremost evangelist, Billy Graham, swayer of umpteen million mostly Republican votes, said his wife would have wept if one of his children confessed to using drugs or having an affair.

The Ford White House reeled in this media firestorm. Betty's answers had challenged the core of Jerry Ford's political persona. As President watchers such as Richard Reeves pointed out, being Mr. Nice Guy, doing his best to avoid making people angry at him, had been the basic idea of his career. His positions on abortion, drugs, and premarital sex reflected the largely conservative Republican Michigan constituency he had represented for almost thirty years.

Most accounts of Betty as First Lady skip this part of the story and blithely tell their readers that people eventually got around to admiring Betty for her frankness. These writers never spent any time inside the White House. Twenty-eight thousand negative letters do not make for laughs or blithe dismissals. If that many people are mad enough to sit down and write a letter, it suggests there may be another

2,800,000 out there sounding off to their friends and relatives. "The President," Ron Nessen told Betty's press secretary, in what was almost certainly an understatement, "is very upset."

What to do? Betty being Betty, she had no intention of changing her convictions. She was—and is—exactly what one of her surgeons described her as: "a gutsy lady." She remained convinced that a majority of Americans agreed with her remarks—or at least felt she had a right to express her opinions. But how to reach them? As she discussed the crisis with her staff, they began to suspect the heart of the problem was a clash between TV and newsprint. Chatting with Morley Safer, Betty had expressed the same personal opinions she might have offered in a conversation with any visitor to the White House. Safer had not debated these issues with her. They had passed on to other subjects. If the remarks had been left in verbal form, they might have caused far less fuss. But the print journalists had turned them into issues and blasted them into people's faces with headlines and reams of analysis.

Betty and her staff decided the only thing to do was fight print with print. They spent weeks drafting what they eventually called "the letter." It is a very interesting document, a veritable masterpiece of First Lady spin control. It also happened to be an accurate description of Betty Ford's views:

> *Thank you for writing about my appearance on the* 60 Minutes *interview. The concern which inspired you to share your views is appreciated. I wish it were possible for us to sit down and talk, one to another. I consider myself a responsible parent. I know I am a loving one. We have raised our four children in a home that believes in and practices the enduring values of morality and personal integrity.*
>
> *As every mother and father knows, these are not easy times to be a parent. Our convictions are constantly being tested by the fads and fancies of the moment. I believe our values to be eternal and I hope I have instilled them in our children.*
>
> *We have come to this sharing of outlook through communication, not coercion. I want my children to know that their concerns—their doubts*

and difficulties—whatever they may be, can be discussed with the two people in this world who care the most—their mother and father.

On 60 Minutes *the emotion of my words spoke to the need of this communication, rather than the specific issues discussed.*

My husband and I have lived twenty-six years of faithfulness in marriage. I do not believe in premarital relations, but I realize that many in today's generation do not share my views. However, this must never cause us to withdraw the love, the counseling and the understanding that they may need now, more than ever before.

This is the essence of my responsible parenthood. It is difficult to adequately express one's personal convictions in a fifteen minute interview. I hope our lives will say more than words about our dedication to honor, to integrity, to humanity and to God. You and I, they and I, have no quarrels.

The letter went out over Betty's signature to those thousands of angry First Lady watchers. One of them sent it to the Associated Press, who put it on its ubiquitous wires, and it was picked up by hundreds of other newspapers, including *The New York Times.*

Slowly, *very* slowly, Betty's poll numbers began turning around. On November 19 a Harris Poll reported more people now approved of her remarks on *60 Minutes* than disapproved. Other polls reported she had come from a bare fifty percent (low for a First Lady) general approval rating to seventy-five percent. At the end of the year, the Gallup Poll ranked her the most admired woman in America. *People* magazine listed her as one of the three most intriguing women in the country.

But this bonanza of goodwill did her husband little good. By the end of the year, his poll numbers had dropped to a subterranean forty-one percent. Was there a connection between Betty's rise and Jerry's decline? No one can say for certain. But there was a rising conservative tide out there, which would crest with Ronald Reagan in 1980. Betty was, according to some headline writers at least, swimming against it—and conservatives have very retentive memories. Perhaps it is no accident that the elephant is the Republican symbol.

By the time Jerry Ford ran for President in 1976, the Ford administration decided Betty was an asset and distributed campaign buttons saying, ELECT BETTY'S HUSBAND. KEEP BETTY IN THE WHITE HOUSE. In the New Hampshire primary campaign, she was a sensational success. Television and print showered praise on her candor, her freshness.

Early on Betty told several reporters that she would campaign for Jerry but might differ with her husband on some issues. "Wow," gasped Ford speechwriter John Casserly in his diary. When the campaign got going, she did no such thing. The Republican platform called for a constitutional amendment to ban abortion, for instance. Betty did not say a word against it.

Instead, like the loving, loyal partner that she was and still is, Betty poured everything she had into her husband's campaign. She tried

The Fords leave the Truman house in Independence, Missouri, after a visit with my parents. My husband, Clifton Daniel, is walking with the President. My mother admired Betty's forthright style. *(Ford Library)*

extremely hard to convince the nation that the decent man she loved deserved to become President in his own right. But she did not like political campaigning. She hated making speeches. Conversation, not oration, was her métier. I suspect she also felt she was out there, doing not her own thing but her husband's thing—and Betty slowly crumbled under this sense of loss of self and the sheer exhaustion that overtakes everyone in a presidential campaign.

Betty began to mess up speeches—at one point she referred to herself as President. At another point, during Jerry's fight with Ronald Reagan for the Republican nomination, she called Reagan the President. She broke down and wept tears of shame and exasperation in hotel rooms. She became more and more dependent on drugs and alcohol to keep going.

As almost everyone knows, Jerry Ford did not win the presidency in 1976. He lost by a heartbreaking two percent of the vote to Jimmy Carter, who had come out of nowhere to win the Democratic nomination as an outsider running against the Washington establishment. The loss sent Betty Ford spinning into a black pit of depression. I am not about to play amateur psychiatrist with a woman I admire and like, but I cannot help but wonder if part of Betty's collapse was caused by a feeling—a fear—that she may have contributed to the loss.

Looking back on it from the perspective of twenty years, Betty does not think this feeling played a part in her depression. In discussing it with me, she pointed—correctly—to many other factors in Jerry's defeat: the overall stench of Watergate; the burden of the Nixon pardon; Jerry's bad luck to be golfing in Palm Springs on the day in 1975 when South Vietnam began its swift collapse, giving the TV news a chance to juxtapose images of a President at play with scenes of blood and horror. But Betty admitted to me that if she regretted anything in her tenure as First Lady, it was the *60 Minutes* interview.

For Betty Ford in 1976, no explanations, however valid, did much to assuage the pain of her husband's defeat—which was also her defeat. Perhaps her best advice came from a previous First Lady, supposedly nonpolitical—certainly one who never said a word in public that disagreed with her presidential husband. In her large scrawl, Mamie Eisenhower wrote:

> *Dear President and Mrs. Ford:*
>   *Words are inadequate from your friends but you can always say: "God I have done my best" Amen*

For the time being, Betty Ford could not say that prayer. As we shall see, it would take another struggle to be honest—this time with herself about her dependency on drugs and alcohol—before she could resume a normal life.

Chapter 11

PUBLIC

PARTNER NO. 1

NOT LONG AFTER JIMMY AND ROSALYNN CARTER TOOK OVER THE White House, a reporter obtained an interview with both of them on the same day. The newsman headed for the mansion with visions of a front-page story dancing in his head. Maybe he could get the new President and his First Lady to disagree over some major issue. Instead, as the scribe shuttled from the Oval Office to the First Lady's office in the East Wing, he found she and her husband agreed on everything—often down to giving the same answers, practically word for word! The bewildered would-be scooper reeled onto Pennsylvania Avenue and gasped to a friend: "I've just met two Jimmy Carters!"

Much of Rosalynn Carter's effectiveness—let's use the blunt word, her power—as First Lady derived from her unique relationship with her husband. She was the first First Lady to go forthrightly, fearlessly public in the role of partner-wife. Other Presidents may have listened to their spouses' political advice behind the scenes, but Jimmy and Rosalynn made a point of their partnership. Not that anyone doubted it. They thought and spoke alike to an almost unnerving degree.

Rosalynn Carter was one of the few First Ladies who enjoyed the job from the moment she entered the White House. One reason may be that she started with a win. For years her friend Betty Bumpers, wife of Senator Dale Bumpers of Arkansas, had been pushing a project to immunize children against measles. She had made very little progress in a discouraging struggle with red tape and federal bureaucracy. With the new First Lady behind her, Mrs. Bumpers soon had access to the wheels within wheels of the Department of Health Education and Welfare. "The results," Rosalynn says, "were astounding." In two years they immunized ninety percent of the children in the nation. By the time Rosalynn left the White House, measles had been virtually eliminated in the United States.

It was a stunning demonstration of the power of the First Lady in the era of big government and big television. Almost casually, Rosalynn mentions another factor in this tour de force—a direct order from President Jimmy Carter to the secretary of HEW. Not many First Ladies could rely on such hands-on cooperation from the Oval Office.

Rosalynn had a solid claim to her almost coequal role. More than any other First Lady except Hillary Rodham Clinton, if push came to shove in the private quarters of the White House (I am sure it never did) Rosalynn could say: "Without me you wouldn't be here!" For almost eighteen months before the Carters reached the White House, she had been out on the campaign trail, asking surprised Americans to vote for Jimmy Carter.

"Jimmy who?" was the early response. Seldom if ever has a candidate started so far back on the list. Not even his own mother thought Jimmy could win. When he told Lillian Carter he was going to run for President, she reportedly said: "President of what?" In my talk with her, Rosalynn recalled, with a nostalgic smile, how Jimmy walked into their bedroom at the Georgia governor's mansion and said: "I'm thinking of running for——."

"He couldn't even say the word, the idea was so awesome," Rosalynn said.

With only a single term (1971–1975) as governor of Georgia and two terms in the state senate on his political résumé, Jimmy Carter was the ultimate long shot. In 1974, when he appeared on the TV show *What's My Line,* he almost stumped the panel.

Rosalynn began her campaign with a staff of exactly one, a friend who drove with her to Florida in 1975 to begin buttonholing Democratic politicians. By the time the primary campaign ended, she had visited thirty states and played a crucial role in piling up the delegates who won Jimmy the Democratic nomination. In the general election against Gerald Ford, she went out on her own again, flying in a chartered Lear jet, speaking in over a hundred cities. "It was like having two candidates," her son Jack said.

Even then reporters noticed something unusual about this small, smiling woman with the soft southern accent: she was tireless— eighteen-hour days seldom fazed her—and she was tough. She could handle any question from the floor, whether it was intelligent or just sarcastic. Very early in her campaign, she encountered a fair number of people who shared Eleanor Roosevelt's opinion that it was "unseemly" for a wife to campaign for her husband and an even larger number of really old-fashioned traditionalists who thought she should be home taking care of her ten-year-old daughter, Amy.

"Do you like to cook?" asked one smarty.

"Yes, I like to cook," Rosalynn replied. "But I'm not doing much of it this year. I'm trying to get Jimmy Carter elected President."

When other questioners baited her about Jimmy's admission in a *Playboy* interview that he had lusted after other women, she replied without a flicker of hesitation: "Jimmy talks too much but at least people know he's honest."

Later a reporter asked her if she had ever committed adultery. "If I had," she replied, "I wouldn't tell *you.*"

One reporter called Rosalynn "a Sherman tank in a field of clover." Another came up with a nickname that stuck—and hurt—"the steel magnolia."

Rosalynn gamely tried to deal with these sideswipes. She claimed she did not mind being called tough—if the word meant "strong." But she did not like the implication that she was insensitive, unfeminine, and determined always to have her own way. She did not see her partnership with Jimmy Carter as a power struggle—and she had deep compassion for the poor and disadvantaged in America.

But Rosalynn did not deny she could often get her own way with her husband. At one point during the 1976 campaign, she promised that if Jimmy was elected, he would create a commission to do something about the deplorable treatment of America's mentally ill. "Then," she says with an almost devilish glint in her hazel eyes, "I went home and told Jimmy."

The Carter partnership had two components which made it unique. It was profoundly religious, and it was intensely ambitious. The religious component meant Rosalynn could simultaneously claim she had her own identity and freely submerge her personality and ideas in her husband's. The ambition was lofted on both religious and secular idealism to an almost dizzying height. The Carters came to Washington with the heady conviction that they could and would change America and the world.

Mental health became a major item on Rosalynn's program. But she did not hesitate to add Mrs. Bumpers's immunization program as well as a concern for older Americans and a determination to do more for woman's rights, including the passage of the Equal Rights Amendment. On top of this load she piled the desire and/or determination to be the President's political partner on almost everything that came across his desk in the Oval Office. It was an agenda that would have exhausted a superwoman. When she announced she was also going to tackle the decay of America's inner cities, one reporter groaned: "She's trying to take on all the problems we have!"

Within a few weeks of entering the White House, Jimmy asked Rosalynn to represent him on an unprecedented diplomatic mission to South America. She was to visit seven countries to explain the administration's foreign policy and explore "substantive" issues with the head of state in each nation. In effect, the President was telling the leaders of these countries that they should listen to the First Lady as closely as they would have listened to him.

Here is how Rosalynn explained that expedition to me: "Every head of state in the world wanted to learn as much as possible about

Jimmy Carter. No one knew him. He couldn't go everywhere. He had made several important speeches on South America, which I had heard and read and thoroughly understood. So we decided I could represent him down there."

The substitution did not work very well. The macho males of Spanish America balked at taking advice and counsel from a woman. Through various back channels their governments communicated their unhappiness to the U.S. State Department, claiming that they found it impossible to evaluate the importance of the First Lady's messages. The State Department was privately irked by Rosalynn upstaging them and leaked these complaints as well as negative comments in the South American press about her unappointed, unelected status.

In several countries Rosalynn's appearance gave local politicians a chance to sound off about aspects of U.S. policy they disliked. Although she had been briefed by top administration officials before she left, Rosalynn was not prepared to debate these policies. All she could do was promise to report the complaints to the President and the Senate Foreign Relations Committee when she returned. The State Department, supposedly trying to defend her against criticism in the American press, put a demeaning label on the trip when a spokesman said Rosalynn's main task was "asking questions."

Although a poll showed the public gave the First Lady's mission a seventy percent approval rating, Rosalynn and Jimmy never again ventured into coequal diplomacy. The next several times she went overseas, it was in more traditional First Lady roles, to extend presidential sympathy at the funeral of Pope Paul VI, or to visit Cambodian refugee camps in Thailand. She returned from the latter trip appalled by the suffering of these victims of the fanatically Communist Pol Pot regime and announced she had another cause to support.

To keep up with the political problems of the Oval Office, Jimmy Carter made sure that Rosalynn was briefed regularly by his national security people, congressional liaison staff, and similar experts. Beginning in 1978, she also took the unprecedented step of sitting in on cabinet meetings. Rosalynn's explanation makes sense in the context of their partnership. "I was constantly asking Jimmy why he or a cabinet officer had made this or that decision," she told me. "I tried to follow these things through the press and TV, but their reports were frequently misleading. Finally Jimmy got tired of explaining the reasons and background for decisions to me and suggested I sit in on the cabinet meetings so I could get the real facts."

Although Rosalynn insists none of the cabinet members was troubled by her presence, a lot of nasty criticism surfaced in the press. Defensively, Rosalynn maintained she made no attempt whatsoever to exercise her coequal authority. She simply sat in the back of the room and took notes. But she learned the hard way that in Washington politics, appearances count for a lot.

Like other presidents, including Harry Truman, Jimmy Carter insisted that he found his First Lady an invaluable sounding board for ideas and issues. They met once a week for a "policy lunch" and spent several hours almost every night discussing their mutual jobs. Except for the Mental Health Act and a few other issues, it is almost impossible to detect Rosalynn's stamp on any major bills or decisions. But that is hardly surprising, when two people think so much alike.

Perhaps the most visible evidence of Rosalynn's coequal status was the size of her White House staff. Instead of the pathetic handful of typists plus a social secretary and an assistant serving my mother in the Truman White House, Rosalynn commanded a cadre of twenty-one, including a press secretary, a social secretary, and a chief of staff who was paid the same salary as the President's chief of staff. Rosalynn's office in the East Wing was another first. Previous First Ladies had operated from a semioffice or study on the second floor. But Rosalynn decided she wanted to keep that area of the White House completely private, a zone of total relaxation for the President and the rest of the family.

As a world-class late sleeper and eternal putter-offer, I can only express awe at this First Lady's energy. *U.S. News and World Report* published the following summary of Rosalynn's first year in the job: she visited sixteen foreign nations and twenty-one U.S. cities; put 250 hours into being the honorary chairperson of her mental health commission as well as its roving spokesperson; presided at thirty-nine White House receptions, twenty congressional breakfasts, and eight state dinners; spent 210 hours learning Spanish and another 71 hours being briefed on problems foreign and domestic—and walked daughter Amy to her public school almost every morning!

The New York Times called Rosalynn "the most influential First Lady since Eleanor Roosevelt." I was intrigued to discover that she was christened Eleanor Rosalynn but preferred the middle name. Once or twice, President Carter referred to her as "*my* Eleanor." Unquestionably, there were similarities. At one point Jimmy remarked: "She never loses an argument. When I think an argument is over and I won it...a week or a month later it revives itself."

But there were also differences, some obvious, some baffling. Unlike the Roosevelts' tormented marriage, the Carter union was a powerful positive force in both their lives, enabling them to keep

Rosalynn Carter rivaled Eleanor Roosevelt as our most energetic First Lady. Here she visits a refugee camp in Cambodia. She tackled a staggering range of issues and problems as our first public presidential partner. *(Carter Library)*

quarrels to a minimum. In an interesting switch, Rosalynn admitted to me that she was "the politician" in their partnership. She wanted Jimmy to postpone until his second term some difficult decisions, such as the controversial treaty with Panama, which gave that nation eventual control of the canal. But he demurred, insisting on putting the national interest first. In another switch, it was she, not Jimmy, who needed protection from overwork. Jimmy seemed to have an inner voice that told him he had done enough for one day. Rosalynn often had to be pried out of her office for a jog, a game of tennis, or a swim in the White House pool.

Rosalynn was also far more thin-skinned than Eleanor Roosevelt, who sailed serenely above the ferocious epithets and accusations flung at her. In a 1984 panel on life in the White House at the Gerald Ford Presidential Library, Rosalynn confessed that the hardest thing for her to do each morning was read the newspapers, with their inevitable criticisms of Jimmy and often of her. She berated the press—always a mistake—when they sniped at her grown children's conduct in and out of the White House. Her son Jack, who steered clear of the Washington publicity maelstrom, said: "Mom [has] always taken every affront to Dad personally. She's a lot worse now." One historian of the Carter presidency criticized Rosalynn's judgment of people because it was based almost entirely on their loyalty to Jimmy—not on an objective estimate of abilities or liabilities.

Enough minuses. Partner Rosalynn can justly claim a lot of the credit for the Carter administration's remarkable record on woman's rights and opportunities. Jimmy appointed three women to his cabinet and named no fewer than forty-one women to lifetime jobs as federal judges. Rosalynn also fought hard—but in vain—for the Equal Rights Amendment, and frequently spoke out on women's issues.

This pioneering First Lady can also claim some of the credit for the biggest foreign policy triumph of the Carter administration, the Camp David accords between Egypt and Israel. This act of daring perfectly suited the Carters' outsider role. An insider might have wavered at the possibility of alienating the millions of Jews who are among the major vertebrae, if not the backbone, of the Democratic Party. Rosalynn told me how, one day when she and Jimmy were alone at Camp David, she suggested inviting Prime Minister Menachem Begin of Israel and President Anwar Sadat of Egypt to confer there. "I said the place was so peaceful and beautiful, if they could not reach an agreement here, they couldn't do it anywhere. A few days later, Jimmy decided it was a good idea."

In spite of her ceaseless efforts on so many fronts, Rosalynn Carter never made it to the top of the lists of most admired women, like some of her far less activist predecessors, such as Pat Nixon and Mamie Eisenhower. One writer who studied her style with the Mental Health Commission blamed it on her "cool" personality—and on the mixed political signals she sent. People found it hard to decide when she was speaking as the compassionate First Lady and when she was being a White House political operator.

Historians, on the other hand, rate Rosalynn highly, in one poll putting her third, behind Eleanor Roosevelt and Lady Bird Johnson, in the top ten of most effective First Ladies. On *another* hand, at a 1993 panel about First Ladies and the Media held at the Smithsonian, the panelists, all women, remarked somewhat ruefully (they obviously wished it were otherwise) that Rosalynn was the least memorable of recent First Ladies.

Whether this tells us something about the American public or about Rosalynn Carter is a tough call. Whether it adds up to more than a hill of beans is also a good question. But as a politician's daughter, I see a connection between being a public partner and the public's perception of a First Lady. The more public the partnership, the more identified the First Lady becomes with all the imbroglios, scandals, and problems of her husband's administration. If the public's perception of his presidency bleeds into the failure zone, the First Lady's popularity sinks with the President's.

This is, to some extent, what happened to Rosalynn Carter. I am not trying to sit in political judgment on the Carter administration here. I am only trying to assess what happened to their presidential partnership. The same historians who rated Rosalynn third among effective First Ladies of modern times rated President Jimmy Carter next to last, barely above Warren G. Harding. Maybe they were trying to confirm the adage that there are lies, damn lies, and statistics—especially polling statistics. But it is a judgment that is hard to ignore.

Unquestionably, the Carters had the best intentions, and they tried to do a great many things. Too many, in the opinion of several recent historians. Seamy friends and relatives, notably banker Bert Lance, who inspired the appointment of a special prosecutor, and Jimmy's brother, Billy, with his off-the-wall attempt to represent Libya's terrorist regime, created disillusioning headlines. The Carters were also unlucky. Inflation soared, the economy stalled. International events, such as the Soviet invasion of Afghanistan, gave them rude shocks, to which their responses seemed inadequate.

The coup de grâce was the Iranian seizure of the American embassy and its staff in Tehran. No President could have done more to cut this Gordian knot—but it seemed the ultimate proof, piled on top of Afghanistan and the all too recent memories of Vietnam, that America had lost its place as a strong, resourceful world leader. One old Washington hand reportedly said to Jimmy in the middle of this crisis: "I think maybe you've used up all your luck getting here!"

Finally, when they submitted their four years to the judgment of the American people in 1980, the Carters found themselves face to face with Ronald Reagan, one of the greatest vote getters in presidential history. In this final struggle, many people felt Rosalynn damaged her image as First Lady and exposed yet another vulnerability of the public partnership. She abandoned mental health and her other good causes to hit the campaign trail for Jimmy again. Grappling with the Iranian hostage crisis, the President felt he had to stay close to the White House. The First Lady's sudden switch from altruism to ambition troubled many people.

The ferocious intensity of Rosalynn's reelection effort was visible in her comment after they lost to Ronald Reagan. Someone remarked that Jimmy did not seem in the least bitter about the defeat. "I'm bitter enough for both of us," Rosalynn said.

I fear that both Jimmy and Rosalynn came to Washington with an exaggerated idea of the power of the offices of the President and the First Lady. These offices can make some things happen, but my father frequently commented on how little even the President can do to get his own way on a dismaying variety of problems. This is even more true for the First Lady. Things are changed in politics not merely by the naked power of the office but by working within the system, having influential friends both inside and outside Washington. Jimmy and Rosalynn painfully lacked these connections. Rosalynn in particular suffered from the lack of a network of powerful women ready to defend, support, and promote her. These hidden but by no means silent backers were among the prime secrets of successful First Ladies such as Eleanor Roosevelt and Lady Bird Johnson.

I know some people want to see a coequal First Lady up to her eyes in politics. But Rosalynn Carter's experience—and Edith Wilson's and Helen Taft's—makes me wonder if this is the best way for every First Lady to achieve maximum effectiveness in her peculiar job. Becoming First Lady does not, after all, endow a woman with magical qualities, enabling her to deal expertly with any and every problem that floats into the modern White House. While I am heartily in favor of women achieving maximum opportunities and power, I doubt that the First Lady is the ideal symbolic vehicle for this ascent. There are too many ambiguities and complexities in her role. To narrow the test of her success or failure to her ability to acquire and wield political power is, in my opinion, a serious mistake.

Again, I am coming down on the side of maximum laissez-faire. First Ladies should all be allowed to do their impossible job their own ways and take their chances with the results. That thought is a good transition to a political partnership as different from the Carters' as the rural roads of Plains, Georgia, are from the elegant streets of Beverly Hills.

Chapter 12

—

THE MOST
PROTECTIVE
PARTNER

Nancy Reagan had a far more difficult time than Jacqueline Kennedy when she tried to bring a touch of class to the White House. She was assailed as a coldhearted snob and an egotistic playgirl by a mélange of critics with a ferocity that must have made her sympathize with Marie Antoinette—and occasionally wonder if she might suffer a similar fate. Seldom has so much vitriol been flung at a First Lady who saw herself as nonpolitical.

Like Jackie Kennedy, Nancy's first reaction to her new job was panic. She called old friends such as the silent film star Colleen Moore and confessed to being "scared and lonely." This anxiety may explain some of the unfortunate remarks and decisions Mrs. Reagan made in her first few months in the White House.

When she was asked if she was going to espouse a cause, like many recent First Ladies, Nancy disdainfully announced she did not have one. For those who knew her, these were strange words. When Ronald Reagan was governor of California, Nancy had been the guiding spirit of the Foster Grandparents Program, which urges older Americans to "adopt" poor children and let them know someone cares.

As First Lady, Nancy Reagan decided to devote her energies to making the White House a "special place." Americans, she said, "wanted it that way." She intended to bring "the best of everything" to the mansion. It helps to put this passion into political perspective. Ronald Reagan had become President at a low point in America's international prestige. Both Reagans felt an intense need to restore American pride.

As Nancy saw it, the Carters' down-home White House style, with its emphasis on informality and cost cutting, seemed part of this negative American image. While the President was telling the American people it was morning in America again, the First Lady decided to remind them that their afternoons and evenings could be wonderful too. All that was needed was some good old Hollywood glamour.

Nancy was trying to help define the Reagan administration's tone by doing what came naturally. Even before the inauguration, contemplating her job, she had told a reporter, "You can only be yourself. If you try to do anything else, it's phony." She was the daughter of an actress who had palled around with the likes of Spencer Tracy and George Cukor. She had been a moderately successful screen star in her own right and had married an even more successful one. Hollywood's lavish style was as natural to her as California sunshine.

Nancy should have seen omens of trouble to come in the criticism of the Reagans' sixteen-million-dollar inaugural. The extravagance had been funded by friendly Republican millionaires, but the Antifeds of 1980, now equipped with press credentials, made Nancy target number one for their aversion to displays of wealth and power. They contrasted the six-year-old blue chiffon gown Rosalynn Carter had worn to her inaugural ball to the one-shoulder white satin sheath by James Galanos that made Nancy the center of attention. "Limousines, white ties, and $10,000 ball gowns are in, shoe leather, abstemiousness, and thrift out," wrote one almost incoherent scribe.

The critics found even more fault with Nancy's White House redecorating. She raised over $800,000 from another batch of rich Republicans to redo the private rooms on the second floor. This too was denounced as outrageous extravagance. Then she decided the White House needed new china, and contracted for a $220,000 order. The Queen Nancy image was born.

By December of 1981, *Newsweek* was telling people that the First Lady appeared to be an "idle rich, Queen bee figure" who was "obsessed with fashion and society." Pollsters reported that sixty-two percent of the American people thought she put "too much emphasis on style and elegance." Megagallons of ink were spilled on how much she spent on her wardrobe. She was roasted for accepting gowns from top designers free of charge. Her plea that she was trying to help the American fashion industry was dismissed with hoots and hisses. Even Republican supporters like Bob Hope joked that when Nancy's childhood nursemaid tickled her, she had said: "Gucci, Gucci, goo." Johnny Carson said she snacked on caviar.

I happened to have lunch with Elliott Roosevelt and Nancy Reagan in the middle of this fusillade. Nancy was extremely upset and bewildered by the media's unrelenting hostility. "Ronnie says I should just forget them, but I can't," she said plaintively.

"Tell them to go to hell!" declared Elliott.

I shook my head and urged Nancy to meet regularly with the press and be as honest as possible with them. "But the questions they ask!" Nancy cried.

"You'll get used to them," I assured her. "Meanwhile, try to stay calm and devote yourself to a cause that people can identify with. Eventually, the public will change their minds about you."

Although we did not agree politically, I liked Nancy personally. In private she is relaxed and full of fun, with a warm quick laugh. She is also far more intelligent and down-to-earth than she has been portrayed by certain journalists. I agreed with her husband (for once) when he said she was getting a bum rap from the press and public. No matter what the pundits thought, the White House needed new china. When the Reagans moved in, the wealthiest nation in the world could not field a complete set of dishes for a state dinner. Every First Lady back to Dolley Madison has exercised her right to redecorate the private quarters to suit her own taste and her family's living arrangements.

When I interviewed Nancy for this book, she still felt bewildered by the flap over the china and the redecorating. "I tried again and again to get someone to explain that the Knapp Foundation was donating the china. Not a cent of taxpayers' money was used. It never got into print," she told me. "As for the redecorating, a lot of money went for basics like plumbing and air conditioning and restoring the marble floor downstairs. It wasn't all spent on the second floor."

Nancy has told people my luncheon advice was the best suggestion she got from anyone while she was in the White House. She talked things over with the President and some of his advisers and decided there was a cause out there she could adopt as her own: drug abuse. She did not pick this out of a hat. In 1981 two decades of the drug culture were cresting with disastrous impact on millions of young Americans. We had been inundated with celebrities and gurus telling us drugs were harmless fun, good for the soul. There was a real need for someone to speak out against this insidious menace.

The Reagan administration launched an all-out assault on drug use. Nancy's program, Just Say No to Drugs, was the centerpiece of the effort. Athletes, movie stars, civic leaders, and numerous private groups pitched in. Nancy attended an endless parade of antidrug conferences and narrated a documentary, *The Chemical People,* for PBS. She convened a conference of First Ladies from other countries in Washington to discuss the drug problem from an international perspective. The bottom line showed significant results. During the years when Just Say No was going full blast, drug use among high school and college students dropped almost fifty percent.

Meanwhile, Nancy was taking a few lessons from that master of spin control, Ronald Reagan, on how to deal with other aspects of her image. At the 1981 Al Smith Dinner in New York, an annual gathering of politicians from all points of the ideological compass, she made an impromptu speech when she was introduced. She said she had

Nancy Reagan's "Just Say No" to drugs campaign was one of the most successful causes ever embraced by a First Lady. It dramatically reduced drug use among Americans of all ages, particularly the young. *(AP/Wide World Photos)*

heard there was a cardboard cutout of her going around, in which she was wearing a crown. "Now that's silly," she said. "I'd never wear a crown. It musses up your hair."

As a chuckle raced through the startled crowd, Nancy said she was taking this opportunity to announce her new charity project: "The Nancy Reagan Home for Wayward China." This time the laugh was long and loud. Nancy was on her way back from the bottom of the polls.

A few months later, Nancy and her husband went to the Gridiron Club dinner, another annual affair in which the high-profile types in the current administration get roasted by the press. As everyone expected, Nancy got a going-over. A reporter dressed in fake high style impersonated her warbling "Second Hand Clothes" to the tune of the Fanny Brice, Barbra Streisand showstopper, "Second Hand Rose." It was a direct hit on the borrowed outfits from Adolfo et al.

When eyes traveled to the dais to see how Nancy was taking it, they found only an empty chair. Even the President looked puzzled. Many thought she had stalked out in a rage. Suddenly onto the stage pranced Nancy as a bag lady, singing her own version of "Second Hand Clothes":

> "Second hand clothes
> I'm wearing second hand clothes
> They're all the thing in spring fashion shows.
> Even my new trench coat with the fur collar
> Ronnie bought for ten cents on the dollar.
> The china's the only thing that's new
>
> Even though they tell me I'm no longer queen
> Why did Ronnie have to buy me that sewing machine?
> Second hand clothes, second hand clothes
> I sure hope Ed Meese* sews."

The applause made the building totter. People got so carried away, one Washington pundit compared Nancy's performance with William Jennings Bryan's epochal speech "You Shall Not Crucify Mankind upon a Cross of Gold." That is going a bit far, but you get the idea. Nancy had found her way back across that perilous gap between upper-class elegance and democratic humility.

Not everything went smoothly for Nancy Reagan or the Reagan administration thereafter. But among First Ladies, Nancy unquestionably rates the Comeback Queen award. By January 1985, just after Ronald Reagan had swamped the Democrats forty-nine states to one for reelection, Nancy was ahead of him in the popularity polls, seventy-one percent to sixty-two percent. *The New Republic,* bastion of oppositionists to almost every President, expressed bewilderment that the woman who had started out as the least popular President's wife in decades could achieve poll numbers that topped Jackie Kennedy's.

All it took was some showbiz smarts and a little Democratic advice. (I was not the only one to offer her my two cents, I hastily add.) But if Martha Washington is watching her successors (and I sometimes

* For those who may have forgotten, Meese was Reagan's attorney general.

think she is), I am sure she was proud of Nancy's performance. It was a class act—in more ways than one.

Nancy also functioned as a political partner in her own way. The old spinmeister Ronald Reagan made this very clear in one of his 1985 weekly radio addresses. "Nancy is my everything," he said. "When I look back on these days, I'll remember your radiance and your strength, your support and for taking part in the business of the nation. Thank you, partner, thanks for everything."

In Rosalynn Carter, the political partner and the wife were so intertwined the result was often a blur. Not so with Nancy Reagan. Out front, she was a wife. This goes back to the roots of her life, when she experienced the pain of her parents' divorce and years of being parked with relatives until her actress mother married a wealthy Chicago doctor and was able to give Nancy a sense of belonging to a family again. Even when she went to Hollywood and launched her own screen career, Nancy made no secret of her desire to marry and have a family.

That probably explains the romantic intensity she brought to her marriage to Ronald Reagan. Ronnie's considerable charm has something to do with it, of course. I was aware of the power of his personality long before he became President. My husband, Clifton Daniel, told me about the day he met Reagan in the early fifties, when Clifton was the *New York Times* correspondent in London. He went down to Southampton to meet his boss, Turner Catledge, the crusty managing editor of *The New York Times*. A chuckling Catledge came down the gangplank with Reagan and introduced him to Clifton. After Reagan said good-bye, Catledge told Clifton he had met Ronnie on shipboard and they had barely parted company during the voyage. "That fellow knows more good stories than I do," Catledge said—a tremendous admission. Catledge prided himself on his prowess as a southern yarn spinner.

Maybe it was those funny stories, or Ronnie's amazingly good-natured ways—but Nancy Reagan adored the man, and he reciprocated with almost gushing emotion. "I pray I'll never face the day when she isn't there," Reagan wrote in his diary. "Of all the ways God has blessed me, giving her to me was the greatest." Unlike George Bush and other Presidents, such as Lyndon Johnson, who loved to organize dinners for twenty on two hours' notice, panicking the White House staff, Ronald Reagan seemed happiest when he was alone with Nancy, watching the news or a favorite show on television, often eating dinner on TV trays. Larry Speakes, Reagan's press secretary, says: "The Reagans have one of the greatest love affairs I have ever seen, in or out of politics. They are truly best friends, as well as husband and wife."

When she became First Lady, Nancy made no attempt to conceal her love, saying things like "My life began when I met my husband." That made her a target for some feminists. Gloria Steinem wrote a particularly nasty article in *Ms.* magazine, condemning Nancy's supposed subservience to her husband. The First Lady compounded this problem with what the press corps dubbed "The Gaze." When Reagan gave a speech, she sat in the first row, watching him with total rapture on her face. She was baffled and not a little hurt when she discovered the press was making fun of her. "It's the way I really feel about Ronnie," she said.

There was another reason for Nancy giving her husband The Gaze. Everyone agreed that her presence had an almost magical effect on his performance. To a degree that approaches mysticism, she and Ronald Reagan are attuned, even invisibly attached, to each other. "She charges his batteries," declared one Reagan aide.

In the 1984 reelection campaign, Reagan did poorly in his first debate with his Democratic challenger, Walter Mondale. Nancy and his campaign advisers decided the problem was the President's attempt to jam too many facts and figures into his head from the massive briefing books that his staff had prepared. But when he started rehearsing for the second debate, they could not get him to relax and be himself. Reagan's confidence seemed badly shaken. He messed up his best lines, forgot favorite jokes, and generally performed like an already beaten man.

When Nancy heard about this, she strode into the room wearing a raincoat, rushed up to her husband, and pulled open the coat as if she had turned flasher. On her sweater were the words "4 MORE IN 84." Reagan broke up, and so did everyone else. "Okay," the President said in his best show-business style, "let's take it from the top." Everyone who was there swears an incredible transformation took place. The relaxed, confident Reagan returned. He beat Mondale in the second debate—and went on to one of the greatest reelection landslides in American history.

That was partnership, Nancy style. There were other small but touching ways in which the Reagans testified to the strength of their alliance. One was the loud plaid suit that the President often wore to press conferences. Aides called it his Mutt and Jeff outfit and began plotting ways to prevent its appearance until they found out that Nancy had selected the material. It was Ronnie's way of taking her into the ring with him.

When the Reagans called on Queen Elizabeth at Windsor Castle in 1982, the President and the Queen left the ceremonial hall together. Ronnie turned and motioned Nancy to join them. "That's a breach of protocol!" spluttered one stuffy British reporter. Larry Speakes lived up to his name and talked fast enough to convince him it was an ancient Reagan family custom for husbands and wives to walk side by side.

When it came to the big issues with which Reagan dealt as President, Nancy's views got a respectful hearing, but they often failed to win her partner's assent. As a politician, Nancy was much too nervous, too eager to adjust to passing public moods to protect Ronald Reagan's popularity. When Reagan gave his famous speech in which he called the Soviet Union an evil empire, Nancy wanted him to tone down the rhetoric. The President refused because he thought it was time to let the Russians know he had no illusions about their totalitarian system.

During the 1984 campaign, Nancy organized a veritable cabal of friends who were invited to dinner to help her talk Reagan out of his stand on abortion. Five minutes into the meal, Reagan said: "Nancy, I know what you're up to. I'm not going to change my mind and that's all there is to it." That was also the end of the argument. Unlike some other First Ladies, Nancy could lose gracefully.

One of their sharpest disagreements was over Reagan's determination to lay a wreath at the Bitburg military cemetery in Germany to commemorate their World War II dead. Many Jewish and non-Jewish spokespeople protested this decision because some SS troops—Nazis—were buried there too. Few were more vehemently opposed than Nancy. "I had a close friend who had spent some time in the concentration camps," Nancy explained to me. She urged the President to persuade Germany's Chancellor, Helmut Kohl, to find another cemetery. When Kohl refused, Reagan decided to go ahead with the ceremony. He was convinced it was time to stop punishing every living German for World War II and testify to the forty years in which West Germany had been a strong and dependable ally.

"Ronnie was right," Nancy says. "The ceremony did become a giant step toward reconciliation between Germany and America. But I still wish Chancellor Kohl had chosen another cemetery."

Looking back on the incident, the President provided a glimpse of how the Reagan partnership operated: "[Nancy] is not one to shout or be [violently] critical when she disagrees with me. Most of the time, she'll just say in her quiet voice something like: 'Do you really think it's a good idea for you to do that?' "

Reagan went on to wonder if a man could be a good President without a wife who is willing to tell him the truth. "If you can't trust your wife to be honest with you, whom can you trust?" he asked. "She'll tell you things no one else will, sometimes things you don't want to hear, but isn't that how it should be?"

To an astonishing extent, Nancy knew Ronald Reagan's strengths, and like every wife, his weaknesses. One of the latter was a dislike, almost an inability, to say no. Most politicians share this trait to some extent. Saying no can make enemies, the last thing a politician wants to do. That is why almost every presidential administration has an abominable no man—someone who takes the heat for making tough decisions about firings, promotions, and the like. In the Reagan White House, Nancy appointed herself to this job.

She frequently exercised near veto power over proposed appointments, when she thought the would-be appointee was trying to push

Reagan around. One story concerns William Simon, the money wizard who was being considered for the treasury. Talking over the job, he laid down a whole set of demands that had to be met before he accepted. Nancy made sure he was a dead duck before he got to the White House gate.

By now I think you can see the leading edge of Nancy's role as partner. She was almost always playing protector. Ronald Reagan's age undoubtedly had something do with it. When he left the White House in 1989, he was the oldest president in history, just shy of his seventy-eighth birthday. The protector tendency magnified as the White House years passed for another much more serious reason. Nancy Reagan is a First Lady whose husband survived an assassination attempt.

As the daughter of a President who was also lucky—far luckier than Ronald Reagan, who was struck by his would-be killer's bullet—I think I understand the impact of this experience on her. I too have felt the inexpressible shock and numbness that an assassination attempt creates in the mind and heart of a President's wife and children. When I first learned members of the Puerto Rican Independence Party had tried to kill my father on November 1, 1950, by rushing the front door of Blair House, where my parents were living while the White House was being rebuilt, I simply could not believe it. My mother, who looked out the window and saw the bodies of the assassins and White House guards bleeding in the street, was far more shaken.

Ronald Reagan's brush with death took place on a downtown Washington street, outside the Washington Hilton Hotel, where he had just given a speech. Nancy was at a luncheon with Barbara Bush a few blocks away. Almost confirming the mystic links that bind the Reagans, she had an intuition that something was wrong and hurried back to the White House early. There she was told that the President had been shot. She rushed to George Washington University Hospital to be at his side, and it may not be an exaggeration to say her appearance helped save his life. With a collapsed lung and a bullet an inch from his heart, he was barely alive when she got there. "Seeing Nancy gave me an enormous lift," he said later.

In my talk with her, Nancy displayed her only flash of bitterness, recalling the anguish of the assassination attempt. "Everyone remembered the funny things Ronnie said after he was hit. No one seemed to want to remember how close he came to dying."

I have always been impressed that Nancy supported her husband's decision to run for a second term, in spite of the assassination experience. The thought that someone—in fact, quite a few someones—out there wants to kill your husband can cast a permanent pall over the power, the glamour, of the presidency. It took real courage on Nancy Reagan's part to back her partner's decision to run in 1984.

But the psychological impact of the assassination attempt on someone as sensitive as Nancy remained profound. Coupled with Ronald Reagan's illnesses in his second term—his colon cancer surgery in 1985, his prostate surgery in 1987—the experience reinforced her instinct to protect him from the stresses and pressures of the job to a degree that caused her and the President serious problems. Nancy clashed head on with Reagan's chief of staff, Donald Regan, who had come to Washington after a successful career as a Wall Street businessman with an autocratic style that was much too indifferent to political nuances—and to the reality of the Reagan partnership.

Instead of understanding and sympathizing with Nancy's role as protector, Regan adopted a confrontational "this is my turf" approach to her requests and suggestions. He ignored her recommendation to keep the President's schedule as light as possible after his surgeries. Worse, from her point of view, he badly underestimated the impact of the Iran-Contra scandal, which revealed a White House–run plan to sell weapons to Iran to rescue American hostages in Lebanon, and to use some of the proceeds to fund the anti-Communist Nicaraguan rebels. Regan exposed an unprepared President to a humiliating press conference about the uproar and then sneered that he would need a shovel to clean up after the mess. Finally, he hung up on Nancy in the middle of a sentence, not once but several times.

The situation swiftly slewed out of control. An enraged Nancy insisted Regan had to go. A dismayed President resisted—then finally consented—giving the Washington press corps irresistible targets.

The New York Times said Nancy had expanded the role of First Lady into Associate President. The *Times*'s resident conservative columnist and every President's gadfly, William Safire, said she was making Reagan look "wimpish." The President called reports that Nancy was running the government "a despicable fiction." Yet a poll reported sixty-two percent of the people thought Nancy had more influence in the White House than any First Lady in American history. Anyone who has read what I have written about Sarah Polk, Helen Taft, and Edith Wilson will thank God history is not written by pollsters—or the polled.

There was worse to come. An infuriated Don Regan did the unforgivable: he wrote a tell-all book that described Nancy Reagan as a ten-foot-tall dragon lady pushing around a President with the brainpower of a Forrest Gump. As I have said already, I do not share many of the Reagans' political views, but I felt sorry for them as this fiasco escalated. I can remember my father saying more than once in his old age that one of the things that pleased him most about his days in the White House was that none of his staff "ever wrote a book on me." In spite of all I have said about the inevitability and pitilessness of the public's demand for information, I believe there is such a thing as White House privacy, and the Reagans, the Bushes, the Clintons, all First Families, are entitled to it.

Donald Regan revealed the existence of a White House astrologer, whom Nancy Reagan had hired to advise her on days or weeks when the President was likely to be unlucky. Regan made this sound as silly as possible, of course. When I interviewed Nancy for this book, she talked candidly about the astrologer. "I consulted her because I was looking for ways to find some comfort, to control my anxiety, every time Ronnie appeared in public," she said. "It made me feel better to be told that certain days were safer than others."

As someone who was in show business, I am amazed by all the speculation about where Nancy got such ideas. Actors are among the most superstitious people in the world, closely followed by politicians and generals. They are all firm believers in Murphy's famous law, if anything can go wrong, it will. The Reagans' final two years in the White House, harried by the Regan revelations and the Iran-Contra scandal, amply demonstrated that Murphy was still very much on the scene. It is more than a little ironic that Nancy's fear of dark forces seemed to produce them in spades.

The Donald Regan debacle was a runaway outgrowth of Nancy Reagan's attempt to protect the man she loved, the husband she almost lost on that terrible November day in 1981. If we view it from that perspective, we can be a little more understanding—and forgiving—toward a First Lady who had one of the roughest rides through Washington since Mary Lincoln.

Chapter 13

THE ALMOST

PERFECT

FIRST LADY

HAS THERE BEEN A FIRST LADY WHO DID IT ALL—WHO WAS A FLAWLESS White House hostess, a loving and protective wife, an astute political partner, and an admired public person in her own right? Such a paragon probably never will be seen at 1600 Pennsylvania Avenue. But a remarkable consensus of historians, reporters, and average Americans seem to agree that there has been one First Lady who came close: Claudia Alta Taylor Johnson, better known to the world as Lady Bird.

Her tenure as First Lady began under the worst imaginable circumstances. She was hurled from pleasant obscurity as the wife of the vice president into a White House riven by the shock of John F. Kennedy's assassination. I have discussed the trauma that an attempted assassination can inflict on those close to a President. I shudder to think of what the actual murder of a President would do to ordinary mortals like me. Lady Bird was totally exposed to the horror of Kennedy's death, from the nightmarish gunshots in that Dallas plaza to the grisly aftermath on the plane back to Washington. In her diary she recalled her visit to Jackie Kennedy's compartment on that funereal plane: "Mrs. Kennedy's dress was stained with blood. One leg was almost entirely covered with it and her right glove was caked, it was caked with blood, her husband's blood."

In those terrible days, these two very different women established a friendship which endured for three decades. It began with Lady Bird's words on the plane: "Oh Mrs. Kennedy, you know we never even wanted to be Vice President and now, dear God, it's come to this." The friendship deepened as Lady Bird watched Jackie take charge of JFK's funeral, indeed become its presiding spirit. During the procession that escorted the slain President's coffin to the Capitol, Lady Bird looked out at the sea of faces on both sides of Pennsylvania Avenue and thought Jackie was achieving something she had never quite attained in the Kennedy years in the White House, "a state of love, a state of rapport between herself and the people of this country."

Two days later Lady Bird had tea with Jackie in the White House. Still in deep shock, her eyes haunted, her face taut with tension, Jackie at first tried to talk to Lady Bird as if this was a normal transition between an outgoing and an incoming First Lady. She dispensed basic lore, such as "Never tell a waiter that you don't like this particular type of cookie because you will never see that particular butler again for two weeks."

Abruptly, Jackie went from household minutiae to the deeply personal: "Don't be frightened of this house. Some of the happiest years of my marriage were spent here—you will be happy here." She repeated this a half dozen times, as if she were trying to exorcise the nightmare of the assassination for Lady Bird.

After a tour of the private quarters on the second floor, Jackie and Lady Bird went down to the East Room to hear Lyndon Johnson give a speech to South American diplomats who had participated in the Kennedy Alliance for Progress—an attempt to export U.S. economic know-how to our Spanish neighbors. Lady Bird realized everyone's eyes were on Jackie. "But all the more my heart went out to the bravery of Lyndon," she told her diary at the end of the day. "[He] marches into this circumstance with so much determination and not all the preparation that one would have sought, if one could have foreseen one's destiny at sixteen."

These are remarkable words. They reveal Lady Bird Johnson's ability to look at her larger-than-life-size husband with an extraordinary combination of affection and objectivity. They also reveal her calm acceptance of Jackie Kennedy's star quality—without a trace of the envy or anxiety that such a predecessor might have stirred in a lesser woman. Lady Bird had no grandiose illusions about her career as First Lady. On the contrary, her dominant note was caution. She told her friend Nellie Connally, wife of John Connally, the Texas governor who was badly wounded by JFK's assassin in Dallas, "I feel like I am suddenly onstage for a part I never rehearsed."

But for Lady Bird, caution did not mean hesitation, or a retreat to timid seclusion. She tackled the First Lady's job with a calm determination that was rooted in the self-confidence she had acquired from almost twenty years in Washington, D.C., as a wife who watched—and frequently helped—her husband rise from obscure Texas congressman to Senate majority leader. It was no accident when she told Jackie Kennedy, "*We* never even wanted to be Vice President." That *we* testified to her profound sense of partnership with Lyndon Johnson.

By the time the Johnsons moved into the White House on December 7, 1963, Lady Bird had put together the nucleus of the best staff any First Lady has yet recruited. For her social secretary, she chose Bess Abell, daughter of a Kentucky senator and wife of the assistant postmaster general—an ultimate Washington insider. Her press secretary and de facto chief of staff was an even more inspired choice: Liz Carpenter, a shrewd, spunky newspaperwoman who had been reporting on Washington's ways and means for decades. Of her Lyndon Johnson once remarked: "She'd charge hell with a bucket of water." Liz was one of the few people in the White House, besides Lady Bird, who had the courage to tell LBJ he was occasionally wrong.

Eventually six full-time assistants worked under Liz in the press section, and Bess Abell had four assistants to handle the social side of the White House. Jackie Kennedy's decision to hire a press secretary

Lady Bird Johnson
was a many-sided
First Lady. Here she
works in her White
House Office.
*(Lyndon Baines Johnson
Library)*

has been hailed by some historians as a great leap forward. But Jackie still largely operated on her own, scrawling long memos on legal pads in her campaign to rehabilitate the White House. Lady Bird converted the leap into a quantum vault from the realm of gifted amateur to the domain of the orderly professional. Among her several talents, Lady Bird was a successful businesswoman; she had run the Johnsons' radio and television properties ever since they acquired these valuable assets early in Lyndon's congressional career. She brought something really new to the East Wing: expertise.

Lady Bird had a long talk with Liz Carpenter about the press. She told Liz she wanted "a workable formula that will allow us to live happily together." Liz conferred with the White House reporters, most of whom she knew personally, and boiled the process down to two basic principles: "Be Available" and "Never Lie. Tell us you can't tell us but never lie." My father's old friend and press secretary, Charlie Ross, who died at his desk in the White House living up to similar principles, would have given Liz Carpenter's version of them his heartfelt approval.

Meanwhile, Lady Bird was engulfed by the thousand and one details of moving into the White House and simultaneously dismantling and selling The Elms, the gracious Washington home where she and Lyndon Johnson had lived for so long. She had to cope with two supercharged daughters, Lynda Bird and Luci, each a very distinct personality, and worry about how life in the White House would affect them. She somehow found time to meet and shake hands with every single member of the White House staff—and managed to begin one of the most important sides of her partnership with Lyndon Johnson—entertaining key members of Congress.

On December 14, 1963, only a week after she moved in, the new First Lady presided at a dinner for a half dozen panjandrums of the House of Representatives and gave their wives a tour of the second-floor quarters. As she watched the guests depart, Lady Bird, with that objectivity that is one of her most remarkable characteristics, thought it was a good evening but "what feelings of warmth it created remains to be seen."

As a vice president filling out the last fourteen months of John F. Kennedy's term, Lyndon Johnson was anxious about getting elected President in his own right. But he courageously pressed ahead with some very controversial legislation, notably the Civil Rights Act, which infuriated southern conservatives. When the Republicans nominated the conservatives' hero, Senator Barry Goldwater of Arizona, as their standard-bearer in 1964, a classic confrontation seemed in the making, with the South one of the principal battlegrounds. Friends told the President he would face pickets and violent demonstrations if he ventured into the land of cotton. "We'll send Lady Bird instead," LBJ said.

This was not nearly as off the wall as it sounds. During the 1960 campaign, Lady Bird had traveled thirty-five thousand miles, mostly in the Deep South and Texas, speaking for the ticket. After the razor-thin victory over Richard Nixon, Robert Kennedy, the manager of

JFK's campaign, paid her a rare tribute: "Lady Bird carried Texas for us." It was an amazing achievement for a woman who in 1954 was too shy to make a speech. When LBJ became Senate majority leader in 1955, considerably upping their public exposure, Lady Bird said she "got really annoyed with myself for being so shy and quiet"—and took speech lessons. She was soon calling the course "one of the most delightful expanding experiences I ever had."

Expanding is a key word here. Growth was at the heart of Lady Bird's very special relationship with her husband. Not a few people have wondered how she managed to stay in love with this driven, abrasive man, who often publicly criticized her taste in clothes, sometimes ordered her around like a servant, and was not always faithful. Liz Carpenter says part of the explanation is genetic. Lady Bird's father, Thomas Jefferson Taylor, was another tall Texan who always expected to get his own way about everything. But I prefer Lady Bird's explanation: "Lyndon stretches you," she said once. "He always expects more of you than you're really mentally or physically capable of putting out."

There is more to any love story than a single idea, of course. Although Lyndon may have wandered to other women more than once, Lady Bird knew she was the center of his life. She found that out the day in July 1955 that Senator Johnson collapsed with a massive heart attack. "Take my hand and stay with me," he said as she rushed him to the hospital. "I want to know you're here while I'm trying to fight this thing." For six weeks, she lived in the room next to his; she was with him literally day and night.

That experience—and a large dose of southern womanhood and the Tall Texan explanation—underlies an extraordinary scene Liz Carpenter recalls from the 1960 campaign. Texas was in the grip of a September heat wave, which means temperatures in the hundreds. Several times Lady Bird was assailed by hecklers who accused her of treason and worse for trying to put John F. Kennedy, a Catholic, in the White House. Early in the day she sprained her ankle, but she kept going until she reached her hotel room late that afternoon and collapsed on the bed with the ankle swollen to three times its normal size.

The phone rang. It was LBJ calling from Washington, to find out how the day had gone. "Just perfectly, dear," Lady Bird said, omitting all mention of the murderous heat, the vicious hecklers, the swollen ankle. Pacing beside the bed, an exhausted, sweat-drenched Liz Carpenter told herself to stay calm and learn something about the arcane art of dealing with a man. But she kept seeing LBJ in his air-conditioned Senate office, blissfully unaware of what his "wimmen," as he probably called them, had gone through for him in the previous ten beastly hours.

"And how are *you*, dear?" Lady Bird said, almost causing Liz to keel over with apoplexy. She decided then and there (and I heartily agree with her) that Lady Bird was unique, and there was no point—or hope—in trying to imitate her.

Four years later, in his own campaign for president, LBJ's respect for Lady Bird increased exponentially with her 1964 invasion of the South aboard "the Lady Bird Special"—an eighteen-car train on which she loaded some 250 reporters and a handpicked staff under Liz Carpenter's unerring eye. "Don't give me the easy towns, Liz," she said, as they planned the trip. "Anyone can get into Atlanta. Let me take the tough ones."

Of course she was snipping a leaf out of the Truman campaign notebook with this whistle-stop tour. Both Johnsons were Truman aficionados; LBJ thought Dad was a great President, and Lady Bird just thought he was great. Early in her First Lady days, she had taken a trip to Greece with him to attend the funeral of King Paul. After the ceremony they met a Greek prince who told them his great-great-grandfather had been an aide to General Ulysses S. Grant in the Civil War. Ex-President Truman, perhaps influenced by several days of listening to Lady Bird's southern accent, decided he no longer had to conceal his true sympathies in that ancient conflict. "Young man," he said, giving Lady Bird a conspiratorial wink, "as far as this lady and I are concerned, your great-great-grandpa was on the wrong side."

Lest this tale upset the uninitiated, perhaps I should add that Dad's mother was an unreconstructed Missouri Confederate until the day she died. When he joined the Army reserve and came home one day in a blue uniform, she told him never to wear it again in her house. She also told him why she felt that way. More than once during the Civil War, her life had been threatened by bushwhacking, barn-burning Yankee guerrillas from Kansas. I can practically guarantee Dad told this story to Lady Bird at some point in their twenty or so hours in the air going to and coming from Greece. To a very small, carefully selected circle, he revealed his southern roots.

Lady Bird did a lot of the crucial advance work for the 1964 tour of the South herself. She personally called most of the congressmen and senators and the governor in each state and asked for their help. "Guv-nuh," she would purr, "I'm thinkin' about comin' down to your state—" She also enlisted a cadre of wives of southern politicians, such as Lindy Boggs of Louisiana and Betty Talmadge of Georgia. Liz Carpenter remarked that they all had the exquisite manners of Melanie in *Gone with the Wind*—and the steel-trap mind of Scarlett O'Hara.

The initial response of the old-boy politicians to this female onslaught was panic and flight. Lady Bird was handed the worst collection of lame excuses in history. One senator said he was still mourning his wife, who had died two years before. A congressman claimed he had a date to go antelope hunting that he could not possibly break. In the early days of our 1948 whistle-stop hegira, the Trumans, written off as losers by every Democrat from Maine to New Mexico, got the same sort of baloney by the carload.

Excuses be damned, the Lady Bird Special rolled out of Washington on October 5, 1964—and began making history. It was, I need hardly add, the first time a First Lady ever went after votes on her own in this totally professional fashion, with advance men—and women—out in front of the scheduled stops rounding up the crowds and lining up the local officials to do the greeting. It was a presidential-style campaign with a First Lady instead of the candidate as the centerpiece.

For four days the Lady Bird Special snaked through the South, making forty-seven stops in eight states from Alexandria, Virginia, to New Orleans, covering an amazing 1,682 miles. Everywhere Lady

Bird delivered a message that was perfectly designed to win southern hearts and even a few minds. She did not spend a lot of time defending the Civil Rights Act of 1964; she simply said she thought it was "right," and in time she was sure most southerners would agree with her. She was really there to tell people that "for this President and his wife the South is a respected and valued and beloved part of the country." She wanted to defend the South against the rest of the nation, against snide jokes about rednecks and cornpone. She wanted to let everyone know she was a southerner and proud of it. "For me," she often said in summary, "this is a journey of the heart."

The first time Lady Bird said that, speaking off the cuff to her advance people, she got a standing ovation from a bunch of mostly cynical pols. From Norfolk to Mobile, she got the same reaction from average southerners—times ten. Day after day, the crowds coming out to wave and listen grew larger. Pretty soon—and once more the memory of a similar experience aboard the Truman train in 1948 made me smile—the skittery governors and congressmen who had been hiding out in the tall timber were fighting to board the Lady Bird Special and get their pictures taken beside the First Lady.

Back in Washington, D.C., an ecstatic LBJ greeted his wife with Texas-size accolades. He called her "one of the greatest campaigners in America" and perhaps surprised himself by exclaiming: "I'm proud to be her husband." I need hardly add that he rolled to a landslide victory over Barry Goldwater in 1964. Half of those contested southern states voted for him, thanks to Lady Bird.

Before LBJ reached that happy climax, however, his campaign was shaken to its foundations by one of those White House tragedies that seem to strike Presidents with the random ferocity of a lightning bolt. Without Lady Bird, the Johnson presidency might not have survived the blow. A few weeks before the election, one of LBJ's closest personal aides, Walter Jenkins, who had worked for him since the 1940s, was arrested in a public men's room performing a homosexual act.

Lyndon Johnson was in New York to give a speech. Reporters besieged him for a comment. He went into hiding and put through a call to Lady Bird. She had already decided what they should do. She would make a statement for both of them. Liz Carpenter was with her when she took LBJ's call. She read him her statement and talked to him in a low, reassuring voice for a long time. Finally she said: "I've never loved you so much as I do this minute."

Lady Bird summoned reporters to the White House and read her statement, which proclaimed the Johnsons' total loyalty to Walter Jenkins and his tormented family. It was a deeply sympathetic, profoundly moving document, which lifted the scandal from vicious gossip to a spiritual plane. Best of all, Lady Bird meant every word of it.

This, I submit, is what a White House partnership is really about— being there for each other when need is paramount. There is a lot more to being First Lady than giving advice on policy. Lady Bird repeatedly proved that matters of the heart are at least as vital.

Along with the campaigning and rescue operations such as the Jenkins affair, Lady Bird concentrated a lot of effort on structuring the White House to give her husband an island of peace on the second floor. When it came to working, Lyndon Johnson made James K. Polk, Woodrow Wilson, and Harry S Truman look like layabouts. The man never stopped long enough to look at a clock; he was immune to orders and exhortations. Only Lady Bird knew how to lure him out of the Oval Office to a quiet dinner with a few friends on the second floor. Without her expert intervention, LBJ might have become a burnout case in his first White House year.

Once Lyndon was President in his own right, Lady Bird felt free to give some thought to other aspects of her job. She was very conscious of the symbolic power of the First Lady, and she wanted to put it to good use. She made a start with "Women Doers" luncheons, which brought together women from Washington and the rest of the country to hear one of their number tell what women were accomplishing in, say, the United Nations. But these luncheons lacked a thematic focus, something that the public at large could respond to and participate in on a national scale.

Typically, Lady Bird found her inspiration in her husband's vision of a greater America, in which not only would poverty be conquered but the natural beauty of the land would be restored and preserved. In his 1964 inaugural address, Lyndon Johnson had called for programs to preserve and enhance America's natural beauty. In that speech and another speech in May of 1964, in which he called on Americans to establish a "Great Society," Lady Bird found what she described as "interests that made my heart sing, the ones I knew most about and cared most about. These were the environment and beautification."

Liz Carpenter once compared Lady Bird Johnson and Eleanor Roosevelt. She noted that Eleanor was an "instigator." She frequently tackled causes on her own, without her husband's endorsement. Lady Bird, on the other hand, was always an implementer, an embellisher and translator of her husband's ideas. "She was a WIFE in capital letters," Liz says.

Cautious as always not to overcommit herself, Lady Bird decided to start her beautification program in Washington, D.C., which was badly in need of a face-lift. Everyone from Secretary of the Interior Stewart Udall to *The Washington Post* had been condemning the capital for its mangy lawns, its crime-ridden parks, its hideous, rat-infested vacant lots. Worst of all was the condition of the 761 miniparks the capital's original planner, Pierre Charles L'Enfant, had inserted into his heroic vision of magnificent avenues and splendid circles. They were mostly, in Lady Bird's words, "gray and dismal, with a little scabrous grass and a couple of leaning benches."

Once more the First Lady demonstrated what a professional approach could accomplish. To her Committee for a More Beautiful National Capital she lured the great names—and great wealth—of Laurance Rockefeller, Mary Lasker, and Brooke Astor. She backed them with Katharine Graham, publisher of *The Washington Post*, plus Stewart Udall and various other government honchos, such as Nash Castro of the National Park Service. Finally she brought aboard leaders of Washington's African-American community, notably Walter Washington, who with Lady Bird's backing eventually became the city's first mayor.

This shrewd mix not only guaranteed top-of-the-line effectiveness but also prevented the committee from turning into an elitist operation that planted flowers and trees in downtown Washington for the tourists and congressmen and ignored the city's eight hundred thousand segregated, often impoverished black residents. This committee planted downtown *and* in the neighborhoods.

Without Lady Bird, the committee might have split into quarreling factions: the neighborhood wing sometimes referred to the downtowners as "the daffodil and dogwood set." The downtowners sometimes opined it was a waste of money to plant flowers and trees for people who did not seem to appreciate them—and occasionally destroyed them. Lady Bird supported both programs with equal enthusiasm.

She also breathed new life into related programs, such as the revival of Pennsylvania Avenue, which had been kicking around Washington since Helen Taft's days. (I exaggerate only slightly.) The architect in charge, Nathaniel Owings, had been supposed to make a report on the project to John F. Kennedy on November 23, 1963. Owings was sure he had been born under an unlucky star, until he met Lady Bird. She not only adopted his plan but also adopted him onto her capital committee. Soon, whenever Owings had a problem getting congressional approval for something tricky, like building a reflecting pool in front of the Capitol, he would procure an endorsement from Lady Bird. "It was like a contract in your file," he said.

Then he would head for the Hill. In the reflecting pool imbroglio (almost everything in Washington is an imbroglio), he approached the austere Speaker of the House, John McCormack, with a roll of plans and sketches a foot thick. "Does Mrs. Johnson like it?" McCormack asked.

"I'm authorized to tell you she approves it completely."

"Never mind the sketches," the Speaker said. "Where do I sign?"

McCormack also found Vice President Hubert Humphrey and the majority and minority leaders of the House and Senate and got them to sign up. In thirty minutes Owings had six signatures it would have taken him a month to obtain on his own. "I was in a dream," he said.

Led by her wealthy members, Lady Bird's Committee for the Capital raised two million dollars and in the next two years landscaped eighty parks, plus nine schools and eight playgrounds, planted 83,000 spring flowering plants, 50,000 shrubs, 25,000 trees, and 137,000 annuals. Mary Lasker, whose generosity had already spread beautiful flowers around New York, was so enthusiastic, she told Lady Bird her only worry now was whether the nation's nurseries would have enough stock to plant "the whole United States."

The neighborhood program evolved into something really worthwhile—Project Pride, which enlisted local residents to "clean up," "fix up," "paint up," and "plant up" some of the most deprived sections of the city. Walter Washington became as enthusiastic about Lady Bird as Nathaniel Owings. "When this program started, there were some who regarded it as Marie Antoinette's piece of cake," Washington said. "After all, how many rats can you kill with a tulip? But it hasn't been that way at all."

With Washington, D.C., on its way to a new look, Lady Bird went national with beautification. She flew around the country, urging all Americans to join her campaign. A tidal wave of speaking invitations poured into the White House. Lady Bird organized cabinet and Senate wives, many of them old friends, to form a speakers' bureau to handle the appearances she could not make without cloning herself. Meanwhile, she began leading "See America" tours to national parks and other scenic sights. These expeditions included several hundred reporters, federal officials, and local folk—the sort of thing that only a pro like Liz Carpenter could orchestrate.

Perhaps the most memorable tour was the trek into the spare, stark Big Bend region of Texas, climaxed by rafting down the Rio Grande. Liz summed up one opinion of this particular outing (with which a comfort lover like me concurs) when she said she preferred the parks where all the concessions were run by the Rockefellers. But Lady Bird loved every minute of the Big Bend adventure. She filled her diary with descriptions of "the awesome spires of the canyon walls pierced by centuries of wind."

Next this tireless woman tackled the legislative side of beautification. She and her staff sponsored and partly wrote a law that LBJ submitted to Congress, to eliminate the proliferation of junkyards and billboards along our nation's highways. Both these industries had

Here Lady Bird
relaxes in a field of
bluebonnets,
reminding us she
was the First Lady
who revitalized
America's love of
natural beauty.
*(Lyndon Baines Johnson
Library)*

powerful lobbyists who battled the bill in every imaginable way—
especially in the West. Some of the more outspoken billboard owners
printed IMPEACH LADY BIRD on their endangered assets.

Lady Bird personally oversaw the White House lobbying for the
bill, making numerous calls herself. LBJ put on the pressure in his
own hell for leather way. The bill was being considered by the House
on the day of a scheduled "Salute to Congress" reception at the White
House. The President sent the solons a message: there would be no
salute if they didn't pass the bill first. It was quite late in the evening
by the time they stopped wrangling and showed up at the White
House with a voted bill. One Republican congressman, a certain
Robert Dole of Kansas, was so annoyed he moved to insert Lady Bird's
name in the language of the bill, as if he wanted to identify her as the
culprit not only behind the controversial measure but also behind the
deflated White House party.

While she was raising the national consciousness about America's natural beauty, Lady Bird somehow found time to be one of the mostest hostesses the White House has ever seen. At everything from formal state dinners to back lawn hoedowns, she and LBJ entertained a staggering two hundred thousand people in their five years in residence. Unlike most White House denizens, Lady Bird never seemed to grow weary of these handshaking marathons. She studied briefing books and consulted aides so she had something friendly and personal to say to almost everyone on the guest list. She topped this hospitality extravaganza by overseeing both her daughters' weddings in the White House, an exercise in press relations and guest list juggling that can safely be compared to restaging D day twice.

Lady Bird's achievements are all the more remarkable for another reason. She played her vibrant, creative role in an administration that was sideswiped by history, almost from the day Lyndon Johnson took office. The Kennedy assassination was only one factor in the creation of a torn country. Northern big city black ghettos seethed with anger, the rural South boiled with racial antagonism, as Martin Luther King and other leaders strove to win basic civil rights for their people. Multiplying the turbulence was the war in Vietnam, which LBJ reluctantly expanded in 1965, when it looked as if our small ally, South Vietnam, was on the brink of defeat by Communist North Vietnam.

As more and more Americans turned against the war, Lady Bird found herself drawn into the controversy. By 1967 protesters gathered whenever she visited a college campus to talk about beautification or the environment. Finally, they invaded the White House. First, the singer Eartha Kitt rose at one of the Women Doers luncheons and ranted against the Johnson administration. According to some reports, she even spat at the First Lady. Then a salute to the nation's writers and artists in the Rose Garden turned into a boycott by some and diatribes by others who showed up only to denounce the President to his face. Day and night, through the windows drifted the chant of protesters in Lafayette Park, across from the White House: "Hey hey, LBJ, how many kids did you kill today?"

Lady Bird watched this nightmare take a fearful toll on her husband. As old Senate friends, such as William Fulbright of Arkansas, turned against him, depression ravaged LBJ's sleep. In her diary, Lady Bird would note with relief that his bedroom light was out at 11:00 and then discover he had awakened at 2:00 A.M. and worked for the rest of the night. She told me how she fought a losing battle with "the night box," in which aides put urgent documents to be signed or reports to be read. No doubt thinking of these latter days, Lady Bird said she really only deserved a B-minus as a First Lady who protected her husband from overwork.

Some mornings, according to an aide, LBJ would lie in bed with the covers pulled up almost to his chin, and the window shades pulled down, reluctant to get up. "I can't read *The Washington Post* this morning," he would groan. As his political partner, Lady Bird felt the vicious accusations, the anguish and frustration and deaths of the endless war, as acutely as her husband. By 1968, she noted ruefully in her diary, when they appeared in public, they moved in what she called "riding in the tumbrel" attitudes, shoulders just a bit squarer, head just a bit higher. One Sunday in March, she wrote: "I have a growing feeling of Prometheus Bound, just as though we were lying there on the rock, exposed to the vultures and restrained from fighting back."

Finally there came a historic moment when Lyndon Johnson and Lady Bird had to decide whether he should seek a second term. Most people have imagined—I know I did until I discussed it with Lady Bird—that they began to ponder this decision in 1968, when opponents of the war such as Senator Eugene McCarthy entered the primaries and demonstrated they could challenge LBJ for the Democratic nomination. In fact, thoughts of a single term had been in Lady Bird's mind since 1965, long before Vietnam became a national obsession. She showed me a passage in her White House diary from that year in which she lamented the "intractable problems" confronting Lyndon. "I am counting the months until March 1968," she wrote, "when, like Truman, it will be possible to say, 'I don't want this office, this responsibility, any longer, even if you want me. Find the strongest, the most able man and God bless you. Goodbye.' "

But the day of decision, when it finally arrived, was more agonizing for the Johnsons than I or almost anyone else has imagined. The ordeal began with Lynda Bird arriving at 7:00 A.M. on the red-eye flight from California, where she had said good-bye to her husband, Charles Robb, as he departed with his Marine company for Vietnam. After church, LBJ went back to work on a speech he was giving to the nation that night, on the war. Lady Bird had spent much of the previous two days reading and rereading it and making suggestions.

Suddenly, as she read the latest draft, Lyndon said: "What do you think about this? This is what I'm going to put at the end of the speech." A pause, and he read a statement which ended with the stunning words "Accordingly, I shall not seek and I will not accept the nomination of my party for another term as your President."

Even though she and Lyndon had discussed it "over and over, hour by hour" in the past, the decision came as a blow to Lady Bird. Struggling for her customary objectivity, she saw there was a part of her that cried out "to go on, to call on every friend we have...to spend and fight, right up to the last." But uppermost in her mind was what she sensed was also dominating Lyndon's mind, the words she had heard him say more than once in recent months: "I don't believe I can unite this country."

In midafternoon of this stressful day, Lady Bird broke the news to Lynda and Luci. Both young women burst into tears. With undisguised bitterness, Lynda said: "Chuck will hear this on his way to Vietnam." Luci's husband, Patrick Nugent, was scheduled to depart for Vietnam in a few days. How could their father do this? they cried. He was betraying the soldiers, betraying in particular the men they loved.

Somehow, Lady Bird calmed her distraught daughters and convinced them to stand by their father. She joined aides in the task of inviting close friends, such as the Clark Cliffords, to the White House for the speech. Again and again she struggled with the temptation to try to change Lyndon's mind, only to realize she more than anyone had played a crucial role in helping him reach this wrenching decision. In the end, she simply told him to make the speech as great as possible. "Remember, pacing and drama," she whispered, as he sat at his desk in the Oval Office.

Until LBJ got to the very end of the speech, which was essentially an announcement that the United States was going to call a halt to the bombing of North Vietnam as part of an attempt to reach a negotiated peace, Lady Bird was not absolutely certain the withdrawal from the presidency would be made. When it finally came, she said she felt an incredible sense of relief, of becoming "immeasurably lighter." She was able to deal calmly with the deluge of phone calls from people like Liz Carpenter, who could not believe it, who begged her to do something, anything, to change LBJ's mind.

"We have done a lot," Lady Bird said, when Liz asked her for a statement for the media. "There's a lot left to do in the remaining months. Maybe this is the only way to get it done."

The First Lady lived up to those brave words. She continued her crusade for beautification and conservation. With her backing, Lyndon persuaded Congress to set aside millions of acres of wilderness for new national parks and wildlife refuges. Lady Bird even managed one more See America trip that took her to Florida and New Orleans and ended in Redwood National Park in California—an appropriate last stop—in the shadow of those unique, gigantic trees, among America's greatest natural treasures.

Back in the White House, every time Lady Bird walked past the portrait of Woodrow Wilson on the wall in the Red Room, she became more convinced that Lyndon had made the right choice. Painted late in Wilson's presidency, it was a picture of a man ravaged by history, the face gaunt, the eyes haunted by wordless pain. Events soon reinforced the wisdom of the decision as well. Within a week, Martin Luther King was assassinated and the nation's cities erupted in orgies of looting and burning. The stature LBJ had gained as a President willing to sacrifice his pride and ambition for the good of the people was invaluable as he struggled to hold the nation together in the aftermath of this tragedy.

As far as the Vietnam War was concerned, LBJ's noble gesture went largely unappreciated, both in America and in North Vietnam. The protesters continued to jeer him, and the Communists paid little more than lip service to peace. But Lady Bird almost magically transcended the atmosphere of rancor and gloom that engulfed the battered administration.

Pundits from Eric Sevareid of CBS to James Reston of *The New York Times* praised her. Reston said she was "probably the most remarkable woman who has presided over the White House in this century." Sevareid said she had created a "new popular consciousness about the precious American land." Shana Alexander, a tough critic of things political, said she was "quite possibly the best First Lady we have ever had." One of her beautification associates called her "the most consummate politician" he has known in Washington.

If there is a secret here, it is in that wonderful phrase this almost perfect First Lady originated when she campaigned aboard the Lady Bird Special in 1964: a journey of the heart. There is no better summary of her five years in the White House. Except, perhaps, the words of one of the members of her staff, as she said good-bye: "You made us all better people, Mrs. Johnson."

—

Chapter 14

THE FIRST LADY
NOBODY KNEW

BEHIND HER BACK JOURNALISTS CALLED HER "PLASTIC PAT" AND "The Robot." Feminists said her subservience to her husband betrayed American womanhood. The British press sneered that her "terrifying poise" was more doll-like than human. "She just doesn't care," scoffed one American reporter. A slightly more charitable columnist opined: "She is really a very nice woman but seems to lack a purpose."

Lady Bird Johnson managed to transcend her husband's unpopularity. Pat Nixon was almost obliterated by the antagonism Richard Nixon generated. The result has been a blank in the public mind about one of the most gifted, hardest working First Ladies in the long history of the White House.

To some extent I shared this miscomprehension until I started work on this book. In my youth the name Nixon ignited sparks in Bess and Harry Truman—and even a few in me, though I tried mightily to distance myself from things political. In one of his less appealing moments on the campaign trail in the 1950s, Dick Nixon accused Harry S Truman of being a Communist. The man who had awakened the country to the realities of Joseph Stalin's horrendous dictatorship and charted the course to eventual victory in the Cold War! It was, perhaps, the ultimate example of the depths of bitter partisanship to which Richard Nixon could sink in his ruthless pursuit of power.

But when Nixon became President of the United States, Dad put aside the memory of that fifteen-year-old gibe and studied his performance with the nonpartisan eyes of a member of the world's most exclusive club. (I know they used to say this about the U.S. Senate, but that has been a misnomer for a long time.) Ex-Presidents see things in a President's performance that the average citizen misses. To Dad's surprise, he liked the firmness with which Nixon set about extricating us from Vietnam on honorable terms. "Every so often," he told me on one of my visits to Independence, "the fellow hits a boomer."

Then Dad added words that to some extent sum up the tragedy of President Richard Nixon and his First Lady: "But no one gives him any credit for it."

We have seen Lady Bird Johnson entering a White House torn by the trauma of assassination. That was in some ways a visible specter that could be exorcised. Richard Nixon brought with him a host of invisible specters—an immense list of enemies hungering for revenge. Coalescing with the passions fueled by the war in Vietnam, they culminated in the presidential disaster called Watergate. Among the many casualties of that upheaval, Dick Nixon dolefully noted in his memoirs that his wife had "not receive[d] any of the praise she deserved. There [was] no round of farewell parties...no testimonials, no tributes. She had given so much to the nation and to the world." Her only reward, he wrote, was "to share my exile. She deserved so much more."

Those are among the truest words Richard Nixon ever wrote. They explain why Pat Nixon is the First Lady nobody really knows. To prove my point, let me tell you a few things about her that will probably surprise you.

She was the first First Lady—and remains the only one—to venture into an overseas combat zone.

She was Jackie Kennedy's equal—some think her superior—in redecorating the White House.

She was the first First Lady to go on record as prochoice on abortion.

She was a woman of great compassion who once said, "Helping another person gives one the deepest pleasure in the world."

A Republican by marriage, Patricia Ryan Nixon was a small *d* democrat in her bones, someone who always preferred to iron her own dresses, wash her own clothes, who instinctively sympathized with the poor and unlucky of this world.

Helen Thomas, the White House reporter who has known all the First Ladies since Bess Truman, said Pat Nixon was "the warmest First Lady I covered and the one who loved people the most."

Without her, Richard Nixon would never have survived Watergate, mentally or physically.

All right, you are probably saying, I'm surprised. Still, when I look at a picture of Pat Nixon with her frozen smile, I can't help thinking those cracks about Plastic Pat and the Robot have a point.

You are right, for the wrong reason. The Pat Nixon Americans saw in public was a woman struggling to play a role she hated, for the sake of the man she loved. People who knew the young Pat Ryan have testified to her being a totally different person. They use words like "approachable," "happy," "enthusiastic," "friendly." She was an incredibly popular teacher of typing and shorthand at Whittier High School, mainly because she never talked down to her students, many of them Mexican Americans.

She was no spoiled daughter of the rich, or even of the middle class. She had been born in a miner's shack in Nevada. Her German-born mother died of cancer when she was fourteen, her Irish-American father succumbed to lung disease when she was eighteen. Pat Nixon never forgot what it meant to be poor and work hard for middling wages. Once, when the journalist Gloria Steinem began asking her about her role models, Pat snapped: "I never had time to think about things like that. I had to work."

Then Pat Ryan married a young lawyer named Richard Nixon, who had enormous energy and large ambitions, and her life changed forever. He plunged into politics, using her life savings to finance his first campaign for Congress. In one of the most meteoric rises in history, in six years he went from congressman to senator to vice presidential candidate. Then came the first of the episodes that would eventually congeal Pat Nixon's smile.

Accused of living on a slush fund from rich Californians, Dick Nixon discovered the Republican Party was inclined to let him swing in the wind. He rescued himself by revealing every humiliating detail of the Nixons' parlous personal finances on national television, while Pat sat silently beside him.

Never again would Richard Nixon trust another politician. Never again would Pat Nixon like one. At a party a few years later, she told Samuel Goldwyn, Jr., that politicians made movie people look like saints. "They [politicians] are the most vicious people in the world," she said. As the daughter of a politician, this strikes me as overkill—but it is grim evidence of the wounds that 1952 ordeal inflicted on Pat Nixon.

Thereafter she loathed politics and dreamt only of the day when Richard Nixon would somehow be cured of his hunger for power and fame. After his failed 1960 bid for the presidency, she made him put in writing a promise to quit politics. A year later, when he told her that he had decided to run for governor of California, she burst into tears. When he announced, without consulting her, that he was going to run for President in 1968, she plunged into a depression and told her daughters she did not know if she could face another campaign.

Yet she faced it, she shook the hands, she answered reporters' questions, she smiled her smile from a thousand platforms. What enabled her to stay in the game? Along with love, it was the conviction that Richard Nixon had gifts, ideas, policies, America badly needed. She wept joyous tears when he won the White House in 1968 because she felt "he was where he could really be of value to the country and to the world."

Incidentally, the American people—unlike the Washington press corps—were unbothered by Pat's frozen smile. If public opinion polls tell us anything, among the voters she was one of the most admired women in America—and she stayed near the top of the polls, even after Watergate. Maybe they intuitively sensed what all but the most compassionate reporters missed: here was heroism in action, a woman doing a job she intensely disliked because fate had handed it to her, and doing it very well.

J. B. West, the White House chief usher who retired soon after the Nixons began their tenure, said it was his "distinct impression" that Mrs. Nixon was not happy in the White House. In later years, when he was more reflective, Dick Nixon himself admitted as much. He said Pat was "very good onstage, so to speak, even though she prefers not to be onstage." I find this deeply moving—and as admirable in its own way as Lady Bird Johnson's consummate performance as First Lady.

Pat Nixon seldom if ever used the word *partner* to describe her relationship with Richard Nixon. "We're a team" was the expression she preferred. It was a team on which Dick was the coach-captain and Pat and to some extent her daughters were players, doing the bidding of the boss. When asked if Richard Nixon ever tried out his speeches on her, Pat said: "He never tries out anything on me."

Yet Pat Nixon worked at being First Lady, even when she was running a temperature of 102. Like the post office, she was never deterred—by snow, rain, or heat—from her appointed rounds. "I never cancel," she said. There was a gritty Irish pride at work here, an inner toughness. But this woman was not cold. Anyone who saw her with a child or a group of children knew that. The political smile was replaced by the real thing, a veritable glow of warmth; her arms opened, she was, for a few minutes, a happy woman.

Once, when a little crippled boy came to the White House for a photo opportunity with the First Lady, Pat saw the youngster was terrified and tried everything to help him relax, to no avail. Suddenly he blurted: "This isn't your house!"

"Why do you say that?" Pat asked.

"Because I don't see your washing machine."

Pat solemnly conducted him to the third floor and showed him the washing machines in the laundry rooms. He returned to the first floor holding her hand, as contented and cheerful as if he were with his own mother. His awed parents said it was the first time he had ever been at ease with a stranger.

Another unknown side of Pat Nixon was the First Lady who tried to read every letter she received and send a personal answer. As the number of letters swelled to over two thousand a day, she realized this was impossible. But she still tried to answer more of her mail than any other First Lady. Again, it was the lowercase democrat at work. She came from a small town and knew what a letter from the White House could mean. "It's shown to all the neighbors, and often published in the local paper," she told reporters. "It's important to people who receive it."

When a letter sounded a note of desperation, Pat often did more than answer it. One young woman told her in grisly detail about her drug addiction and said she was going to commit suicide. A phone call from the First Lady persuaded her to change her mind, and it

Reporters called her Plastic Pat and ridiculed her frozen smile. But behind the scenes, Pat Nixon was a warm and caring woman–especially when children visited the White House. *(The Richard Nixon Library & Birthplace)*

was followed up by psychiatric help, which soon had her on the road to stability.

Although Dick Nixon had semirebuked her when she said their White House entertaining would not be limited to big shots, Pat made good on that promise. Her most innovative idea was a Sunday prayer service in the East Room, to which several hundred Washingtonians were invited every week. It was not only deeply religious in the Quaker tradition Pat had embraced when she married Dick—it was profoundly democratic. African-American clerks from the Bureau of Printing sat beside cabinet members and senators and their wives. All received a personal greeting and a warm handshake from the President and his First Lady.

This people-to-people contact was the side of politics that Pat Nixon valued. What she did not like was being displayed as an icon before screaming thousands in an arena, or to millions on television. That was when she froze, when she saw politics as a horrendous violation of her private self. She was happiest when she could escape from being a prisoner of the White House. She even treasured small escapes, like walking a hundred paces or so ahead of her Secret Service guards.

She frequently bridled at the constraints of protocol and red tape and occasionally insisted on doing things her way. Perhaps the most dramatic example was her visit to Vietnam. It was part of a longer trip to Southeast Asia, which allotted only a day to embattled Saigon. When Pat was told she would spend most of the time having tea and shaking hands with the wives of Vietnamese officials, she shook her head in a way that got everyone's attention. "I want to see some wounded Americans!" she said.

Before anyone in the Secret Service could do more than stutter an objection, the First Lady was in a helicopter, flying over eighteen miles of jungle rife with potential Vietcong sharpshooters to an American evacuation hospital. The Secret Service and Army gunners crouched in the open hatches of the helicopter, loaded machine guns poised to return fire. At the hospital the doctors had a lecture ready to give the First Lady on how well they were running the place. Again, Pat Nixon shook her head. "I want to see the boys," she said.

She spent two hours going from bed to bed, talking with each wounded man in tones too low for frustrated reporters to overhear. More than once she got down on her knees beside a man who could not sit up in bed. Like Eleanor Roosevelt three decades earlier, she made careful notes of names and addresses, and when she returned to the White House wrote letters to parents, telling them she had seen their sons and how much she admired their sacrifices for their country.

Another mission of mercy saw a Pat Nixon who could think in large political terms. It was a glimpse of the First Lady who might have found a larger stage, with a different presidential husband. When Peru was ravaged by an earthquake in May 1970, Pat persuaded Dick to let her fly to Lima with an aid mission that brought tons of supplies and medical help. The presence of the First Lady, personifying American compassion, made the mission historic. Pat toured the devastated areas with the wife of the President of Peru. The result was a vast improvement in relations between the two countries. One correspondent who made the trip observed that not even Eleanor Roosevelt had combined diplomacy and a mission of mercy so astutely.

In 1972 Pat repeated this triumph with a four-nation trip to Africa that began with the inauguration of the new President of Liberia. American and foreign reporters who covered the trip expressed amazement at how smoothly the First Lady handled the diplomacy and the press conferences in each country. When she returned home, Nixon aide Charles Colson prepared a seven-page memorandum on the trip, thick with praise from newspapers and TV commentators. Colson concluded that after three years of the staff trying to project the human side of the Nixon presidency, "Mrs. Nixon has broken through where we have failed. She has come across as a warm, charming, graceful, concerned, articulate person."

Pat Nixon never adopted a cause or a project with the success that gave Jackie Kennedy and Lady Bird Johnson a special aura. She felt that approach narrowed the First Lady's role, excluding all sorts of people and organizations who could use her help. The closest she came to espousing a broad project was something she called "Volunteerism." Pat liked it because it left her free to visit the aged, the blind, the orphaned, the handicapped—to give as many people as possible the benefit of the First Lady's power to attract sympathy and help. Again and again, obviously speaking from the heart, she reminded Americans that government is impersonal. For help to really work, it "needs the personal touch." This was the real Pat Nixon speaking.

One of the most moving stories of Pat's White House years was her invitation to Jacqueline Kennedy Onassis to view the portraits of herself and John F. Kennedy that had recently been hung in the White House. Jackie responded that she could not face a public ceremony. She wanted to bring John Jr. and Caroline but feared the visit would revive grisly memories—especially if the press was swirling around them, asking personal questions.

Pat Nixon scrapped plans for a ceremony. Instead, she launched an operation as secret as anything the CIA has ever put together. There was no publicity whatsoever connected with Jackie's visit. Only four people on the entire White House staff knew anything about it. No one in either the West Wing or East Wing press office was told, so they could honestly plead ignorance to the reporters.

Pat and her daughters, Julie and Tricia, greeted the Kennedys on the second floor. Julie remembers being struck by how much Jackie resembled her photographs—the large, haunted eyes, the pale skin, the perfectly coiffed hair. They went downstairs and looked at Jackie's portrait first. The artist, Aaron Shikler, had created an otherworldly creature, with the long, tapering fingers of a fairy queen. John Jr., ten, and Caroline, thirteen, were unimpressed and said so with refreshing frankness.

From there they went to John F. Kennedy's portrait by the same artist. His arms crossed, his head bowed, he is struggling with the forces of history. The Nixons and Mrs. Onassis watched nervously as John Jr. and Caroline studied it. Without a trace of the anguish the adults had feared the portrait might arouse, both said they liked it and asked what was the next stop on the tour. For them, this was a visit to a fabulous place, the White House, which they had been told about many times but barely remembered. They wanted to see the whole thing.

Pat put Tricia and Julie in charge of their tour while she took Jackie through the recently redecorated state rooms. The Kennedys stayed for dinner with the President, who later took them into the Oval Office, where young John had played as a toddler, and up to the Lincoln Bedroom, where he sat John on the huge bed and told him if he made a wish, it was guaranteed to come true. (This is a piece of the Lincoln legend I had not heard before.) It seemed to work for John, who reported in a thank-you letter he had had great luck the next day in school.

With a depth of emotion only another First Lady would appreciate, Jackie thanked Pat for her top-secret hospitality. "The day I always dreaded turned out to be one of the most precious ones I have spent with my children," she wrote.

In her tour of the redecorated state rooms, Jackie found nothing to criticize and a great deal to praise. This was a remarkable tribute to Pat Nixon, who had undertaken nothing less than a major overhaul of these rooms. In the six years since Jackie had decorated them, over seven million tourists had tramped through; hundreds of receptions, lunches, and dinners had wreaked added havoc on draperies, wallpaper, and rugs.

Pat Nixon made redecorating these rooms one of her priorities. She recruited a first-class art historian and preservationist, Clement Conger, to be the White House curator. He had done some outstanding work at the State Department. Together they toured the White House from top to bottom, discussing what needed to be done. Conger recalls how impressed he was by the First Lady's preparation for this tour. In three hours she did not refer to a single note. Together they chose wallpapers, fabrics, wall colors. Often Pat Nixon displayed a remarkable combination of good taste and historical appreciation. When Conger acquired a portrait of Dolley Madison from the Pennsylvania Academy of the Fine Arts and learned that it had once hung in the Red Room, Pat decided to hang the portrait there again and paint the room in the exact shade of the red velvet draperies in the portrait. She also pursued hundreds of eighteenth- and nineteenth-century pieces of American furniture, paintings, and other objets d'art to add to the White House collection. As usual, Congress was in its no-real-money-for-the-White-House mode. Acquiring these treasures called for major private fund-raising.

By the time Pat Nixon left in 1974, the Executive Mansion's antique and art collection had become one of the finest in the nation. Only a third of the furnishings were authentic antiques when the Nixons moved in. When they left, two-thirds were vintage treasures. Clement Conger often urged the First Lady to seek a little publicity for this accomplishment. But she refused to say a word about it. She did not want anyone to think she was trying to steal Jackie Kennedy's glory.

Pat never stopped thinking of ways to help Americans and foreign visitors appreciate the White House. She launched the idea of printing well-diagrammed pamphlets in different languages so foreigners would know what rooms they were going through. Even when Watergate was haunting her, she arranged for the first time for visitor tours of the gardens. Probably her crowning achievement in this department was the decision to illuminate the White House every night. The artfully deployed lights made the mansion seem doubly majestic. In the shadows beyond their glow seemed to lurk decades of half-forgotten history.

I remember being in Washington not long after the nightly illumination began. As I walked past it, I had an unnerving experience. I turned to the friend I was with and said: "You know, the Margaret Truman who lived in that house is a complete stranger to me. She seems like a totally separate person." I have often wondered whether Pat Nixon's illumination has had a similar effect on other former White House residents.

This portrait of Pat Nixon is all the more remarkable if we pause to consider what was happening in the nation her husband was attempting to govern. In the first year of the Nixon administration, America was racked by no fewer than forty thousand protests, bombings, and assorted acts of violence as the leaders of the antiwar movement, convinced they had driven Lyndon Johnson from office, sought to break

President Nixon too. Wherever Pat Nixon went, protesters shouted vile names at her. Another trick was showering her with confetti, then shouting: "If that was napalm, you'd be dead."

The peace movement came to Washington for huge demonstrations on October 15, 1969, when a quarter of a million protesters gathered for Moratorium Day. The protests became more and more violent, until they reached a searing climax in the spring of 1971. This time, two hundred thousand marchers tried to shut down the federal government. They bombarded motorists with rocks and bottles, blocked traffic, fought pitched battles with police. At the White House, buses were drawn up in the surrounding streets in a protective cordon. Armed guards with loaded weapons and canisters of tear gas swarmed behind the fence. "It was like a war," said one of Pat Nixon's staff.

Any First Lady who was in the White House during such days might acquire a somewhat frozen smile. Throughout these tension-filled years, Pat Nixon also had to deal with something even more unnerving: her inability to communicate with the lonely, brooding man she had married. Again and again throughout his presidency, Richard Nixon revealed almost incredible gaps in his personal relationship with his wife. When Pat returned from Africa loaded with media praise, she talked to H.R. Haldeman and John Ehrlichman, Nixon's two top aides. Neither so much as mentioned the trip to the President. When she complained to her husband about this affront, he simply noted it in his diary as a sort of oddity.

Even when Pat tried to reach out to Richard Nixon, he managed to convert the attempt into a negative. In early 1972, when he was grappling with a treacherous Communist offensive in Vietnam and violent protests at home, she told him she did not know how he was able to withstand the pressures of his job. The President noted this remark in his diary and added that Pat's questions were "not intended to hurt." She simply did not understand the problems he was facing.

There is a lot of hidden anguish in those words. They spring, I think, from the root quarrel in the Nixon marriage—Pat's loathing for politics, which made her husband feel that he was perpetually engaged in a profession that caused her pain. Unquestionably they tried to love each other across this gulf, but the gulf remained, a kind of black hole that sucked into it the good feelings that might have made Richard Nixon a more human, more stable President.

Yet the Nixons continued to function as a team. The historical record is undeniable on this point. Richard Nixon refused to submit to the protesters' demand for an immediate, unilateral withdrawal from Vietnam, and his wife displayed an equal toughness. "We are not going to buckle to these people," she told her press secretary. On one of the 1971 protest's worst days, she went ahead with a luncheon for congressional wives. On other days she maintained her full schedule.

From a political point of view, this toughing out produced the greatest payoff in American history: Richard Nixon's stupendous victory in his run for reelection in 1972. The protesters turned off the vast majority of American voters—and they unglued the Democrats, impelling them to nominate Senator George McGovern, a candidate who simply did not represent the moderate majority of the party. I remember my mother saying, distress in her voice, during that tumultuous election: "This isn't the Democratic Party that I knew." As it turned out, our party got clobbered so badly, the corpse was barely recognizable by anybody. The Nixon team garnered 520 electoral votes to McGovern's 17, winning 61 percent of the popular vote to his 38.

For the Nixons, the real victory came in January, when the North Vietnamese finally accepted terms that ended the war. In his memoirs, Henry Kissinger tells of calling Nixon to congratulate him, and how pleased he was when Pat took the phone to congratulate Kissinger in return for his years of patient negotiation. Kissinger added a remarkable tribute to Pat—words that might, if fate had been kinder to Richard Nixon, served as a eulogy of her White House years: "What a gallant lady.... With pain and stoicism she had suffered the calumny and hatred that seemed to follow her husband.... Her fortitude had been awesome and not a little inspiring because one sensed it had been wrested from an essential gentleness."

This pinnacle of success, as Mr. Kissinger dolefully noted at Richard Nixon's funeral, suddenly turned into a precipice called

Watergate. As the President stonewalled and lied to cover up the facts of the Republican break-in at Democratic Party headquarters, Pat Nixon could only watch in mute horror. The gulf between them created by her loathing for politics became part of the abyss that swallowed Richard Nixon's reputation. From a politician whose every calculation seemed uncannily apt, he became a blunderer who could not do anything right. When Pat discovered that he had been taping every conversation in the Oval Office, she was appalled and urged him to burn the tapes immediately. He ignored her and went his lonely, dogged way to political destruction.

In the end, after eighteen months of battering revelations and denunciations in the newspapers and on television, an exhausted, demoralized Richard Nixon became the first President to resign his great office. Once more, he ignored his wife's advice. She wanted him to fight it out to the end in an impeachment trial—to drag out of the White House closets the skeletons of bugging and manipulation of the FBI by other Presidents, all the way back to Franklin Roosevelt. It was heroic advice—but I fear it sprang from Pat's loathing for politics, from her desire to prove how vicious politicians could be, as much as from a desire to vindicate her husband.

To his credit, Richard Nixon preferred resignation. He saw that such a carnival of mudslinging could and probably would damage the presidency beyond repair. As it was, Watergate inflicted wounds from which the office has yet to recover.

So the Nixon presidency dwindled to that hot day in August 1974 when Richard and Pat Nixon and the man and woman who would replace them, Gerald and Betty Ford, walked to a waiting helicopter on the White House lawn. The ex-President gave a rambling, almost incoherent farewell speech in which he praised his mother, while Pat, standing behind him, fought back tears. Of his First Lady, Richard Nixon in that tormented farewell said not a word. Yet Julie Nixon, looking back on the eighteen-month ordeal, said it was Pat Nixon's inner strength that had held her husband and the whole family together. His omission was one more mute witness to the gulf that had separated them since that trauma of abandonment and alienation in 1952.

In Pat Nixon's final White House words, it was the old wounded loathing that spoke. Betty Ford, struggling to say something benign, remarked on the length of the red carpet that had been rolled across the lawn to the helicopter. Pat Nixon replied: "You'll see so many of those, you'll get to hate them."

Chapter 15

—

THE

GENERALS'

LADIES

THE MORE I STUDIED FIRST LADIES, THE MORE CONNECTIONS I SAW between them. One of my better brain waves linked two who were separated in time by almost a century, Julia Dent Grant and Mamie Doud Eisenhower. Studied in isolation, they do not seem to have much in common, beyond being Republicans. But when you see them both as army wives, a whole world of associations comes to life—and with them a lot more understanding of how they handled the role of First Lady.

We have just finished reading about a First Lady who hated politics and barely managed to tolerate the White House, although she did a good job. There have been other First Ladies who hated the job so much they seldom came out of their bedrooms for their husbands' entire terms. President Andrew Johnson's wife, Eliza, was one of these recluses. Bewildered and horrified by her spouse's all-out war with Congress over how to deal with the defeated South, which led to his near impeachment in 1868, she came downstairs to receive visitors only twice in four years.

Julia Grant and Mamie Eisenhower, on the other hand, liked being First Lady and managed many aspects of the job quite well. They were not their husbands' political partners. But they ran the White House with flair and dispatch and did a better than average job of keeping their Presidents healthy and happy.

The secret of their success was their long careers as army wives. From the beginning of their marriages, they were expected to entertain their husbands' fellow officers and their wives at dinner parties as soon as they arrived on a post. Meeting strangers and making small talk, a major part of the First Lady's job, soon came naturally to them. As their husbands moved up in the Army, they acquired larger houses and more money, enabling them to give bigger and better parties— good training for White House receptions.

Finally, they had in common something rare in First Ladies. They were unfazed by the White House's splendor. To some extent they felt they had it coming to them. They had put in their junior years of pinching pennies and cutting corners as wives of underpaid lieutenants and captains. Talent and luck had made their husbands generals—and then winning generals on a grand scale. When they contemplated the breadth of their husbands' triumphs—Grant, the savior of the Union in the Civil War; Eisenhower, the savior of Europe in World War II—the White House seemed a perfectly logical and well-deserved next step.

That was unquestionably Julia Grant's attitude. In fact, she was far more interested in living in the White House than her husband, who saw himself as a soldier with little concern and less aptitude for politics. The leitmotiv of the Grants' tenure was struck on inauguration day in 1869. After he took the oath of office and gave his speech, the new President walked across the platform to his wife and whispered: "Well my dear, I hope you're satisfied."

In her memoirs, Julia downplayed her role as power broker but did portray Grant as a reluctant candidate. Their good friend General William Tecumseh Sherman may have had something to do with this stance. After the Republicans nominated Grant, Sherman warned Julia that now she would find out she was married to "a very bad man."

Julia was indignant. "Why, General," she exclaimed. "General Grant does all things well. He is brave, he is kind, he is just, he is true." "Oh my dear lady," Sherman replied. "It is not what he has done but what *they will say* he has done. . . . You will be astonished to find out what a bad man you have for a husband."

Recalling this story after she left the White House, Julia said: "I was astonished too, but I grew not to mind it."

Having seen how attacks on their husbands caused other First Ladies so much pain and anguish, you may be surprised, as I was, by Julia Grant's flippant dismissal of the critical slings and arrows that are an inevitable part of the presidency. To understand her attitude requires further recourse to her unique position as the wife of Ulysses S. Grant. These days Grant has faded from popular memory. His tomb on Riverside Drive in New York, once one of the major tourist attractions of the city, has been allowed to molder into a defaced, abandoned wreck, to the justified indignation of his descendants and the disgrace of the National Park Service, which is supposed to maintain it.

In 1868 Ulysses S. Grant was as close to a sacred figure as any American had come since the death of George Washington. Unassuming, reticent, he was another small *d* democrat in Republican clothing whose appeal cut across all parties and classes. No one completely understood how this stumpy, silent man had saved the Union as it teetered on the brink of defeat in the Civil War. But he had saved it—and the slogan he offered to the exhausted nation seemed heaven-sent: "Let us have peace."

Another reason for Julia's immunity to criticism of her husband was the simple fact that she adored him—and he adored her—with an extravagance seldom seen again in the White House until the Reagans arrived. The mansion has its share of touching love stories, but the Grants' saga is the stuff of storybook romance. From the day she met him, Julia was convinced her laconic lieutenant was destined for "great things." Her wealthy Missouri father did not think so—nor did Grant's superiors in the U.S. Army, who handed him a series of dead-end assignments that drove him to drink and finally to resignation from the service. But Julia's faith in him apparently never wavered, and she followed "Ulys" from one discouraging job to another with a resolution that was doubly amazing for a woman raised in a mansion. It was named, incidentally, White Haven, perhaps another reason why Julia felt at home in the White House.

The Grants had four children, and they added youthful good cheer to the aura of triumph the General and Julia brought to 1600 Pennsylvania Avenue. Two older sons spent most of their time away at college, but thirteen-year-old Nellie was pretty and high-spirited like her mother. Ten-year-old Jesse was a hell-raiser who was constantly playing pranks and sneaking stories to reporters.

Julia doted on Jesse, who, she claimed, "had an answer for everything." In her autobiography (the first by a First Lady) she told how smoothly the scamp could outwit his father. One day Jesse showed up late for breakfast, and Grant gave him the standard parental lecture. (As a chronic late sleeper, I heard the Truman variation more than once.) "Jess, how is this? Nine o'clock and you just down to breakfast? When I was your age I had to get up, feed four or five horses, cut wood for the family, take breakfast and be off to school by eight o'clock."

Jesse smiled sweetly at his father and said: "But you did not have such a papa as I have."

When the whole family was in residence, the Grants frequently assembled in Julia's bedroom at the end of the day for a half hour of teasing and storytelling. In her autobiography, Julia wrote a charming description of the scene. She lay on her bed, one of the boys often stretched across the foot, and the President sat next to him smoking a cigar. Nellie sat in a cushioned chair, "radiant in the beauty of youth and a full dinner dress," while jokes and gossip flew back and forth. "These half hours were the [White House] times we really enjoyed most," Julia said.

Julia also thoroughly enjoyed taking charge of the White House. She was the first First Lady in decades to do something about its dilapidated condition. With a little help from her victorious General, she browbeat Congress into voting funds for a thorough overhaul. One of her innovations caused Congress to rumble and growl about the First Lady wasting money on a newfangled idea: closets. The more things change, the more Congress remains the same.

The First Lady also took charge of the mansion's servants with a firmness worthy of her military background. Discipline had disintegrated under the distracted Lincolns and Johnsons. Ushers, sweepers, and messengers hung around the north door, chatting with the doormen, smoking pipes, and heating their lunches as if they were on bivouac. Julia banned the hangers-on forthwith and ordered the doormen to start wearing black dress suits and white gloves. They were to stand at attention while on duty, and smoking was strictly forbidden.

The staff groused at first, but they soon learned that the First Lady practiced another army tradition: she cared about the welfare of the lower ranks. Warmhearted and kind, Julia seldom gave unreasonable orders. She fretted about their low pay and was always ready to help if anyone needed a loan because of a family illness or some other misfortune. Often she advised the staff to invest their spare cash in real estate, which was selling at bargain rates in the expanding capital. One of the black staffers, Henry Harris, declined to take this advice. Julia nagged and pestered him and finally *ordered* him to buy some land. When he died, his wife and children inherited a substantial estate.

Succeeding White House families were grateful for another change Julia Grant made in the mansion's rules and regulations. In 1869 the grounds were still open to the public, as a sort of park. When the First Lady went for a stroll with one of her children, she was often followed by "a crowd of idle, curious loungers." She persuaded Ulysses to close the gates and post guards at them. Passersby could still peer at the First Family sitting on the South Portico, but that was a major improvement over having John Q. Public literally breathing down their necks.

Along with launching major redecorations of the East Room, the Blue Room, and other state rooms downstairs, Julia Grant purchased new china, 587 pieces in an earth color called Grecian. In the center was a cluster of various American flowers, with no two plates exactly the same. Julia also strove to banish bureaucratic stuffiness and make the old house warm and cheery. She put bright silk tydie bows on the backs of the parlor chairs and colorful pillows on the sofas. Lively prints decorated the walls.

To this stylish White House, Julia invited foreign diplomats, members of Congress, and permanent and temporary Washingtonians for glittering receptions and elegant twenty-nine-course dinners. She had spent enough time in Washington as a general's wife to perceive that if the First Lady chose to be, she was the social leader of the city. Julia chose to be. She prevailed on the President to come to her receptions, which quadrupled their attendance; everyone wanted to get a close look at the nation's hero. Soon there was scarcely a man or woman in Washington who was not panting for invitations to the White House.

Julia laid down strict rules for her guests, and she enforced them with military rigor. Ladies outside the Grant official family were expected to wear hats. In her autobiography, Julia wrote that sometimes a caller imposed upon her "good nature" by declining to wear

Julia Grant was the first First Lady to write her memoirs. She tried to get her reluctant husband elected to a third term and almost succeeded. *(American Heritage Library)*

one. But this "little maneuver was never repeated by the same person." Some guests encountered plainclothesmen Grant hired to make sure no one showed up with a gun or knife. Memories of Lincoln's assassination still haunted the White House. These forerunners of the Secret Service were not above probing the contents of a lady's purse or frisking surprised gentlemen.

Thanks in part to Ulysses Grant's stupendous fame, during his eight years in the White House the press discovered the Executive Mansion made good copy. Julia gave interviews, and her husband's fondness for risking his presidential neck behind the two fastest horses in the district became national news. Pretty Nellie's high jinks at midnight dancing parties were eagerly devoured by millions of readers. Descriptions of the incredibly elaborate dresses of the period all but exhausted the reporters' supplies of adjectives.

Julia's affability and self-confidence made her one of the most popular First Ladies in White House history. She sometimes teased her famous husband in public and liked to show him up now and then. Once, when young Jesse vaulted over the porch railing of their summer cottage at Long Branch, New Jersey, Grant observed that it was a good way to get out of the house if the place caught fire. But he wondered how Julia would escape a conflagration. She stood up, put her hand on the railing, and vaulted over it in a perfect imitation of Jesse. "That way," she said.

There was a political purpose at work in the Grants' relaxed, comfortable style. In Washington, D.C., nothing, however seemingly innocent, is completely devoid of politics. Both Grants saw their wholesome family, their lavish entertaining, as a projection of his slogan, "Let us have peace." They were trying to steady the nerves and soothe the anxieties of a nation shaken by a civil war that had left in its wake a million dead and wounded and almost as many widows and orphans.

For a while Julia and Ulysses succeeded admirably. The General was elected by a landslide for a second term in 1872. Then the Democrats won control of the House of Representatives in the 1874 midterm elections and began investigating the Grant administration.

They uncovered scandal after scandal. Millions in graft had gone to federal officials administering government contracts; the stench reached into Grant's cabinet and White House staff. The President himself was not implicated. But the public discovered he was much too naive and trusting in his choice of subordinates.

Before the political roof fell in, Julia managed an extravaganza which hypnotized the nation: her daughter Nellie's wedding to a wealthy Englishman, Algernon Sartoris. They had met when eighteen-year-old Nellie toured Europe in the summer of 1873. Julia tried to talk her out of the union, but Nellie was as strong willed as her mother. After months of feverish speculation in the newspapers, the wedding was set for May 21, 1874. Julia and Nellie, followed by swarms of reporters, traveled to New York by special train to select her wedding dress. It was a traditional white satin gown covered by a great wavy overskirt of Brussels point lace that spilled into a six-foot train.

At 11:00 A.M. on the great day, the bride descended the grand staircase preceded by eight bridesmaids in white satin, with overskirts of white illusion. Through the Blue Room and the Green Room the procession marched to the spacious East Room, where the groom met Nellie and escorted her to a platform beneath the central chandelier. The ceremony was performed there so it could be seen by all 250 guests.

The White House was turned into a garden for the occasion. Masses of blossoms and ferns were banked against the walls. A wedding bell of white roses hung from the ceiling. Nellie's veil was held in place by a wreath of white orchids and orange blossoms. Her gift from the groom was a loose bouquet of rare flowers that had been rushed from New York on a night train. Algernon, in a gesture of gender equality a hundred years ahead of his time, upset the Grants by insisting on carrying a bouquet of his own.

After a reception and a viewing of the wedding presents in the upstairs Oval Room, the doors of the State Dining Room were thrown open to reveal a fantasy world full of ropes of flowers, with more banks of blossoms piled on silver trays at the end of the banquet table. The food was not as overwhelming as a twenty-nine-course state dinner, but it was enough to threaten any modern diner with indigestion. The guests started with softshell crab and worked their way through lamb, beef, wild duck, and chicken. The multi-tier wedding cake was served with chocolate pudding and baskets of chilled fruits. All this, plus descriptions of the gowns of the guests, many of them wives of the nation's burgeoning crop of millionaires, pushed the rest of the news off the front pages of the newspapers.

Afterward, the newlyweds drove to Union Station in a White House carriage while tens of thousands lined the streets and applauded. It would be nice to report that they lived happily ever after, but Sartoris turned out to be a cad and a bounder. However, he had the decency to die in 1893, leaving Nellie a very rich widow.

Julia Grant enjoyed the White House so much, she hated the thought of leaving it in 1877. She brushed aside the numerous scandals as mere blemishes and urged the General to run for a third term. Grant demurred. He felt personally humiliated by the lapses of his appointees and yearned to escape politics.

This led to a first-class contretemps between the President and his First Lady. The Pennsylvania state legislature—Republican controlled, of course—had passed a resolution urging Grant to run for a third term. Numerous Republican newspapers were voicing similar sentiments. One Sunday in the spring of 1876, Grant summoned the cabinet to the White House and read them a letter he had written to the Pennsylvania pols, declaring he would not be a candidate.

Julia Grant noticed the cabinet members coming and going and wanted to know what they were doing in the White House on Sunday. Grant said he would tell her as soon as he "lighted his cigar." He went off, supposedly in search of a match, and was gone several minutes. When he returned, he told her about the letter.

"Why did you not read it to me?" Julia cried.

"I know you too well. It would never have gone if I had read it."

"Bring it and read it to me now!" demanded Julia.

Grant shook his head. "It is already posted. That's why I waited to light my cigar, so it would be beyond recall."

"Oh Ulys! Was that kind to me? Was that just to me?"

"I do not want to be here another four years. I don't think I could stand it," Grant said. "Don't bother [me] about it, I beg of you."

Julia felt "deeply injured" for a while but she soon recovered her good cheer, and the presidential couple, deserted by the last of their children when Jesse went to college, often spent the evening in one of the upstairs parlors holding hands and chatting like a pair of youthful lovebirds. But Julia still had trouble tearing herself away from the White House. She hung on as hostess right through inauguration day, presiding at an elaborate luncheon for incoming President Rutherford B. Hayes and his wife, Lucy, which had them wondering if she was ever going to depart. Julia barely kept her composure until she was in the privacy of the railroad car, where she hurled herself on her General's broad chest and wept bitter tears.

To console her, Grant suggested a trip around the world. Julia instantly accepted, foreseeing it would be a perfect way to wangle Ulysses into a third term: As we shall see in a later chapter, strong-willed Julia almost succeeded, with disastrous consequences for the Republican Party.

—

JULIA'S GRIEF ON LEAVING THE WHITE HOUSE WAS UNDERSTANDABLE if we recall the nomadic existence of the army wife. Number 1600 Pennsylvania Avenue was the closest thing to a permanent home the Grants had ever known. Mamie Doud Eisenhower's experience in the U.S. Army replicates this roving life—and then some. She moved thirty-four times—seven times in a single year—before reaching the White House.

Like Julia Grant, Mamie grew up in very comfortable circumstances, one of three sisters whom well-to-do parents showered with money and attention. In a prophetic touch almost as good as Julia growing up in a house called White Haven, the Douds had a red carpet running down the front steps of their Denver home, apparently because there was always a party in progress.

Cupid's dart found its mark in Mamie's heart when lithe, strong-jawed Lieutenant Dwight David (Ike) Eisenhower met nineteen-year-old Mamie while the Douds were spending the winter in San Antonio, Texas, in 1915. He's about the handsomest male I've ever seen, she thought. Ike, known as the woman hater of nearby Fort Sam Houston, succumbed almost as instantaneously.

Behind his Texas-size smile, Ike was a much sterner character than Ulysses S. Grant. When his bride began to sob because he was leaving her to go on maneuvers less than a month after their wedding, Ike sat her down and said, as she recalled it a half century later, "Mamie, there is one thing you must understand. My country comes first and always will. You come second."

Mamie retaliated by going home to Denver whenever she found the Army too much to handle. For a while it looked as if the Eisenhower marriage might founder. It suffered a body blow when their firstborn son, Doud Dwight Eisenhower, nicknamed Icky, died of scarlet fever in 1921. Only with the arrival of a second child, John Sheldon Doud, did good feelings return. But in the 1930s Mamie let Ike spend a year in the Philippines without her because she did not like hot climates. Unlike the vigorous, robust Julia Grant, Mamie suffered from a number of illnesses—insomnia, dizzy spells (from an inner ear disorder, Ménière's disease), a heart which beat with violent irregularity if she became fatigued or upset. These woes entitled her to spend a lot of time in bed—or justified yet another retreat to Denver.

In World War II, Dwight Eisenhower soared to fame while Mamie sat home, lonely and unhappy and letting Ike know it now and then. While many of his letters to her are full of endearing sentiments, others are on the short side. A great many people believe General Eisenhower had an affair with his attractive Anglo-Irish secretary-driver, Kay Summersby, although the lady herself, in her two books on the subject, was evasive to the point of obfuscation. Mamie was worried enough about the rumor to ask Ike bluntly if there was any truth to it. He emphatically denied it.

At any rate, by the time Ike and Mamie reached the White House, they were definitely not lovebirds like the Grants. Possibly thinking of Kay Summersby, Mamie confided to Julie Nixon, after Julie married her grandson, David Eisenhower, that there were a lot of times when Ike broke her heart. But the Eisenhower union was still much more than a marriage of convenience. No matter what may have happened in Europe, Mamie had a strong sense of being the significant woman in Ike's life.

But it was a marriage without even a semblance of equality. While Julia Grant was not in the least shy about giving her general political and even military advice (which he seldom took), Mamie never dreamt of doing such a thing. When reporters asked her in 1952 how she would describe her life, she replied she was "thankful for the privilege of tagging along by Ike's side."

On the way to the White House, Mamie had to cope with several challenges Julia Grant never had to worry about. In the Grants' day, candidates stayed home and let others campaign for them. The Eisenhowers had to fight both Republicans (Senator Robert Taft of Ohio challenged Ike for the nomination) and Democrats for the presidency, a struggle which involved flying all over the country. Mamie hated crowds—and planes. But her devotion to Ike overcome her nerves, and she soon became a key player in the Eisenhower road show. She seldom said a word, but her signature bangs, her youthful figure and her cheerful smile were worth fifty electoral votes, in the opinion of one Ike staffer.

Eventually, Mamie began to enjoy herself. "Seeing thousands and thousands of people adoring Ike, believing in his leadership, kept me cloud high all the time," she told one reporter. She was also buoyed by a solemn promise Ike made to her, that once they got out of the White House, he would never ask her to fly anywhere again.

To Harry Truman's chagrin, Ike won in a landslide. By the time the election ended, so many nasty charges about McCarthyism, Communism, and the supposed mess in Washington had been traded back and forth, the incoming and outgoing Presidents were barely speaking to each other. But my mother liked Mamie. She had gotten to know her when Ike served as Army chief of staff under Dad. For a year Mamie had come to the White House once a week to study Spanish in a class that Mother organized to promote inter-American friendship. The two First Ladies had no trouble remaining friends. Mother invited Mamie to tea and gave her a tour of the mansion. After Mamie left, Mother cast a wry eye on one of the White House staff and said they could look forward to "plenty of pink" in the new First Lady's decorating plans.

Bess did not need a crystal ball for that prediction. Pink was Mamie's favorite color. She wore pink dresses, pink suits, pink shoes, pink bows. She even had pink cloth covers on her lipstick tubes. Sure enough, Mamie splashed pink all over the White House. Pink cushions, pink furniture for her bedroom. Since pink is usually considered a little girl's color, some psychohistorians have suggested that Mamie saw herself as Ike's little girl. I say bosh. The real Mamie Eisenhower was a lot more complicated.

There was nothing little girlish about the way Mamie took charge of the White House. The staff swiftly found out they were dealing with a general's lady. The chief usher, J. B. West, discovered she gave orders that were "staccato, crisp, detailed and final." Whenever she left the White House, Mamie told Mr. West, she wanted to be "escorted to the diplomatic entrance by an usher. And when I return, I am to be met at the door and escorted upstairs."

J. B. West reported Mamie could also display a "spine of steel." She meticulously reviewed menus and seating arrangements for luncheons and dinners. One day West showed her a luncheon menu she had never seen before. "What's this?" Mamie demanded. West explained the President had approved it several days ago. "I run everything in my house," Mamie said. "In the future all menus are to be approved by me and no one else."

Early in their marriage, Mamie and Ike had worked out a division of labor. He handled the "office" part of their life together with no interference or comments from her. She ran the home on the same basis. She had always handled their household finances with a thrifty eye, and she applied it to their White House living expenses, which come out of the President's pocket. Every morning she scanned the local newspapers for bargains and hustled the staff around the city to nail down the good buys.

Mamie Eisenhower liked life in the White House with Ike. "I've got my man right here where I want him," she told one staffer, contrasting this with her years of separation as an army wife. *(Bettmann Archive)*

Mamie was equally firm about staff conduct. White House employees were banned from the family elevator. If they wanted to get from one wing of the house to the other, they were told to use the basement or go outside. J. B. West became "Mr. West," but his subordinates were addressed by their first names. Within a few weeks, Mamie had mastered the Executive Mansion's table of organization and knew not only every job but who held it.

As with Julia Grant, the staff soon discovered the General's lady was also intensely interested in their welfare. If someone fell ill, a bouquet from the First Lady cheered him or her toward recovery. The White House chef had a standing order to supply every staffer with a scrumptious cake on his or her birthday. For Christmas Mamie spent days selecting and wrapping presents for all of them.

Simultaneously, she hostessed and hostessed, averaging seven hundred visitors a day in 1953. (My hand aches just thinking about it.)

When sixteen hundred members of the Federation of Women's Clubs tried to wangle an invitation to tea on about twenty-four hours notice, Mamie compromised by driving to their convention center and shaking hands there. Some other First Ladies would have used the short notice as an excuse to stay home and take a nap. Mamie's broad smile, her bright clothes (green was another favorite color), her bubbly good cheer wowed the visitors. Ike was so delighted, he burst into uncharacteristic praise, declaring that Mamie's "intelligence and charm" had made the White House "meaningful" to guests.

Beyond that remark, there is considerable evidence that Mamie's performance as First Lady earned her new respect from Ike and did a lot to restore their badly strained marriage. Mamie seemed to sense this—and it became another reason why she liked the White House. "I've got my man right here, where I want him!" she told J. B. West.

One day Mamie arrived late for dinner. Ike, punctual like most generals, felt a reprimand was in order. "Do you realize you've kept the President of the United States waiting?" he huffed, only half humorously.

"Why no," Mamie said. "I've been busy making myself pretty for my husband."

Stories like this may explain why Ike shunned the Washington party circuit. "For years my evenings have been somebody else's," he told a friend. "At last I've got a job where I can stay home nights and by golly, I'm going to stay home." Mamie persuaded him to take up as a hobby what used to be his household chore: cooking. In their peripatetic Army years, Mamie never got familiar with a stove, mainly, she claimed, because Ike was a much better cook. She ordered a kitchen installed on the second floor, and President Ike regularly whipped up their favorite dishes.

As a hostess, Mamie gradually found she could not maintain her 1953 pace. Her weak heart and her dizzy spells required a number of long vacations from the White House and a lot of bed rest. I learned from Julie Nixon that Mamie was also influenced by a skin specialist who told her that if she spent one day a week in bed, she would never get a wrinkle. She spent so much time in her White House bed one of the maids nicknamed her "Sleeping Beauty."

Mamie's daughter-in-law, Barbara Eisenhower, often played substitute First Lady for her. Barbara even accompanied Ike on his historic trip to India, when Mamie, dreading the long flight, decided to pass. I wish I had room to say more about being a surrogate First Lady. I did a bit of it myself when my mother lingered in Independence. It is hard work but sort of fun, if you don't mind getting your hand mashed.

Ike too found the presidency a stressful job. In 1955 he suffered a heart attack, which left many people unsure whether he should run for reelection in 1956. His brother Milton and a number of other close advisers urged him to quit. But Mamie, unwittingly borrowing a leaf from Edith Wilson's book, demurred. She felt Ike would deteriorate without a challenge to his will to live—and cast her vote for a second term.

Ike made the final decision, of course. But it was the start of Mamie performing another traditional First Lady's role—protector. She became the guardian of Ike's schedule, constantly urging him to take vacations, worrying every time he gave a speech, because the effort invariably raised his blood pressure to unnerving heights. In his second term, Ike was stricken by another heart attack and an intestinal disorder, ileitis, which required serious surgery, redoubling Mamie's concern.

In her protector role, Mamie Eisenhower, unquestionably the least political of the modern First Ladies (in her eight White House years, she only entered the Oval Office four times), may have changed the course of American history. As John F. Kennedy and Richard M. Nixon came down to the wire in 1960, they were in a dead heat. Both sides knew that the most contested state—the one that would make or break the election—was Illinois. Dwight Eisenhower, one of the greatest vote getters in the history of the Republican Party, had agreed to make two appearances in southern Illinois for Dick Nixon in the final week of the campaign.

After a previous appearance for Nixon, Ike's blood pressure had shot up alarmingly. Without consulting anyone, Mamie telephoned

the Nixons and begged them to release Ike from the Illinois assign-
ment. Of course they agreed. She then went to work on Ike and talked
him out of it too. A week later, John F. Kennedy carried Illinois by a
hairbreadth nine thousand votes and won the presidency.

I remember reading in a book about West Point that generals were
"in the history business"—which may explain why we have had so
many of them as Presidents. As First Ladies, Julia Grant and Mamie
Eisenhower, seemingly uninterested in politics, proved that now and
then they could match their soldier husbands in the same momentous
trade.

Chapter 16

—

THE WORST

FIRST LADY?

ACCORDING TO A POLL OF THE NATION'S HISTORIANS TAKEN BY
Marist College, Nancy Reagan should be ranked near the bottom of
the list of First Ladies—grim tribute to her bad press notices. But
there is one First Lady beneath her—consigned, as it were—to history's version of hell. In an incredible paradox, she is the wife of the
man most people regard as our greatest President, Abraham Lincoln.

I majored in history at George Washington University, but I never
went on to earn the M.A.'s and Ph.D.'s sported by the voters in that
poll. Nevertheless, I beg to disagree with these learned ladies and
gentlemen about Mary Lincoln. I think I have made it clear that I also
disagree with their opinion of Nancy Reagan, who overcame some
major obstacles to give a better than average performance in the
White House.

One day in 1962, my good friend historian Arthur Schlesinger
asked President John F. Kennedy to participate in a poll that compared presidents. Arthur was working in the Kennedy White House at
the time, and the President readily, in fact eagerly, agreed to con-

tribute his opinion. As the author of *Profiles in Courage*, JFK was intensely interested in presidential performance. But when Arthur spoke to him about the poll a few days later, he found a frustrated Chief Executive. Kennedy said he had no difficulty rating the greats: Washington, Lincoln, FDR. But when it came to the lesser figures, it was impossible to judge a President unless you made a fairly intense study of his administration and had a grasp of the problems he confronted and his options for dealing with them.

I have been trying to apply that principle to First Ladies. We should judge each First Lady not on some abstract scorecard but on the basis of what she accomplished in spite of the obstacles, personal and political, with which she had to cope during her White House years. Viewed in that more generous light, I believe Mary Todd Lincoln emerges as a First Lady who did her job moderately well under incredibly trying circumstances.

Almost from the day Abraham Lincoln was elected president in a four-way race with only forty percent of the popular vote, he began collecting death threats. Nevertheless, Mary Lincoln courageously insisted she would accompany her husband to embattled Washington, D.C. To add to their worries, the South made it clear that they were not going to tolerate a "black Republican" in the White House and began making good on their vow to secede from the Union. Mary at first thought that she and her husband, as Kentuckians, with ties to neither North nor South, would be ideally suited to reconcile the hostile sections.

Her task as First Lady, as she saw it, was to add dignity and even grandeur to the Lincoln administration—something that large parts of the North and South thought no "westerner" was capable of achieving. It is hard for us to grasp the intense snobbery with which the older sections of the country regarded Americans on the wrong side of the Appalachian Mountains in those days. It was an antagonism that went back to Andrew Jackson's presidency, when the men of the West first seized power in the name of expanding democracy.

In eastern newspapers and magazines, westerners were regularly portrayed as illiterate, tobacco-spitting boors. Whiffs of this prejudice have lingered into our own times. Not a little of Lyndon Johnson's

White House travails could be traced to comparisons of supposedly uncouth Texans with the theoretically ultracivilized denizens of New York and New England. Harry Truman had similar problems when people compared his Missouri accent with FDR's Harvard-honed inflections.

Mary Lincoln thought—with a great deal of justification—that her husband's presidency needed all the help it could get. Lincoln himself was ridiculed in Northern Democratic newspapers as "the brainless bob-o-link of the prairies." In the South the adjectives were barely printable. Mary was all too aware that her ungainly, awkward-looking spouse, with his thick Kentucky accent, did not make a good impression on many people—that he was, in fact, too western for eastern tastes. One of her first moves, after the election, was a trip to New York to buy materials for sixteen expensive gowns. She was determined to show Washington and the world that the President's wife could dress as fashionably as any easterner, North or South.

This approach came naturally to Mary. She had always dressed well, first as the daughter of one of Kentucky's wealthier planters and later as the wife of one of the most successful attorneys in the Midwest. The urge to democratize Lincoln after his death has more or less obscured the fact that he was a very prosperous lawyer, who represented railroads and other major corporations in many lucrative cases.

Moreover, Mary had no trouble visualizing herself as Abraham Lincoln's presidential partner. Throughout their marriage, her ambition had been a major force in her moody husband's career. Politics fascinated Mary. She discussed the subject constantly with Abraham and urged him to run for public office. When he was elected to Congress in 1846, she moved to Washington with him and enjoyed every minute of it. On November 6, 1860, when Lincoln learned he had won the presidency, he burst through the door of their Springfield house shouting: "Mary, Mary, we are elected." That *we* came as naturally to him as Lady Bird Johnson's pronoun when she talked about Lyndon Johnson becoming President.

Mary Lincoln went to Washington hoping to make the White House a rallying point for peace, civilization, and sanity. Even with-

Mary Lincoln here displays one of the expensive gowns that sent her husband into a rage about "flub-a-dubs." She was trying to overcome Abraham Lincoln's image as an uncouth westerner. *(American Heritage Library)*

out this motivation, the mansion badly needed an overhaul. Neglected by our only bachelor President, James Buchanan, and his feckless predecessor, Franklin Pierce, it was a sorry mess of peeling wallpaper, cheap, often broken furniture, and threadbare rugs that according to one visitor looked as if nothing had been changed or repaired "since Washington's day." Mary discovered that Congress allotted each President twenty thousand dollars for redecoration— the equivalent of at least two hundred thousand dollars today—and she embarked on a vigorous search for the finest rugs, china, wallpaper, and crystal in America. In no time she had spent the twenty thousand dollars, which was supposed to last four years—and a lot more.

At first Mary's campaign to enhance her husband's authority and prestige seemed to be succeeding. *Leslie's* magazine applauded the "exquisite taste" with which she redecorated the White House and entertained social and political Washington. Mary was described as a

"Republican Queen," whose elegance and witty conversation had transformed "the dingy sprawling city on the Potomac." The correspondent for *The Times* of London dubbed her the "First Lady" of Washington, one of the early uses of the term.

Alas, good taste and dignity were incapable of solving the national crisis that confronted Mary's husband. For a while, it seemed as if a political solution could be found. Lincoln called on both sides to heed "the better angels" of their natures and said he was eager for a negotiated peace. But the President's refusal to compromise the integrity of the Union clashed head-on with the secessionists' insistence on a virtually separate country. Soon thousands of men on both sides had guns in their hands, and in July 1861 the Union Army reeled back in defeat from Bull Run. The attitude toward Mary Lincoln's role as First Lady underwent a disastrous change. She rapidly became the target of critics who claimed her extravagant gowns and elegant dinners were in bad taste when the nation was fighting a horrendous war.

Most of these critics were trying, to borrow a Harry Truman phrase, "to upset the applecart." They were out to wreck Lincoln's presidency. What baffles me is why so many latter-day historians have agreed with them. I fear it is very difficult for later generations to comprehend the day-by-day lives of those who have preceded them or to appreciate the rude shocks they encountered as they fumbled into the future. Imagine, for a moment, how we would regard Mary Lincoln if her husband had negotiated the Southerners back into the Union, or decisively crushed their rebellion at Bull Run. These same historians who vilify her might very well be hailing the way she created a bastion of prestige and peaceful refinement in the White House in trying times.

Instead, thanks to the fortunes of war, Mary Lincoln was slammed in the newspapers as vain, egotistical, extravagant, tyrannical. In a move that may remind some of newspaper exchanges about our current First Lady, on August 1, 1861, the *Chicago Tribune* cried "ENOUGH!" No previous First Lady, they protested, "has ever been so maltreated by the popular press."

A sensitive woman who craved approval, Mary Lincoln was deeply hurt by these assaults. She was also mortified to learn how much money she had spent on the White House. The expenses had been handled by a bureaucrat in charge of a typical Washington "commission"—and, in true federal government style, he had not so much as blinked as they went "overbudget," to use modern D.C. groupspeak.

President Lincoln did a lot more than blink. He had an uncharacteristic temper tantrum, raging at Mary that her "flub-a-dubs" had embarrassed him with Congress and the people at a time when the Union armies were losing battles with monotonous regularity and his political capital was dwindling toward zero. A lot of wives would have retreated to their bedrooms and stayed there. Instead, Mary set out to beat the Washington system with the help of some shrewd advice from the White House gardener, John Watt.

Watt was no ordinary gardener, I should add; historians of the White House consider him a genius who turned the haphazard plantings around the mansion into near perfection. He also created greenhouses that supplied the President and his family with flowers year round. I am sure you will not be surprised to learn that he did not work these miracles without spending a lot of money.

Watt calmed the First Lady's fears by assuring her that federal budgets were easily adjustable. All you had to do was find the right formula. Under his tutelage, Mary deftly disposed of her original commissioner as a sacrificial offering to her critics, obliquely blaming him for the red ink. Then she found another commissioner, an old Washington hand named Benjamin French. They hit it off immediately. "She is a smart intelligent woman who likes to have her own way pretty much. I am delighted with her independence," French told a friend. "She bears herself in every particular like a lady."

French's commission was responsible for the upkeep of the Capitol and other federal buildings, as well as the White House, and it had a budget of a half million dollars. He soon found it easy to reassign money from such projects as gas lamps on Capitol Hill to finance Mary's overbudget wallpaper and rugs. Commissioner French smoothly advised his boss, the secretary of the interior, that such transfers were legal under a statute passed in the presidency of Martin Van Buren. To the flummoxed secretary, who was, like many cabinet officers before and since, a Washington newcomer, that was almost as far back as the reign of King Tut. When more red ink oozed onto the White House ledger, French persuaded a friendly congressman to noodle an extra $4,500 into an appropriations bill. It passed without a demur.

Stung by Lincoln's threat to pay for her redecoration out of his salary, Mary meanwhile instituted a cost-cutting program for routine White House expenses. For a woman accused of reckless extravagance by contemporaries and historians, she managed the Lincolns' personal expenses with remarkable skill, saving two-thirds of the President's $25,000 salary each year, building up a retirement fund of almost $70,000 by the end of Lincoln's first term.

Mary Lincoln had two problems: one was the Civil War; the other, less acknowledged, was the prejudice against independent, strong-willed women in the America of her day. In the smaller world of Springfield, Illinois, Mary had functioned as her husband's political partner with no difficulty. Now, as President, he became a remote figure, engulfed day and night by visitors, walled off by two brash young secretaries, John Hay and John Nicolay, who treated Mary with the same sort of condescension that H. R. Haldeman and John Ehrlichman would later display toward Pat Nixon. Mary was reduced to asking near strangers to influence her husband on matters about which he used to seek her advice. Some of the men around Lincoln—especially Hay and Nicolay—resented her intrusions and leaked nasty versions of her attempts to remain her husband's partner. The result was another sneering epithet: "Mrs. President."

Much of the time, Mary was doing exactly what hordes of males were doing in the White House—looking for government jobs for themselves or their relatives. In those pre–civil service days, the spoils system, instituted by President Andrew Jackson, left the whole federal government up for grabs when a new party won power. Mary saw no reason why the President's partner was not entitled to a few pieces of the action for her friends and family. Many of her critics were competing for the same positions.

Lincoln's anxiety about how much money Mary spent was to some extent his own fault. She had always run the family's finances. Money made Lincoln uncomfortable; he had no interest in it and even less aptitude for handling it. The President acknowledged this in calmer moments. There was no question that he enjoyed the sight of Mary in expensive clothes. At one White House reception he remarked: "My wife is as handsome as she was when a girl and I, a poor nobody, then fell in love with her and ... have never fallen out."

In an era when most women were so poorly educated that they panicked at the thought of conversing with a man through a long state dinner, Mary Lincoln was a striking exception. She had both a good education and a passion for politics, and she had no qualms about displaying either one. She also worked at the less charming aspects of the First Lady's job. Commissioner Benjamin French used to go into hiding on "handshake days," as he called them. But Mary was always there with a smile and a warm greeting.

Not a few of the guests went away charmed. George Bancroft of Massachusetts, a man who had studied the history of the country more thoroughly than any other American of his time, arguably making him a better than average judge of a First Lady, found Mary Lincoln remarkably well informed on the war and the politics of Washington. She told him she was a "conservative" and had no sympathy for secession, even though several of her Kentucky brothers were serving in the Confederate army. She also discussed her redecoration of the White House and urged him to return for another visit. "I came home entranced," Bancroft said.

Alas, Mary Lincoln's ability as a hostess played a part in irreparably damaging her reputation. At one of her early receptions she encountered "Chevalier" Henry Wikoff. A name-dropper with an eye for juicy gossip, he was one of those European adventurers who show up periodically in America and live quite successfully on their wit and charm. Mary was by no means the only Washington hostess who seized on the chevalier to enliven her parties. It did Wikoff no harm that he was a good friend of White House gardener John Watt.

Unfortunately, Washington was a city under siege, with Confederate armies only a few miles away in Virginia and Confederate sympathizers everywhere. To root out spies, Congress created the Special Committee of Investigation of the Loyalty of Public Officers. One of the accused was John Watt, whom Mary defended with a barrage of outraged letters. Watt convinced Benjamin French that he was true to the Union, and he became even more favored by the First Lady.

Then came an unnerving leak of the sort that can rattle the entire White House. The *New York Herald,* a paper dedicated to destroying Lincoln, printed the text of the President's State of the Union address while it was still in draft form on his desk. The editors naturally accompanied their scoop with a few columns of uncomplimentary remarks. Some vigorous detective work revealed Henry Wikoff had passed the speech to the *Herald* for a fat fee. In jail under threat of a firing squad—penetrating the President's office was considered high treason—Wikoff confessed he got the speech from John Watt, who had memorized portions of it in the course of several visits to Lincoln's office and recited them to Wikoff. Watt was forced to admit this grisly truth before the congressional committee on loyalty—and Mary Lincoln's reputation in wartime Washington received a devastating blow.

Henceforth she was widely regarded as disloyal, possibly even a Confederate spy. Her brothers in the Confederate army were offered as proof—along with her viscous Kentucky accent. On top of this scandal came a personal tragedy that further unraveled Mary Lincoln's stability. Her favorite son, eleven-year-old Willie, the brightest and most effervescent of her four boys, died of typhoid fever. Ironically, he was a casualty of the same Civil War that destroyed Mary Lincoln's reputation. The White House drew its drinking water from the Potomac River. The thousands of troops camped along its bank used the river as a latrine, filling the water with typhoid and other deadly bacteria.

Mary had lost another son, Eddie, during the Lincolns' Springfield years. The death of a child was not unusual in 1862—but the loss of Willie, combined with the accumulating rumors and gossip about her disloyalty and sneers about her sometimes impulsive, supposedly tyrannical attempts to get her way in the White House, was more than Mary could handle. In a pathetic attempt to regain Willie, she began consulting spiritualists. Again, it was something thousands of other Americans, in anguish over the loss of loved ones in battle, were doing at this tormented time. But Mary Lincoln's desire for consolation came to be seen as one more proof of her deficiency as a First Lady.

Although her private behavior became erratic (she often broke into tears at the mention of Willie's name), Mary continued to work hard as First Lady. In February 1863, Benjamin French wrote in his diary: "Mrs. Lincoln and the President had such a reception as I have never seen before in the day time. The rooms were crowded with 'fair women and brave men.' Mrs. Lincoln appeared unusually lively and gracious, and received with an air of grace and dignity, surpassing her ordinary self."

From French we know that after one of these ordeals, the Lincolns usually retired to the Oval Room, where Mary soaked and rubbed her husband's hand. Apparently Lincoln never acquired the art of the trick handshake that has helped other Presidents survive receiving lines. His big hand was often blistered and swollen. In those days ladies did not shake hands, so Mary escaped this sort of damage. But she still had to stand beside her husband for two or three hours in a room that became all but depleted of oxygen.

Some people thought Mary did a better job than her husband at another White House chore—reviewing the troops. With the war in full swing, all sorts of divisions and brigades paraded past the White House, and the Lincolns were required to come out and inspect them. One critic warned the President that too often he slouched and turned his head to talk to friends, when he should keep his eyes on the brave men in blue. Mary, on the other hand, "had savoir faire and was charming enough to make up for all your deficiencies."

Mary's performances as a hostess and parade watcher became sporadic, however, as the war ground on and the casualties multiplied endlessly. Spilling across half the continent, the conflict absorbed, even consumed, the President. His wife retreated into a shell of private grief, haunted by imaginary fears and nightmarish dreams. She passed most of the day in her sitting room on the second floor, waiting for her exhausted husband to appear, which he rarely did before midnight.

In her loneliness, guilt began mingling with Mary's sorrow. She, the ambitious one, had been the driving force behind Abraham's ascent, and God had apparently punished her with Willie's death. The ambition that drives a man or his wife to the presidency can do terrible things to them when tragedy strikes down one of their children.

Mary's grief multiplied when she learned that two of her brothers, Samuel and Alexander, her favorite, had died fighting for the Confederacy. Even worse, somehow, was the news that General Ben Helm, husband of her youngest sister, Emilie, had been killed leading an attack on the Union Army at the Battle of Chickamauga. When Emilie attempted to return to Kentucky with her two young children, federal officials arrested her. Lincoln ordered her sent to the White House. Among the mean-spirited, this ignited another spate of rumors about Mary Lincoln's Southern sympathies.

I am more interested in Emilie's reaction to Mary's deterioration. She could not believe this frightened, haunted woman was the happy, lively older sister she had left with protestations of love when they parted in 1861. Mary's fears, her dreams were "unnatural and abnormal," Emilie said. Lincoln begged Emilie to stay on in the White House, in spite of the fact that she was an irreconcilable Janey Reb. He felt she was the companion Mary badly needed. But Emilie, after several ferocious exchanges with Northern senators and congressmen—she shared the hot Todd temper and sharp tongue—went home to Kentucky, leaving Mary even more bereft.

Gradually, Mary Lincoln began to hate the White House. It was haunted by Willie's ghost, and by her present but preoccupied husband. She spent more and more time at a summer residence, the Soldiers' Home, on Rock Creek Road, about three miles north of the Capitol. Built in the 1850s to house retired federal veterans, it had a charming cottage on its five hundred wooded acres that several Presidents used to escape Washington's ghastly humidity and foul smells.

By the time victory emerged from the slaughter in early 1865, Mary Lincoln was a deeply depressed, isolated woman. Her mental state became apparent in an episode which did almost as much to ruin her reputation as the mess with Chevalier Wikoff. On March 23, 1865, she accompanied her husband to Virginia to review General Ulysses S. Grant's Army of the Potomac and be on hand for what looked like the imminent end of the war. The day after they arrived, Lincoln left Mary aboard the side-wheeler that had brought them up the James River and rode off with his generals to visit the battlefields around Richmond. Later in the day Mary and Julia Grant climbed into an army ambulance that had been converted into a makeshift carriage. Bouncing over the atrocious roads, Mary became more and more infuriated. When she reached the field where the review was to be held, she found herself relegated to a seat far in the rear, while the President sat on his horse in the front row, beside an extremely pretty woman, the wife of a Union general.

Mary's Todd temper erupted. This was not the way Abraham should treat his political partner. She had stood beside him as a near equal at the White House, reviewing hundreds of parades. Why, in the hour of victory, was she being treated like a nobody? She waded across the muddy field and assaulted the President with every irate verb and adjective in her vocabulary, while the ranking generals of the Army of the Potomac gaped with disbelief.

The story spread through Washington, certifying Mary Lincoln as something close to a madwoman. I make no apologies for it—beyond the explanations already given. It was atrocious behavior. But Mary soon calmed down and was thoroughly ashamed of herself. She barely spoke to anyone for the rest of the trip, sequestering herself with her youngest son, Tad, and her oldest son, Robert, who had become an officer on General Grant's staff. Eventually she returned to Washington, mortified and even more alone.

While others tut-tutted, Abraham Lincoln was not particularly upset by Mary's outburst. He had encountered her temper too often to take it seriously. He knew Mary quickly regretted her explosions and did her best to make amends with soothing words and her ample feminine charm. A little over two weeks later, on Palm Sunday, she stood smiling at a White House window while Lincoln spoke to a joyous crowd, celebrating the news that Robert E. Lee had surrendered his army to General Grant at Appomattox Court House.

With peace at hand, Lincoln started trying to be a husband again. He wrote Mary tender, playful notes and invited her for rides around Washington in one of the White House carriages. The President's good humor—and his desire to share it with Mary—led him to suggest they go to Ford's Theater on Good Friday, April 14, to see a comedy, *Our American Cousin*.

That afternoon they went for another carriage ride. Mary wanted to invite some friends, but Abraham said he preferred to be alone with her. "We must both be more cheerful in the future," he told her. "Between the war and the loss of our darling Willie, we have both been very miserable." Here is evidence that the man who understood Mary Lincoln best was well aware of what had happened to her. He was taking part of the blame, admitting he too had been depressed and unable to help her.

At the play that evening, Mary impulsively took Abraham's hand during the third act. With them were a young couple, Major Henry Rathbone and his fiancée, Clara Harris. They were deliriously in love. "What will Miss Harris think of my hanging on you so?" Mary asked.

"She won't think anything about it," Lincoln said, airily comparing them with the young lovers.

Ten seconds later a madman named John Wilkes Booth burst into the presidential box and shot Abraham Lincoln in the head. From that moment Mary Lincoln ceased to be a balanced woman. Can anyone blame her?

—

THE
(PROBABLY)
WORST
FIRST LADY

I HAVE MY OWN CANDIDATE FOR WORST FIRST LADY. WHEN THE Trumans used to discuss former denizens of the White House, Warren Harding's name was seldom spoken with respect. Dad did not hesitate to call him our worst President. As I began delving into the lives of First Ladies, I found myself wondering if Florence Kling Harding was just as bad. I soon discovered they were a matched pair.

You could argue that Florence's first mistake was marrying Warren Harding. But that would be a bit unfair. When Florence Kling met the affable Ohioan, she was a desperate woman with a failed marriage. Her first spouse had been a playboy who abandoned her and her infant son. She was determined, if she married again, to choose a man she could keep in line.

Warren may have struck her as a bit vacuous, but that was a minor problem. Her quarry (she pursued him relentlessly) was unquestionably handsome, and he had high if vague ambitions. Florence was almost thirty-one and Warren was twenty-five, no doubt another reason why she thought he would be easy to control. She should have listened more closely to Warren's mother, who told her if she wanted a happy marriage, she should keep the icebox full and both eyes on Warren.

Harding was the owner and publisher of the Marion, Ohio, *Star*, a newspaper that was barely breathing. Florence appointed herself circulation manager and head bookkeeper and in eighteen years of hard work built the *Star* into a profitable small-town paper. As one of the neighbors observed, Florence "runs her house; runs the paper ... runs Warren, runs everything but the car."

Meanwhile Warren wrote editorials full of platitudes about God and country and home and mother and recited them in speeches up and down Ohio. Pretty soon the local Republicans decided his eloquence and his matinee idol profile made him a likely candidate for the state senate. There he met a political operator named Harry Daugherty, who said to himself: "That man looks like a president."

Florence had mixed feelings about Daugherty. Perhaps she sensed, from the start, that "Wurr'n," as she called him, was not qualified for high office. Maybe she feared that politics would make it harder for her to keep her eyes on him. Both fears turned out to be well grounded, although Warren did not need politics as an excuse to stray. For over two decades he conducted a passionate affair with Carrie Phillips, the wife of one of their best friends in Marion. Many people who knew about it did not blame Warren too much. Florence never stopped nagging him about money and other matters, and from all accounts her nasal, peremptory voice would have driven even a devoted husband out of earshot. Warren's attitude is probably summed up in the nickname he pinned on her: "The Duchess."

In spite of her misgivings, Florence allowed Daugherty, a less than successful lawyer, to become Warren's alter ego and perennial promoter. Thanks to this eager beaver, Harding was elected to the U.S. Senate from Ohio in 1914.

Florence liked being a senator's wife. She enjoyed the capital's social scene and was thrilled when the millionaire hostess Evalyn Walsh McLean befriended her. Florence's fears about her husband's incompetence proved groundless. There were many senators as dumb as Warren, without his personal charm or gift for platitudes.

Harry Daugherty was still lurking in the wings of Senator Harding's career, and as the Wilson administration collapsed into illness and political disarray, it became more and more apparent that the Republicans were going to win in 1920. Moreover, the nomination was wide open because Theodore Roosevelt, the most likely candidate, had died in 1919. At first Florence reacted coolly to the idea of Warren becoming President. This time maybe she was sure he was not up to the job. In any case, she told Daugherty she preferred to remain a senator's wife.

There were other more serious reasons for saying no. Warren had high blood pressure, a heart condition, and a long record of "breakdowns" which required him to retreat to a sanitarium at Battle Creek, Michigan, to recuperate. Florence had lost a kidney in 1905 and was frequently forced to retreat to her bed with attacks of nephritis. Neither was in any condition to handle the stresses of the White House.

Harding himself was less than enthusiastic about running for President. He had no great opinion of his talents; in fact, he was a modest man, aware of his limitations. He was also lazy. He spent a lot more time on his extramarital affairs than he devoted to politics. He was now conducting two of them, one with his long-running flame, Carrie Phillips, the other with Nan Britton, a curvaceous twentysomething blonde who bore him an illegitimate child in 1919. No wonder Warren missed two-thirds of the votes in his five years in the Senate.

Florence's doubts about a presidential race were deepened by a visit to Madame Marcia, one of Washington, D.C.'s more popular astrologers. Florence told Marcia only the time and date of Warren's birth and asked for a reading on his destiny. Marcia declared the man was a "great statesman" and was destined to become President. But he would die in office. She also said his life was full of clandestine love affairs and he was subject to melancholia.

Harry Daugherty pooh-poohed Madame Marcia and overcame Florence's doubts by convincing her that the presidency was no more trouble than a Senate seat. He dangled the First Lady's social power before the Duchess's susceptible eyes. During her Washington years, Florence had begun keeping a list of people who had snubbed her. The chance to even scores with these adversaries swept her away. Need I say this is not a very good reason to persuade an ailing husband to run for President?

Nevertheless, Florence and Harry Daugherty soon had "Wurr'n" in the race. At first, he was a horse so dark he was all but invisible. There were several leading Republican contenders, but none had enough votes to win the nomination. The canny Daugherty said he did not expect Warren Harding to win on the first ballot or the second or the third. He was going to be a compromise candidate when the deadlocked convention had nowhere else to go.

Harding's lack of enthusiasm for the run made him a less than energetic candidate. When he faltered at rounding up delegates in Ohio and Indiana, he decided to withdraw. Florence arrived just as he was placing the call and snatched the telephone out of his hand. "Wurr'n Harding, what are your doing? Give up? Not until the convention is over," she cried.

The Republican Convention played out exactly as Daugherty had predicted. The leading contenders deadlocked, and Daugherty and his Ohio cohorts pushed Harding until the bleary-eyed party leaders finally accepted him at 2:00 A.M. in a room full of cigar smoke at Chicago's Blackstone Hotel. The bosses asked Warren if he had any skeletons in his closet. He thought it over for ten minutes and said "No." He had concealed his love life as senator. Why not as President?

As the final ballot neared, Daugherty joined Florence Harding in a box in the balcony. She had taken off her hat and was clutching two enormous hatpins in her right hand. "Warren will be nominated on the next ballot," Daugherty said.

Florence whirled, a maniacal light in her eyes, and drove the hatpins deep into Daugherty's side. The mastermind of Harding's presidency staggered away, wondering if he were mortally wounded, while the roll call of the states put his man over the top. What inspired this extraordinary act of violence? We will never know, but I tend to suspect that Florence Harding sensed in her deepest self that making

"Wurr'n" President was the worst mistake of both their lives. She yielded to an unconquerable urge to wreak harm on the man who had set the fatal machinery in motion.

Harding won the election by an astonishing seven million votes, and the Republicans did almost as well in the House and Senate. It was not an endorsement of Harding, of course; it was a repudiation of Woodrow and Edith Wilson. But no one stopped to think about that. Harding instantly became a "popular" President. He gave the disillusioned American people what they wanted in the White House at that moment: a nice man with a big smile and no ideas whatsoever. He or one of his speechwriters chose a word to sum it up: normalcy.

Florence soared on Warren's bubble. She saw herself as the queen of Washington and with Evalyn Walsh McLean's help planned the most expensive inauguration gala the country had ever seen. The Republican National Committee, true to the party's tightfisted tradition, refused to foot the bill. So Mrs. McLean and her husband paid for the bash out of their own pockets and held it at their estate, Friendship, outside Washington. Needless to say, the guest list was studded with millionaires. It was a harbinger of things to come.

Sixty and in poor health, Florence tried to conceal her haggard appearance with layers of powder and rouge. Edith Wilson gave her a brief White House tour and invited her to tea. She was so appalled by her successor's déclassé style, whining voice, and overbearing manner, she rang for housekeeper Elizabeth Jaffray and left without saying good-bye. Florence, knowing a snub when she saw one, retaliated by firing Jaffray. A week later, when she realized the complications of running the Executive Mansion, she rehired Jaffray and let her handle that side of the White House with scarcely a word of comment. Florence had little interest in housekeeping.

By this time she also had little interest in Warren. During the campaign she had found out about his long-running romance with her friend Carrie Phillips. The Republican National Committee gave Carrie and her husband twenty thousand dollars to leave the country and stay away for the next four years. That left the Harding partnership very close to a marriage of convenience.

Warren sat in the Oval Office, scared half out of his wits, wondering what to do next. He confessed to an amazing number of reporters that he did not think he was up to the job. He told one, Bruce Bliven of *The New Republic,* that he wanted Congress to pass a bill that would make the U.S. tariff wall high enough to help Europe's industries recover from the war—demonstrating he had one of the big issues of the era exactly backward. When another newsman returned from a trip across the war-ravaged continent and offered to tell the President what he had seen and heard, Warren said he had no interest in that "Europe stuff" and referred him to his secretary and chief speechwriter.

Needless to say, Florence was not equipped to fill this vacuum in the oval office. She had no political ideas either, beyond a mindless hostility to Democrats. One of her few interventions concerned a speech Warren planned to give in which he semiendorsed Wilson's League of Nations. Florence made him remove the kind words. She could still run "Wurr'n," but she did not have a clue about where they should go.

The only political program that occurred to either of them was a spurious populism. At a White House reception shortly after Evalyn Walsh McLean's million-dollar inauguration party, Florence noticed the servants were lowering the window shades to prevent the public from goggling at the guests. "Let 'em look in if they want to!" she cried. "It's their White House."

Tourists traipsing through the public rooms were sometimes startled to find the First Lady in their midst, shaking hands and acting as an impromptu guide. Warren too was eager to shake hands by the hour. This touch of democracy, after the austere Wilson White House, with its barred gates and unused state rooms during the war and the eighteen months of the President's illness, struck many people as charming. For a while Warren and Florence enjoyed a honeymoon with the people and the press.

Behind the scenes, Florence remained mean-spirited, evening scores with the snubbers on her list by excluding them from the White House and exalting her favorites. She was also ferociously hostile to anyone she perceived as a potential competitor for Warren's share of the political limelight. When the widow of Senator John B. Henderson of Missouri tried to donate her handsome house on Sixteenth Street as a vice presidential residence, good-natured Warren had no objection to asking Congress to appropriate a few hundred thousand dollars to maintain the place for Calvin Coolidge and his pleasant wife, Grace. The Duchess exploded when she heard about it and ordered "Wurr'n" to kill the bill. "Do you think I am going to have those Coolidges living in a house like that?" Florence shouted. "A hotel apartment is plenty good for them!"

It would take another forty-some years and the generosity of Nelson Rockefeller for the vice president to get a decent house. When Dad became vice president in 1945, we stayed in the same two-bedroom apartment we had lived in while he was a senator. Although Dad was only vice president for three months, it would have been nice to get some training in a sort of minor-league White House before being thrust into the real thing.

All sorts of machinations were taking place behind the scenes in the Harding White House, none of them very nice. Warren had made Harry Daugherty his attorney general, and this dime-store Machiavelli started collecting on his long years of toil to make Harding President. One of his first moves was to get a presidential order giving him control of the corporations confiscated from German owners under the Alien Property Act during World War I. He and his pals began selling off these assets at bargain rates and pocketing bonuses paid under the table. Another crony skimmed millions from the Veterans' Bureau, selling alcohol and drugs needed for soldiers still recuperating from their World War I wounds to bootleggers and narcotics dealers. The secretary of the interior, Albert B. Fall, an old Harding Senate pal, allowed oil companies to tap into the Teapot Dome oil reserve and other government-owned fields for a half million dollars in "loans" which Fall never bothered to repay.

The only political plum Florence demanded was the appointment of Dr. Charles Sawyer as surgeon general. She credited this quack, who believed in "nature food" as a sovereign remedy, with keeping her alive and hoped he could continue to work his miracles on her and Warren in the White House.

Having nothing else to do, Warren spent incredible numbers of hours answering the mail. He composed personal replies to innumerable appeals for help and warnings of imminent national disaster, the two chief reasons people write to the White House. One night the president of Columbia University, Nicholas Murray Butler, visited Harding in his office and found the President groaning over a huge pile of letters on his desk. Butler glanced at them; their triviality boggled his mind. He urged Warren to put a clerk in charge of this mundane chore.

Butler did not realize that Warren had to fill his time somehow. He never read a book. He had no interest in art or the theater, except for the Gayety Burlesque, which he visited regularly to watch the bumps and grinds in a special box that concealed him from the public. During the day he played a lot of golf, and the nights when he was not at the Gayety he tried to fill with poker and booze. While the rest of the country wrestled with the idiocy of Prohibition, for which Warren's party was chiefly responsible, he and Florence were serving hard stuff on the second floor of the White House to his poker-playing buddies.

Florence tolerated—she even encouraged—Warren's poker playing and golf. But there was one recreation that she would not condone. That was why she became the first President's wife to demand her own Secret Service agent—launching the unhappy tradition of imprisoning the First Lady as well as the President in their eternal vigilance. Florence's Secret Service man was acquired not to protect her but to keep Warren's remaining inamorata, Nan Britton, out of the White House.

The agent did not do a very good job. According to the bestseller Nan wrote a few years later, she swiftly established communication with Warren via the mails, and soon he was sneaking her into the Oval Office, where they enjoyed themselves in a five-foot-square clothes closet. Once the First Lady almost caught them. Tipped off by her Secret Service man, she rushed downstairs and demanded access to Warren's sanctum. The Secret Service agent who had escorted Nan from Union Station was guarding the inside door, which he refused to open "by order of the President."

An infuriated Florence raced around and invaded the office of George Christian, one of the President's secretaries, adjoining the Oval Office. Sensing what was up, Christian stalled her with double-talk about his boss being busy, while the Secret Service man guarding the other door extracted Nan from the closet and hustled her out a side exit. When Florence finally charged into the Oval Office, "Wurr'n" was at his desk, reading a letter. That did not save him from a ferocious tongue-lashing. "She makes life hell for me!" he told Nan later.

Other Presidents have been unfaithful to their wives. But none has perpetrated the kind of French farce the Hardings performed in the White House. Beyond the gates another drama was beginning to unfold that would transform the farce into tragedy. Honest men started telling the President what Daugherty, Fall, and others were doing to his administration. The appalled Harding did not know what to do or say. He spent his nights staring into the darkness and his days in a sleep-starved fog. Whenever possible he consoled himself with Nan, who listened tearfully to his troubles after another rendezvous in the closet.

Meanwhile, Florence collapsed with a near fatal attack of nephritis that left her bedridden for months. Recovered, she hobbled around on swollen ankles, looking more and more like a walking corpse. Both the First Lady and the President were desperately in need of someone to protect them from each other—and the huge uproar that was gathering around them. Harding finally found the nerve to ask one of Daugherty's top aides, Jess Smith, to resign. He was the alien proper-ties operation's bagman, and all sorts of witnesses were ready to tes-tify that they had deluged him with bribes. Smith went home to Ohio and blew out his brains. The crook who had been looting the Veter-ans' Bureau soon imitated his example.

Like other Presidents before and since, Harding finally decided the best answer to the mounting scandal was a campaign-style trip across the country to let the people see their President was undaunted by the nasty things the newspapers were printing about him. If patriotism is, as they say, the last refuge of scoundrels, populism is unquestionably the final refuge of tottering Presidents. The roar of the crowd will, they hope, wash them clean.

Harding's Voyage of Understanding, as he called it, whistle-stopped across the country with Florence and Surgeon General Sawyer at his side. It never seemed to occur to them that they were exhausting a man with high blood pressure, a weak heart, and acute insomnia. The President hurled his platitudes at the voters at literally dozens of stops from Washington, D.C., to Alaska, where he was welcomed with acclaim by the natives because he was the first Chief Executive to acknowledge their existence by visiting the place.

En route to Alaska aboard a U.S. Army transport, Harding received a coded message from Washington with more bad news about the deepening scandals he had left behind him. For several hours the President looked dazed; he muttered incoherently about false friends. A few days later, when the ship collided with one of her escorting destroyers in a heavy fog, Harding was heard to say: "I hope the boat sinks."

In Seattle, on his way back from Alaska, Harding tried to give a speech, but he faltered in the middle of it, turned green, began slurring his words, and called Alaska "Nebraska." Another speech later that day finished him. In a state of collapse, he was rushed aboard a train, complaining of severe stomach cramps and indigestion. He was almost certainly having a heart attack, but Surgeon General Sawyer diagnosed the President's condition as food poisoning. In San Francisco he was hurried from the train to the Palace Hotel with a fever of 102 and a racing pulse.

Two days later he seemed to rally and even began making plans for a fishing trip to Catalina Island. On the evening of August 2, Florence sat by his bed, reading him an article in the *Saturday Evening Post* which praised him extravagantly. Warren liked what he was hearing. "That's good. Go on, read some more," he said.

Those were his last words. His head fell back on the pillow. Florence thought he was asleep and tiptoed out of the room. A few minutes later, a nurse came in and saw that Warren Harding was dead. At first the nation was plunged into mourning, but grief rapidly turned to indignation as Daugherty, Fall, and other crooks went on trial for their various malfeasances and people began to realize Warren Harding had been a hollow President.

The woman who put him in the White House mourned him with words that can be read several ways. The night before the funeral, Florence went into the East Room, where Harding lay in state, and said: "No one can hurt you now, Warren." She may have been bearing witness to the treachery of his friends. She may also have been confessing that she had been one of the hurters. Evalyn Walsh McLean, who was present, said she sounded more like a mother talking to a lost son than a wife saying farewell to her husband.

Florence's final scene as First Lady was not pretty. Although it was August at its most beastly in Washington, D.C. (and air conditioning had yet to be invented), she ordered a fire built in the fireplace of the President's second-floor study and spent the next five days going through Warren's papers, burning potentially incriminating evidence. The President's horrified secretary George Christian managed to hide some papers in the basement pantry. Otherwise our knowledge of the Harding administration would be close to zero.

Suddenly, Florence could not bear another minute in the White House. She packed the remaining papers in boxes and trucked them out to the McLeans' estate, where she spent several more days burning evidence on the lawn. All in all, it was a performance more suitable for the bereaved mistress of a South American dictator than the widow of the President of the United States.

Sixteen months later Florence Kling Harding was dead of nephritis, and the sorry story of the First Lady with no judgment and the President with no brains came to an end—except in the courts, where various members of the Harding administration continued struggling to evade the punishment they so richly deserved.

Chapter 18

—

DANGER:
PRESIDENT
AT WORK

THE HARDING STORY—AND TO SOME EXTENT MARY LINCOLN'S tragedy—underscores one aspect of the presidency that few people understand: it is dangerous work, loaded with emotional and physical stress that can destroy the body and maim the mind. One First Lady triumphed over formidable obstacles to achieve a rare serenity in the White House—while doing her job with a finesse that won plaudits from Americans in both parties. But for reasons beyond her control, Grace Coolidge could not communicate this serenity to her deeply troubled husband.

There have been other serene First Ladies, notably Edith Roosevelt, but she did not have to overcome as many challenges as Grace Coolidge. First, Grace was married to Calvin Coolidge, a man who would have driven me—and most other women—to despair. Not only was this laconic, moody Vermonter, known even to his friends as "Silent Cal," Grace's total opposite in temperament and attitudes but he was a domestic dictator who insisted on running her private life.

Those with good memories will recall the letter I mentioned earlier, from Grace Coolidge to Bess Truman, assuring Mother that she would survive the shock of waking up one morning and discovering she was no longer that invisible personage, the vice president's wife. This was, of course, another obstacle for both the Coolidges. In their case, along with being catapulted into the White House, they were saddled with a huge political-financial scandal perpetrated by the scoundrels in the Harding administration.

Yet thanks to Calvin Coolidge's unflinching Yankee honesty and Grace's smiling serenity, the Coolidges pulled off a political miracle and survived the Republican Party's disgrace to win a startling victory in the 1924 presidential race. The Democrats helped, of course, by publicizing the deep divisions in their party at their nominating convention, where they took over a hundred ballots to name a cardboard compromise candidate.

After Florence Harding, a First Lady who made people wince every time she opened her mouth, Washington discovered a woman who made people feel good every time they met her. Willowy Grace Coolidge had a magical smile and a warm greeting for everyone. She was gregarious, cheerful, outgoing—the opposite of her diffident, poker-faced husband, who seemed to make it a rule not to smile more than once a month. While Coolidge's unblemished reputation was helpful in weathering the crisis that confronted his party, he utterly lacked the personal warmth that wins votes. Most people agree that without Grace Coolidge, Calvin would not have risen beyond mayor of Northampton, Massachusetts, where he practiced law before going into state politics.

Along with filling the void in conversations at dinner parties and receptions, at which Calvin would sit or stand mute by the hour, Grace told funny stories about his taciturnity, helping to make him into a character. She was the source of the tale about a determined woman who sat next to Coolidge at a dinner, vowing she could make him talk to her. "Mr. Coolidge," she said, "I made a bet today that I could get more than two words out of you."

"You lose," Cal said.

Another of Grace's stories dealt with two men who were overheard discussing the President and his wife. One of them remarked that Grace had been a teacher in a school for the deaf before her marriage. "She taught the deaf to speak," he said.

"Why didn't she teach Cal?" the other man asked.

Grace was not above teasing her husband for his verbal parsimony. One night at dinner on the presidential yacht, he sat between two women friends who were staying at the White House and did not say a word to either of them. The next morning, when they came into the dining room for breakfast, they overheard Calvin asking Grace where their guests were. "They're probably still in bed, exhausted from your conversation last night," she answered.

Grace was also an expert mimic and gave a wonderful imitation of her husband's Vermont accent, which added three extra syllables to the word *cow*. She told people how, in the early years of their marriage, he forbade her to attend any of his speeches, perhaps suspecting what her reaction would be. One day she disobeyed him and had to hide behind a pillar to control her laughter at his Yankee twang. Here, too, Grace helped turn a potential minus into a plus.

She even made a joke out of Coolidge's frugality, which was one of his major political assets. In private, however, it must have been one of his more trying traits. When a Northampton hotel went out of business, Coolidge purchased a supply of their towels and silverware, emblazoned with the words NORWOOD HOTEL, and insisted on Grace using them.

From the start people puzzled over what had brought the Coolidges together. When they attended his college reunion not long after their marriage, the wife of a classmate wondered aloud "how that sulky redhaired little man ever won that pretty charming woman." Her husband said Coolidge was bright and ambitious and would make a name for himself someday. "Yes, but through Grace," his wife replied.

Love is a very mysterious potion. There is no doubt that the Coolidges loved each other. While Grace was frolicsome and even a little rebellious in her youth, she had grown up under the eye of a strong-willed father, who ran her life much the way Calvin did when he took over. She and Calvin shared a puckish sense of humor, which expressed itself in constant teasing. When he was governor of Massachusetts, he said he was going to send the crust on Grace's pies to the road commissioner for testing because it seemed superior to concrete. He sometimes dropped one of her biscuits on the floor and stamped his foot to make it sound as if a lead weight had struck the rug.

Grace began charming Washington in her days as the vice president's wife. Tall, dark haired, with big gray-green eyes and that winning smile, she carried herself regally but was totally unaffected. She loved people and parties, and her enthusiasm warmed everyone around her. Calvin's determination to accept any and all invitations helped widen Grace's popularity. (The reason for this uncharacteristic sociability became apparent when he remarked: "Got to eat somewhere.") One member of Washington society said no other vice president's wife had ever seemed to enjoy herself so much—"and give so much in return."

In the White House, Grace went from popularity to acclaim. President Coolidge could not bring himself to give callers more than a curt nod and a quick handshake. Grace remembered everyone's name and was a genius at small talk—hardly surprising after almost twenty years with Silent Cal. She had a refreshingly down-to-earth attitude toward White House pomp and ceremony. Once a tourist wandered into one of her receptions and confessed her crime. Grace invited her to stay. "I know I'm going to do something wrong," the poor woman quavered.

"That will only make you more interesting," Grace assured her.

The list of Grace's accolades could fill the rest of this book. Chief Justice William Howard Taft (appointed by President Harding) pronounced her "*very* nice," perhaps a comment on his sharp-tongued Nellie. Comedian Will Rogers, an admitted Democrat, said she was "chuck plumb full of magnetism." A foreign diplomat who did not understand a word of English said he did not mind conversing with her because "to look at her is gladness enough."

Every day Grace's picture seemed to be on the front page of half the nation's newspapers, embracing Boy Scouts, puppies, handicapped children. She told one of her friends if she kept it up she was going to be named "National Hugger." Her passionate interest in the ups and downs of the Boston Red Sox became part of her charm. She entertained Marie, the Queen of Rumania; transatlantic hero Charles Lindbergh; the Rockefellers; and movie stars like Douglas Fairbanks and Ethel Barrymore. Always, that golden smile showered cheer on everyone. The White House staff nicknamed her "Sunshine."

How did she do it? Here was a woman who seemed to be utterly tyrannized by her husband, to the point where Calvin drew up her schedule of appointments for the week without telling her what they were. At breakfast one day, she made a rare protest. "Calvin, look at me," she said. The President's face was buried, as usual, in the daily paper. Grace demanded the weekly schedule from the Secret Service, so she could be more prepared for where she was going and whom she was going to meet. "Grace," Calvin said in his presidential voice, "we don't give out that kind of information promiscuously."

There was an element of teasing in that answer—but Grace never saw a schedule. She was reduced to having a variety of dresses and accessories ready for every imaginable occasion. Coolidge also insisted on monitoring other aspects of her life. When she took up horseback riding, he made her stop after the first lesson. If she stayed out after 6:00 P.M., he had no hesitation about calling her up and telling her to come home. He forbade her to dance in public, which was a pity, because she was an excellent dancer.

If he were my husband, I might have become the first First Lady to assassinate a President. But nothing—or almost nothing—Calvin said or did could alter Grace's affection and respect for him, and her smiling equanimity with everyone else.

Calvin's frank admiration for his wife's beauty may have had something to do with her amazing tolerance. Even after he became President, his favorite hobby was buying clothes for Grace. He often went shopping with her and was not hesitant about expressing his opinion about what looked good on her and what didn't. He urged her to spend so much money on clothes, his reputation for frugality would have been permanently exploded if the reporters had told all they knew. You could hardly blame the man. Grace Coolidge's slender elegance and nineteen twenties fashions were made for each other.

At Calvin's urging, Grace abandoned her restrained New England styles and bought gorgeous lamé gowns with long trains of gold lace and satin and silk dresses decorated with rhinestones, feathers, and fur. As for colors, her secretary, Mary Randolph, said: "Very few things were unbecoming to her; white, pink, yellow, blue, red, orchid, old rose... suited her equally well." She wore her hair in a "horseshoe marcel" that instantly became the preferred style for half the women in America. As always, Calvin's dictatorial style intruded. While he loved to see Grace dressed to the nines, he forbade her to wear slacks, culottes, shorts, and other kinds of casual clothes.

Grace handled this regimen in various ways. Like Eleanor Roosevelt eight years later, she decided the First Lady was not her. She was a "personage" that Grace Coolidge was assuming for the duration of her stay in the White House. This enabled her to put up with a lot of otherwise meaningless rules and regulations and constant demands on her time and patience. When she became really distressed, she turned to her knitting. She said she often found her needles a compass, "keeping me on my course."

It will probably surprise no one to discover that Calvin Coolidge never discussed politics with his wife. Early in their marriage, they had agreed that the ideal union called for two separate spheres, with the wife in charge at home and the man in the office. This division was hardly original with Coolidge, but he never hesitated to invade Grace's bailiwick. In the White House he often went over her menus and guest lists, peremptorily changing dishes and crossing out people he did not like.

By the time the Coolidges completed their first year in the White House, Grace had become one of the most popular First Ladies in memory. Chief Usher Ike Hoover pronounced her "ninety percent of the administration." Will Rogers practically abandoned his allegiance to the Democratic Party and called her "Public Female Favorite No. 1."

I love this portrait
of Grace Coolidge
in one of those
marvelous 1920s
gowns her husband
selected for her.
Posing with her is
her famous white
collie, Rob Roy.
*(White House
Historical Society)*

Even a frozenpuss like Housekeeper Elizabeth Jaffray pronounced her "warm and friendly." Coolidge himself was forced to admit to his father: "She is wonderfully popular here. I don't know what I would do without her."

Then came a tragedy that tested Grace Coolidge's serenity to its utmost. The Coolidges had two sons, eighteen-year-old John and sixteen-year-old Calvin Jr. Like many parents, they each had a favorite. Grace doted on John, who had her penchant for fun and sunshine, and the President adored Calvin Jr., who was not a little like him. When Calvin Jr. received a letter addressed to the "First Boy of the Land," he fired off a stiff reply, telling the writer the title was a mistake, since he had done nothing to deserve it. The First Boy of the Land should be "some boy who had distinguished himself through his own actions."

One hot day in July 1924, Calvin Jr. played a game of tennis on the White House courts. He did not bother to wear socks and acquired an ugly blister on his big toe. Like any boy his age, he ignored it until his whole foot was inflamed. The Coolidges called in the best doctors in the country, but they had no sulfa drugs or penicillin to fight such an infection. They and the agonized parents could only stand helplessly beside his bed while Calvin Jr. slowly died of blood poisoning.

Grace was grief stricken—but her sorrow could not compare with her husband's devastation. In my account of Mary Lincoln's troubled White House tenure, I mentioned how the death of a child can mortally wound the morale of a President or a First Lady—or both. Probably the most grievous example is the case of the Franklin Pierces. Jane Means Pierce was strongly opposed to her husband running for President. In 1853, shortly before he was inaugurated, their only surviving son, Benjamin (they had lost two other boys to illness), was killed in a train wreck. Jane Pierce regarded the loss as the judgment of God on her husband's presidency and spent the next years in her White House bedroom writing maudlin letters to her dead son. The equally distraught Pierce, to quote Harry Truman, "didn't pay any more attention to business as President of the United States than the man in the moon."

Calvin Coolidge did not undergo that sort of collapse. But there was a stark, dismaying contrast between the President who resumed his tasks after Calvin Jr.'s funeral and the energetic, decisive man who had taken charge of the executive office and masterminded the policies that enabled his party to retain the White House in spite of the Harding administration's corruption. Coolidge told his father he would never run for public office again. Later he wrote that, when Calvin Jr. died, "the power and the glory of the Presidency went with him."

The laconic, seemingly undemonstrative man had loved that power and glory during his first year in office. Ike Hoover recalled in his memoirs how Coolidge had positively exulted in being the center of attention, with news photographers' flashbulbs exploding on all sides. He even liked the swarms of Secret Service agents around him—and riding alone in his limousine in motorcades while his aides followed him in less glamorous cars. Hoover said Coolidge had displayed "more egoism, self consciousness or whatever you call it" than any of the nine other presidents he had served.

There was absolutely nothing wrong with this. The presidency is an office rich in ego satisfaction for a man who thinks he can do the job. But now this personal satisfaction returned to haunt Calvin Coolidge as guilt. He convinced himself that his vaulting ambition had been the cause of his beloved son's death.

Even after he was elected by a handsome majority in 1924 Coolidge remained a deeply wounded man. He talked obsessively about Calvin Jr. "When I look out the window, I always see my boy playing tennis on that court out there," he told one of his aides. He seemed particularly tormented by the incongruity of being President, with all the pomp and power of the office, yet having lacked the power to help his dying son. "When he was suffering, he begged me to help him, I could not," he lamented to the journalist William Allen White.

From a President who was a strong believer in being the country's "chief legislator," Coolidge sank into an aimless passivity in his second term. His contact with key members of Congress became, in the words of one historian, "infrequent and perfunctory." He let his cabinet members run their departments as if they were separate countries, snappishly telling them to make their own decisions when they came to him for advice or direction.

Calvin Coolidge also withdrew from the presidency in a less obvious way. He began to sleep—or at least stay in bed—eleven hours a night. Each afternoon he took a long nap. He was soon working only four and a half hours a day—and doing little or nothing while he was at his desk besides fret about his health. He grew so hypochondriacal, he often had an electrocardiogram taken twice in the same day.

Ironically, Grace's long apprenticeship in obedience and resignation as Calvin Coolidge's wife enabled her to accept Calvin Jr.'s death. She was immensely helped by a deep, almost mystical religious faith. Soon after the funeral, she wrote to her close friend, Mrs. R. B. Hills: "As we stood beside the grave, the sun was shining, throwing long slanting shadows and the birds were singing their sleepy songs. Truly it seemed to me God's acre.... I came away comforted and full of courage." That Christmas, in a note to Lou Henry Hoover, whose husband was Calvin Coolidge's secretary of commerce, Grace said that she felt a "peace which passeth understanding" as they sang carols "thinking of our Calvin singing them in his heavenly house."

Unfortunately, the peculiar configuration of the Coolidges' marriage made it impossible for her to help her husband. Calvin Coolidge had dominated Grace so thoroughly that she—having abandoned all semblance of equality—was in no position to give him advice or comfort. The man who seldom spoke was also a man who never listened to his wife.

Grace Coolidge was able to resume her busy White House schedule within a few months of her son's death. She continued to hug visitors, kiss babies, and shake thousands of hands, apparently with the same wonderful enthusiasm. She also tackled a task that may have been a covert attempt to cheer her depressed husband: she decided to redecorate the White House. Mrs. Taft and the first Mrs. Wilson had made a stab at battling the drab, virtually unfurnished state of the family quarters, which looked as if they belonged in a second-rate hotel rather than the First House of the land. Grace decided to start with these rooms.

The American wing of the Metropolitan Museum of Art had opened on November 10, 1924, beginning a revival of interest in our national arts and artifacts. Grace Coolidge became the vanguard of a line of First Ladies who decided the White House should be a museum containing the best available examples of American design. Congress obligingly passed a resolution permitting the First Lady to accept gifts of furniture and artwork and astonished everyone, including themselves, by raising the appropriation given to each incoming

President for redecorating from twenty thousand to fifty thousand dollars. A delighted Grace Coolidge put together a committee of distinguished names from the art and museum world to accelerate the collection process.

Then came the uproar. As the Trumans can testify, any President or First Lady who tries to change anything in the White House is liable to get caught in a cross fire that resembles Armageddon. Grace's committee issued a broadside about their goals for the White House which went far beyond her modest plans to redecorate the family quarters. They wanted to eliminate the supposedly European influences that had infiltrated the mansion when Theodore Roosevelt sponsored a major overhaul in 1902 in the then universally popular beaux arts style. The American Institute of Architects, who thought beaux arts was just as good in 1925 as it had been in 1902, called on the President to stop this desecration.

Newspaper stories blossomed while the Coolidges were on summer vacation in Massachusetts, picturing an artistic civil war raging at 1600 Pennsylvania Avenue. Calvin Coolidge solved it in typical fashion—typical, I regret to say, of the depressed man who had lost interest in being President. He simply announced there would be no redecoration of the White House. Grace Coolidge's ambitious plans came to an abrupt end. Nothing was done beyond some painting in the family rooms.

In the same sad year, 1925, the Coolidges were also harassed by the widespread rumor that Grace was pregnant. It was a tribute to her youthful good looks—but she was forty-six years old. No matter how often she denied it, Grace could not prevent a deluge of caps, blankets, pillows, socks, and afghans from pouring into the White House. It was another way for Americans to express their sympathy for Calvin Jr.'s death, but it must have only redoubled the pain of their loss for Grace and particularly for the stricken President.

Few if any Americans were aware that the presidency was on cruise control. The stock market was booming, the country was at the height of the frenzied prosperity that came to be called the Roaring Twenties. The United States did not seem to need a strong President. It did not even seem to need a government. The businessman was king, and everyone seemed ready to shout Yes! when bandleader Ted Lewis asked his trademark question: "Is everybody happy?"

In 1927, while the White House was undergoing some badly needed renovation of the roof and the third floor, the Coolidges vacationed in the Black Hills of South Dakota. They stayed at a twenty-room state-owned game lodge, which was inevitably christened the summer White House. Grace loved the scenery, which reminded her of New England's hills. She began taking long walks in the woods around the lodge. Coolidge insisted on a Secret Service agent for an escort.

One sunny day in June, she set out with a young, handsome agent named James Haley. City bred, he knew nothing about the woods, and he and the First Lady soon got lost. Back at the summer White House, the President grew more and more alarmed. When Grace and her escort did not appear for lunch, Coolidge became almost frantic. He was sure she had been bitten by a rattlesnake and was dying or dead. He was only minutes away from ordering the U.S. Army to conduct a search when Grace and Haley came strolling out of the woods, none the worse for wear.

Coolidge proceeded to tear the hide off the quivering agent, calling him an incompetent idiot and demanding to know what "you and my wife" had been doing for the better part of five hours. While reporters watched and Grace winced, the President made himself sound like a husband who suspected the worst possible scenario. He compounded this blunder by ordering Haley transferred immediately to a trivial job elsewhere in the government. He made matters even worse by refusing to speak to Grace for the better part of a week. Stories of jealous, not-so-silent Cal sprouted in newspapers across the nation.

One can only wonder if this imbroglio had anything to do with an extraordinary announcement the President made on August 2. Early that morning, Calvin Coolidge casually remarked to Grace that the date meant he had been President for "four years [as of] today." Later in the morning, he summoned reporters to his temporary office in nearby Rapid City and handed out slips of paper on which was written a single sentence: *I do not choose to run for president in 1928.*

At lunch, Senator Arthur Capper of Kansas was one of the guests. He expected Grace Coolidge to say something about her husband's startling decision. She never mentioned it, and neither did the President. Coolidge went off to take a nap and Capper said: "Quite a surprise the President gave us this morning."

Grace, settled with her knitting in a leather chair before a great stone fireplace, gave Capper a blank look. The senator described the pandemonium among the reporters when they saw the announcement. "Isn't that just like the man!" Grace said. "He never gave me the slightest intimation of his intention. I had no idea."

Later the head of the Secret Service detail, Edward Starling, asked her what she thought of the President's decision. "I have such faith in Mr. Coolidge's judgment," Grace said, "if he told me I would die tomorrow morning at ten o'clock I would believe him."

When you put the extravagance of that statement in the context of the lack of judgment Coolidge displayed in the Haley incident, one can only surmise that Grace's serenity was under severe strain. She was talking to herself as much as to Starling. I would not be surprised if she resorted to her knitting a great deal during these troubled weeks, hoping her needles would keep her on course.

The Haley incident started an even more disturbing rumor that Grace planned to divorce Calvin Coolidge the minute she left the White House. The gossip became so serious that some of Coolidge's aides urged the couple to make more public appearances together. But these performances, to which the President grudgingly assented, did little good because Coolidge was as incapable as Richard Nixon of expressing affection in public. Nor would he tolerate the idea of letting Grace kiss him or hug him.

The depressed President vetoed personal appearances by Grace alone. In the fall of 1927, a friend invited her to the Army-Navy game. "Of course, if I went I should have to go with 'bells on' and there's no fun in that," she wrote, meaning that her fame as First Lady would attract too much attention. "Couldn't get permission anyhow," she added. "I guess nobody but you knows how shut in and hemmed about I feel."

In her later White House years, Grace retreated to a room which she had suggested adding to the White House when the government renovated the third floor, the Sky Parlor. This glassed-in sunroom on the roof of the South Portico had a magnificent view of the Washington Monument and the Mall. It contained a couch, a writing table, porch furniture, a phonograph and portable radio. Only the President and her closest friends visited her there.

Grace's restriction to the White House renewed her interest in leaving some sort of mark on the mansion. She persuaded her husband to allow her to form another committee of experts and antiquarians, who operated with more stealth and political smarts than the previous group. Even more helpful was Lieutenant Colonel Ulysses Grant III, grandson of the President, who had been in charge of the renovation of the third floor and roof. He not only handed over the surplus cash from that operation but helped locate lost Lincoln treasures at the Soldiers' Home. Under his supervision, they transformed the Green Room from a beaux arts extravaganza to a chaste colonial parlor, featuring a reproduction of a settee owned by George Washington, delicate Hepplewhite tables and chairs, and a striking portrait of Thomas Jefferson.

Grace Coolidge left the White House proud of this contribution, her smiling serenity intact. But she was never able to share her inner peace with her wounded, brooding husband. He could not find a good word to say for his successor, Herbert Hoover, beyond a bitter epithet: "the wonder boy." Workmen erecting the reviewing stand before the White House for Hoover's inauguration thought Coolidge acted like a prisoner watching "the building of a scaffold for his [own] execution."

Back home in Northampton, Calvin Coolidge continued to be a depressed, unhappy man, tormented by constant bouts of indigestion, allergies, and asthmatic attacks. In his autobiography, he again lamented his son's death and linked it to his ambition for the presidency. He wrote almost the same tormented words he had spoken to William Allen White: "In his suffering he was asking me to help him and I could not."

A year after she left the White House, Grace Coolidge awoke one night with a poem alive in her mind. She had been writing poems since she was a girl. But this one had a special message—one that I think she was desperately trying to share with her husband:

THE OPEN DOOR

You, my son,
Have shown me God.
Your kiss upon my cheek
Has made me feel the gentle touch
Of Him who leads us on.
The memory of your smile, when young,
Reveals His face,
As mellowing years come on apace.
And when you went before,
You left the gates of Heaven ajar
That I might glimpse,
Approaching from afar,
The glories of His grace.
Hold, son, my hand,
Guide me along the path,
That, coming,
I may stumble not,
Nor roam,
Nor fail to show the way
Which leads us—Home.

"The Open Door" was the ultimate expression of Grace Coolidge's serenity. But Calvin Coolidge, if he read it, could not accept the message. Four years after he left the White House, he was dead at sixty. His wife knew why. "The death of our younger son was a severe shock and the zest for living never was the same for him afterward," she said.

Chapter 19

—

MURDER BY
NEWSPRINT

Some readers are aware that I am an aficionado of murder mysteries and have even written a few set in Washington, D.C. But I never thought I would find myself exploring the sudden and unusual deaths of two First Ladies. Nor did I expect to find they were both done in by the same unique weapon.

The first death is what the old cliché experts in the murder mysteries of the nineteen thirties used to call an open-and-shut case. There is no doubt that Rachel Jackson, wife of President Andrew Jackson, was murdered by the nation's newspapers before she even reached the White House.

Anyone who thinks the public's interest in political sex scandals is a twentieth-century phenomenon may be surprised to learn that Rachel's virtue—or lack of it—was the chief issue in the presidential campaign of 1828. The incumbent President, John Quincy Adams, was a stiff, superdignified son of the second president, John Adams. John Quincy's presidency had been a political calamity—Congress had ignored virtually every proposal he sent them—but the forces of respectability (read snobbery) in the original thirteen states regarded him as the last bastion in their losing struggle against the wild-eyed Democrats of the West. Adams's opponent, Andrew Jackson, personified this rough, tough, swaggering breed—although he lived in a Nashville mansion, The Hermitage, as impressive as any house in the country.

President Adams's backers correctly foresaw that Jackson was unstoppable on the high road. The country was disgusted with John Quincy's inert presidency. So they opted for the lowest of low roads—the somewhat messy details of how Rachel and Andrew Jackson met and married. On March 27, 1828, the *Daily National Journal*, an influential Washington paper, announced that Jackson was not only a wastrel who had spent the prime of his life in gambling, cockfighting, and horse racing but also a libertine who had "torn from a husband the wife of his bosom."

With quivering indignation, the newspaper demanded to know how the public would react if President Adams or his secretary of state, Henry Clay, "were to take a man's wife from him pistol in hand." It all came down to a question of character, the Adamsites maintained. If Andrew Jackson had indeed seduced another man's wife, he was not fit to be President of the United States. It was "an affair in which the National character, the National interest, the National morals" were all deeply involved.

In Nashville, Andrew Jackson did his utmost to shield his sixty-year-old wife from the ugly details of this mudslinging. But it was impossible to prevent her from hearing something about it. Rachel knew that the circumstances of their marriage were more than a little unusual. When Jackson first met her in 1788, she was a married woman—a deeply unhappy one. At the age of seventeen, high-spirited Rachel Donelson had married Kentuckian Lewis Robards, who quickly became a walking, talking—and snarling—disaster. He was pathologically jealous and flew into a rage if she so much as said hello to another man. At the same time, he did not regard the marriage vow as binding on his side of the bed.

Rachel had a sharp tongue and gave Robards the whatfor he deserved. In a fit of exasperation, he sent her back to Tennessee, where she went to work for her widowed mother, also named Rachel, who ran a boardinghouse in Nashville. One of the boarders was an energetic young lawyer named Andrew Jackson, who soon could not keep his eyes off the younger Rachel. Unfortunately, neither could Robards, who showed up at the Widow Donelson's to declare he could not live without his darling wife. Still jealous, he grew testy about the attention she was getting from Jackson and warned the junior attorney to keep his distance.

Men said such things to Andrew Jackson at their peril. Jackson reportedly hoisted Robards aloft by his gizzard and announced he would cut his ears off if he ever cast another slur on Rachel's reputation. The panicky Robards sought the protection of the courts, and Jackson was escorted to the local magistrate under guard. Knowing he was among friends, Andy suddenly called for his hunting knife. That got everyone's attention, especially Robards's. Jackson ran his thumb down the knife's gleaming edge while Robards began to quake. Ten seconds later he was out the door with Jackson on his heels. When Andy returned, the magistrate dismissed the charges against him because the complainant had "vanished." Obviously, the courts in frontier Tennessee gave some prisoners a lot of leeway to defend themselves.

Robards went home to Kentucky but again found life without Rachel intolerable. He wrote her a letter, announcing his intention to take her back to the Bluegrass State. Horrified, Rachel decided to flee to Natchez in Mississippi Territory. Andrew Jackson volunteered to escort her through the wilderness. In Natchez they heard that Robards had gotten a divorce and decided they were free to marry. Only when they returned to Tennessee two years later did they learn that Robards had delayed getting the divorce until he found out Rachel and Andrew were living as husband and wife. He then obtained a permanent severance on the grounds of adultery.

The Jacksons were dismayed and reluctantly accepted the advice of several friends that they should remarry. By doing so, however, they more or less admitted their previous marriage was invalid and they had been living in adultery. The accusation returned to haunt Jackson several times before he ran for President. In 1806 he killed a man in a duel for saying it to his face. But he could do little about newspaper stories. The tangled affair had left a rich lode of evidence from eyewitnesses and court papers.

As the 1828 campaign escalated, Rachel Jackson was called "an American Jezebel," "a convicted adulteress," and "a profligate woman." The Adamsites studiously ignored the almost three decades of fidelity and domestic happiness in which Rachel had lived with Andrew Jackson. She was irredeemable, a forever fallen woman. Jackson's infuriated supporters tried to counterattack along the same low road, dredging up flimsy rumors that President Adams and his wife had had sexual relations before they married. A bellow from Tennessee stopped this onslaught. "I never war against females and it is only the base and cowardly who do," Old Hickory thundered.

The Jacksonites regrouped and counterattacked with their own version of the marriage story, which portrayed a gallant Andrew Jackson rescuing a forlorn and beautiful woman from a life of misery. They found a man who had been living in the Donelson boardinghouse at the time to bolster their account. They obtained affidavits from politicians who had voted on the divorce decree in the Kentucky legislature, affirming they only wanted to liberate Rachel from the beastly Robards. Finally they cited the way all the respectable women in and around Nashville accepted Rachel as their equal in virtue and reputation.

This Democratic defense was distributed throughout the country in pamphlet form. A hefty share of copies went to Tennessee, where, paradoxically, Jackson was both loved and hated with maximum intensity. The original smear campaign had, in fact, begun with a pamphlet by a home state rival. Inevitably, this meant Rachel heard still more about the campaign. "The Enemyes of the Genl have dipt their arrows in wormwood & gall and sped them at me," she told a friend in the summer of 1828.

Possibly because of their tangled marital background, Rachel had repeatedly urged Jackson to forswear politics and retire to The Hermitage. In her middle years she had grown religious, and the pursuit of fame seemed so much worldly nonsense to her. "I had rather be a doorkeeper in the house of God than live in that palace in Washington," she declared.

The news that Jackson had won the presidency in a landslide only made Rachel anxious and depressed. Except for her journeys to Natchez and Kentucky, she had seen little of the world and severely doubted her ability to cope with Washington, D.C. She pleaded with her husband and his advisers to let her at least skip the inauguration, where she would be on maximum public display. She wanted to tiptoe into Washington and take refuge in the White House when the uproar had subsided.

Nonsense, declared the exultant Jacksonians. If she acted in such a furtive manner, her persecutors would "chuckle and say they have driven you from the field of your husband's honors." They were almost certainly right about that; political hatchet men were much the same in those pre-Beltway days as they are now.

Rachel reluctantly began acquiring a wardrobe for the inauguration. Early in December 1828, she went shopping in Nashville. She stopped to rest in the office of a cousin who happened to be a newspaper editor. There she found the pamphlet which Jackson's friends had written to defend her against the Adamsites. It was full of the grisly specifics of the charges and countercharges. When friends arrived to pick her up, they found the once and future First Lady sobbing hysterically.

Rachel Jackson never recovered from the shock of reading that pamphlet. Back at The Hermitage, she took to her bed and died a few days before Christmas. Andrew Jackson uttered a typical homily at her grave. "In the presence of this dear saint, I can and do forgive all my enemies," he said. "But those vile wretches who have slandered her must look to God for mercy." One hopes the wretches did look heavenward because for the eight years Old Hickory was President they found no mercy in Washington, D.C.

———

RACHEL JACKSON'S DEMISE MIGHT BE CALLED SIMPLE, PREMEDITATED murder by newsprint. The attack was made on her directly, with malice aforethought. The other First Lady who suffered a similar fate is a more complex story. The plot, you might say, is thicker, but the conclusion is, I think, equally inescapable.

No one would have dreamed anything but happiness and glory awaited Lou Henry Hoover in the White House. Few First Ladies seemed better prepared for the job. The same seemed true of her husband, President Herbert Hoover. Between them, in 1928, they appeared to be supreme examples of all that was wise and good in American civilization.

Lou Henry was the first woman to get a geology degree from Stanford University. She married Herbert Hoover, a fellow geology major, in 1899 and followed him around the world while he amassed a fortune as a mining engineer. When World War I broke out, the Hoovers were living in London. Together they hurled themselves into the chaos that erupted, helping over 120,000 Americans fleeing the war zone to get back to the United States. All told, they loaned these often frantic fugitives $1.5 million out of their own pockets—the equivalent of $100 million today. All but $300 was repaid, forever convincing them, Herbert Hoover liked to say, of the basic honesty of ordinary Americans.

On the European continent, the entire country of Belgium, occupied by the Germans, blockaded by the British fleet, was close to starvation. Herbert Hoover, with Lou at his side, plunged into an emergency effort to feed 7.5 million people. Lou braved German submarines to return to America to raise money in a cross-country speaking tour. Herbert set up the world's first international relief agency in London. While Lou was being called "the most capable woman alive" for her vivid appeals for American aid, Herbert assembled a fleet of forty ships and five-hundred canal boats, at a cost of $25 million a month, to carry food to the beleaguered country. The success of this stupendous operation made the Hoovers world famous.

When America entered the war in 1917, Woodrow Wilson brought Herbert Hoover back to America and put him in charge of the Food Administration. His job was to persuade Americans to produce more and eat less, so the United States could rescue England and France from

starvation. With Lou's help, Hoover once more succeeded magnifi-
cently. He organized the farmers and shippers with his usual efficiency.
She told the nation's housewives how to "Hooverize" a family's diet by
cutting down on meat, wheat, and sugar, and encouraged the nation's
Girl Scouts to increase food production by cultivating war gardens.

After the war Herbert Hoover accepted still more international
relief assignments, funneling millions of tons of food to the starving
women and children of Germany, Eastern Europe, and Russia. By
1920 *The New York Times* ranked Hoover among the ten greatest living
Americans. Woodrow Wilson reportedly said he hoped the Great
Engineer, as the newspapers called him, would succeed him as President. Franklin D. Roosevelt, Wilson's assistant secretary of the navy,
said he would be proud to run as Herbert Hoover's vice president.
Too late, they found out the Great Engineer was a Republican.

At the 1920 Republican Convention, Hoover was brushed aside by
the conservatives in the party, who wanted Warren Harding and the
status quo. But Hoover had been bitten by the presidential bug. He
accepted an appointment as secretary of commerce in the cabinets of
Harding and Calvin Coolidge. While both administrations drifted
into passivity, Hoover converted commerce into the most dynamic
department in the government, topping his performance with another
miraculous rescue operation when the Mississippi overflowed its
banks in 1927, leaving thousands homeless and penniless. Meanwhile,
Lou entertained like a First Lady in waiting at the Hoovers' opulent
home on S Street in Washington and made speeches urging American
women to chart new paths by combining marriage and careers. When
Calvin Coolidge chose not to run in 1928, there was no serious
Republican competition to keep the Hoovers out of the White House.

Herbert Hoover's only obstacle to the Oval Office was the
Democrats' 1928 "cherce"—Alfred E. Smith, the first Catholic to run
for the presidency. Al's sidewalks of New York accent and assaults on
Prohibition ignited almost as much opposition as his Catholic faith. It
was a nasty campaign, in which vicious things were said by some of
Hoover's backers, leaving the Democrats more than ordinarily furious
about losing by another landslide.

On inauguration day, advertising executive Bruce Barton accurately forecast the public mood when he told Hoover: "People expect more of you than they have of any other President." Hoover's inaugural address did little to diminish this soaring optimism. He envisioned a nation of homeowners and farmers "insured against death and accident, unemployment and old age," a future "bright with hope" in which every American could count on "security from poverty and want." Completing his image as a combination white knight and miracle man, Hoover announced he would serve without pay.

Lou seemed the perfect First Lady for the Great Engineer. Finding the White House "bleak as a New England barn," she rearranged the furniture and brought from California some lovely pieces she had collected in her world travels. She also hired Signal Corps photographers at her own expense to take pictures of every piece of furniture in the White House and embarked on a vigorous search for authentic American antiques, continuing the tradition her friend Grace Coolidge had launched. The President may have had some doubts about this eagerness to restore the past after he sat on a chair that had supposedly belonged to Dolley Madison and it collapsed under his bulky six-foot frame.

Lou's long years as a hostess enabled her to cope with any and all entertaining emergencies. She even provided the cook with a recipe that became known as White House Supreme—croquettes of ground ham, beef, lamb, and whatever else happened to be in the refrigerator. The dish was Lou's answer to the frequent discovery that her dinner guests would number forty rather than four. When someone asked the weary housekeeper to sum up the Hoovers' regime, she groaned: "Company, company company!" Lou and "Bert," as she called him, had guests for lunch and dinner every day of the year except February 10, their wedding anniversary, when they dined alone.

On these occasions, guests sometimes encountered a Herbert Hoover who was a less than gracious host. If he decided the company was insufficiently stimulating, or was failing to give him the information he had expected, he would lapse into a glum silence worthy of Calvin Coolidge. Fortunately, Lou was adept at keeping the conver-

Lou and Herbert Hoover relax at their camp on the Rapidan River in Virginia's Blue Ridge Mountains. Lou designed this forerunner of the current presidential retreat Camp David. Protecting the President from stress is one of the First Lady's primary responsibilities. *(Herbert Hoover Presidential Library-Museum)*

sation alive. She was also deft at changing the subject if she saw a topic was starting to embarrass or annoy her husband. Although she never made the kind of extravagant statements about her absolute faith in Herbert Hoover's judgment that Grace Coolidge made about Silent Cal, it was evident to everyone that Lou not only loved Bert, she admired him deeply.

A devoted outdoorswoman who had grown up riding and camping in the California hills, Lou used the First Lady's star status to call for more and better school athletic programs for women and urged parents to enroll their daughters in the Girl Scouts as an ideal way to get them in touch with nature and the beauty of the American countryside. She persuaded her husband to buy 164 acres for a camp on Virginia's Rapidan River, 109 miles from Washington, where they could fish and relax, beyond the reach of the White House's formalities. Lou personally designed a little village of log cabins where, her younger son Allan remarked, everyone could "rough it in perfect comfort."

When the Hoovers discovered that the children in the area had no school, they donated the money to start one and went to considerable trouble to find a teacher for it. That was typical of their private generosity. Both Quakers, they were devout believers in voluntary charity. Lou fretted over the illnesses of the White House staff. One butler, unable to afford the cream he needed for a stomach ulcer, found bottles of it on his doorstep each morning, paid for by Mrs. Hoover.

Lou made some enemies below the Mason-Dixon line when she invited Mrs. Oscar DePriest, wife of an African-American congressman from Chicago, to tea. Some of the other guests refused to shake Mrs. DePriest's hand. Southerners reviled the First Lady for desecrating the White House; the Texas legislature passed a formal rebuke. Lou not only refused to waver—she invited the choir of the black college, Tuskegee Institute, to perform at the White House. These gestures were part of the Hoovers' mutual determination to do their utmost to eliminate injustice and deprivation from American life.

In the Oval Office, the President unleashed a whirlwind of programs to reform America's creaky banking system, improve the farmers' lot, and launch an old-age pension plan. Newspapers showered praise on him, comparing him with Theodore Roosevelt and other presidential dynamos. Then the nation's economic roof collapsed on top of Herbert Hoover—and everyone else. On October 24, 1929, seven months after he became President, the stock market crashed with a rumble heard around the world. By 1930 six million people were out of work, banks were failing, and businesses were going bankrupt by the hundreds. Similar things were happening in Europe.

The Great Engineer, the man who saw the presidency as primarily a managerial problem, struggled to cope with the catastrophe. But his public personality, with its penchant for statistics and facts, its emphasis on the head rather than the heart, lacked a crucial ingredient for political leadership in hard times. Herbert Hoover had a tender heart, and his First Lady had an even more tender one—but they were loath to reveal their private feelings to the American voter and were appalled at the thought of publicizing them for political gain.

A perfect example was the story of three children from Detroit, the oldest thirteen, who showed up at the White House gates to ask the President to help get their father out of jail. The man had stolen a car to keep his family from starving. President Hoover ordered a meal for the children from the White House kitchen, sat them in chairs around his desk, and talked to them about their father. He told them he was sure he was a good man, if he had children who loved him enough to travel all the way from Detroit to Washington for his sake. After the children left, Hoover called in his secretary, who saw tears on the President's face. "Get that man out of jail," Hoover said. "I don't care how you do it."

The secretary succeeded in quashing the conviction—and asked the President if he could release the story to the press. "Of course not!" Hoover said.

Instead of searching for words and gestures that could lift the hearts of the growing numbers of bewildered defeated Americans, Herbert Hoover tried to conquer the worldwide Great Depression with work. Eighteen hours a day, he sat at his desk in the Oval Office, conferring with aides and experts, ordering studies, and forming commissions to cope with the mounting crisis. Lou Hoover tried to contribute, making speeches to women's groups, urging them to help those in need. "The winter is upon us," she said in a radio broadcast from the White House in 1931. "We cannot be warm, in the house or out, we cannot sit down to a table sufficiently supplied with food, if we do not know...every child, woman and man in the United States [is] sufficiently warmed and fed."

Both Lou and the President gave thousands of dollars of their own money to strangers who wrote to the White House begging for help. Always, the gifts were anonymous, delivered through friends who were asked to investigate the pleas to make sure the money was needed. But the scale of the nation's misery was too vast for individuals to comprehend, much less solve. The Hoovers' good intentions, coupled with their stubborn resistance to sympathetic publicity and their inaugural promise to create Utopia, soon transformed the White House into hell.

The Democratic Party played a major role in this metamorphosis. The Democrats' publicity director was a shrewd, ruthless man named Charles Michelson. He correctly discerned that the Great Engineer presented a perfect target for dirty tactics and even dirtier tricks. As one biographer has put it, "The public barely knew him. To most Americans [Hoover] was a rubber face perched above a stiff size 17 collar." From Democratic Party headquarters in Washington flowed a stream of vituperation, blaming this synthetic Herbert Hoover for the Depression, and portraying him as a cold, cruel, uncaring servant of the ruling class.

The stories ranged from scandals to smears to fantasy. An Interior Department employee took a twelve-thousand-dollar bribe to reveal another supposed Teapot Dome oil scam. The President's older son Herbert was forced to resign from his job when he was accused of profiteering because the airline he worked for had a government con-tract to fly the mail. Thousands, perhaps millions, believed the whop-per that the real cause of the Depression was the theft of the nation's gold supply from Fort Knox by Secretary of the Treasury Andrew Mellon, with the President's help.

Soon even Republican-aligned *Time* magazine was calling Herbert Hoover "President Reject." Comedians ridiculed him. H. L. Mencken called him a "fat Coolidge." A Pennsylvania congressman persuaded twenty fellow statesmen to vote a bill of impeachment. Everywhere people recited ditties such as this one:

> Mellon pulled the whistle,
> Hoover rang the bell,
> Wall Street heard the signal,
> And the country went to hell.

Hoover later claimed that his Quaker background enabled him to tolerate this abuse. He simply refused to let it penetrate the center of peace he had cultivated in the core of his self. Perhaps that was true. Nevertheless, his hair turned white and twenty-five pounds vanished from his frame. Beside him, Lou Hoover suffered even more. The President could at least lash back at the "gangster tactics" of Charles Michelson and his allies. The First Lady had to maintain a smiling silence. White House staffers often saw Lou accompany her husband to the door of the Oval Office, where, in a desperate gesture of sympathy, she smoothed his hair with her hand and turned forlornly away.

In the spring and summer of 1932 came the imbroglio that totally ruined Herbert Hoover's reputation. Some twenty thousand unemployed World War I veterans marched on Washington to demand the immediate payment of a long debated bonus for their services in France. They pitched a makeshift camp across the Potomac on the Anacostia Flats and sent flying columns into the city to demonstrate in front of the White House and other government buildings.

Lou Hoover sent coffee and sandwiches to the veterans, but the President decided sterner tactics were in order. With strict instructions to avoid bloodshed, he ordered the U.S. Army's chief of staff, General Douglas MacArthur, to disperse the marchers. MacArthur assembled a thousand men, including a detachment of saber-wielding troopers from the Third Cavalry and six tanks, to assault the unarmed veterans. The only military man with any common sense was MacArthur's aide, Dwight Eisenhower, who advised the chief of staff to play down the operation.

Instead, MacArthur, justifying all the things President Harry Truman said about him twenty years later, reveled in the chance to seize the spotlight. When Herbert Hoover decided a show of force was enough to disperse the marchers, and ordered the troops not to cross the bridge to Anacostia, MacArthur flagrantly disobeyed a President for the first but not the last time. The general sent his men surging into the encampment, which they put to the torch. In the melee a child was badly injured and later died. Hoover, unaware that his orders had been flouted, announced he was "pleased" by the results—hammering the final nail in the coffin of his reputation.

In Albany, New York, when Governor Franklin D. Roosevelt heard the news, he turned to his adviser Felix Frankfurter and said: "Well, Felix, this elects me."

FDR was right, of course, but Charles Michelson and his cohorts took no chances. They continued to batter Hoover with every negative adjective and nasty accusation they could find. Not even Lou was exempt from their dirty tricks. When she attempted to give a radio speech to the nation at a Girl Scout encampment in Virginia, some enterprising Democrat slashed the wires, cutting her off the air.

The embattled President refused to surrender. He accepted the Republicans' nomination in 1932, and with Lou beside him as usual, crisscrossed the nation by train, attacking Roosevelt's solutions to the Depression, defending the Hoover record in the White House. It was a bitter campaign. Voters flung insults and rotten eggs at him. In Kansas—Republican Kansas—a barrage of tomatoes almost finished him. "I can't go on with it anymore," he said to Lou.

She could only put her arm around him in silent sympathy. She did not have the authority to urge him to make a dignified withdrawal, or suggest a change of tactics. She had never been an equal political partner. The man who had worked miracles in her life and in the greater world was being destroyed before her eyes, and there was nothing she could do.

The net result was one of the most humiliating rejections in presidential history. Forty-two out of forty-eight states repudiated President Herbert Hoover. Only two out of five Americans voted for him. Lou Henry Hoover could not believe it. She told friends it was the most vicious, the most unfair campaign she had ever seen. On her last day in the White House, as she said good-bye to her personal maid, tears filled her eyes. "Maggie," she said, "my husband will live to do great things for his country."

This became the faith to which both Hoovers clung. They refused to go quietly into the night. For the next ten years, Herbert Hoover flailed at Franklin D. Roosevelt and his New Deal. Not only were his efforts futile but he did not seem to realize he gave the Democratic Party's flacks more opportunities to attack their favorite target. In each of FDR's three bids for reelection, he ran against the synthetic Herbert Hoover—the rubber face above the size 17 collar.

Lou Hoover supported her husband loyally. But no one seemed to realize the depths of her private sorrow, as she watched him humiliated again and again. Only a few close relatives, such as her niece Hulda Hoover McLean, saw how deeply she had been hurt in 1932, how "broken hearted she was by the injustice of it all."

One other person knew: Grace Coolidge, watching from retirement in Massachusetts. Grace had become close to Lou Hoover during the Coolidge White House years. The two women had exchanged gifts, particularly flowers, and Grace had playfully adopted nicknames from their favorite blooms. Hers was Lily. Lou Hoover became Bleeding Heart. Was this latter choice evidence of Grace's loving perceptiveness? I think so.

For eleven years Lou Hoover waited in vain for her husband's vindication. Instead, Franklin Roosevelt went on from triumph to triumph. When World War II began, Herbert Hoover offered his services to his government. FDR rejected him with contempt, remarking to Bernard Baruch that he was not "going to raise him from the dead." Compounding his cruelty, the President leaked old slanders against Hoover—that he had led investors astray as a mining expert and that he had collaborated with the Germans in some of their World War I atrocities, such as the murder of the English nurse Edith Cavell.

On the surface, Lou Hoover seemed reasonably contented. She spent most of her time in their beautiful hilltop home in Palo Alto, overlooking the Stanford University campus, where she and Bert had met. A glimpse of how much she loved that place is visible in an impromptu poem she sent to Grace Coolidge, inviting her out for a visit:

> *The Spring has come up from the ocean*
> *And started east over the peaks.*
> *The lilacs are wild on the mountain,*
> *Nearly gone are the almond and peach.*
>
> *The humming birds rise from the cherries*
> *To be lost in the blue overhead.*
> *Wisteria drips from its trellis*
> *Pomegranate blooms show their red.*

So Lily, 'tis time you were moving,
Packing up for a picnic or two,
The whole world's before you for wand'ring,
But westward's the right thing to do.

There's a glimpse of the Bay from your bed, dear,
The college chimes drowse in your ear.
You golf or you swim or you wind 'round the rim
To see the sun sink in the sea.

Herbert Hoover scorned this tranquillity. Still embroiled in his feud with FDR, he spent so much time in the East he acquired an apartment in the Waldorf Towers. Lou seldom accompanied him there. She was elected president of the Girl Scouts and became active in the Salvation Army. But her central role, helpmate of the Great Engineer, the man the whole world admired, had been destroyed. In the last year of her life, she confessed to a would-be biographer a yearning for a lost career of her own: "All kinds of projects I should like to have put through. A number of callings or professions I should like to have followed, and was prepared to begin. But always duties, interests or activities of the moment pushed farther back the moment for taking up any long-to-be continued cause or profession."

In 1943 Herbert Hoover finally persuaded Lou to join him in the Waldorf Towers. He was girding for another assault on FDR in 1944, and he felt Palo Alto was too remote from the center of the action. Lou came east with great reluctance. For her Palo Alto had been a refuge from the bitter memories of 1932. Fragments of the trauma still lingered. In her desk she kept a stack of checks from people she had helped in the depths of the Depression. They had tried to pay her back, but she never cashed their checks.

As Christmas 1943 approached, she sent a generous check to her White House maid, Maggie, with a note suggesting she buy presents for her children. Two weeks later, on January 7, 1944, Lou went to Carnegie Hall to hear Mildred Dilling, a gifted harpist who had performed several times at the Hoover White House. On the way back to the Waldorf, Lou felt ill and hailed a taxi. When Herbert Hoover went to her bedroom to kiss her good night—he was on his way out to a dinner honoring an old friend—he found Lou unconscious on the floor, her heart fluttering spasmodically. By the time he lifted her to the bed, Bleeding Heart was gone.

Recent studies at Johns Hopkins University have convinced doctors that the old wives' tale is true: people can die of broken hearts. Researchers have discovered links between the limbic nervous system, which deals with the emotions, and a small spot in the section of the brain called the insular cortex, which controls the heartbeat. Repeated stimulation of the cortex by an intense emotion can cause the heart to fibrillate—beat wildly out of control—leading to cardiac arrest. The fact that Lou Hoover went to a concert that carried her back to the anguish of her White House years may well have been a factor in her sudden death.

Admittedly, it is not an open-and-shut case. But I think that ultimately Lou was killed by the same weapon that sent Rachel Jackson to her death. There is nothing inherently wrong with newsprint, of course. But in the wrong hands, it can have tragic consequences for some inhabitants of the White House.

Chapter 20

—

CAN AMBITION

REPAY SUCH

SACRIFICES?

WHAT A PITY LOU HENRY HOOVER DID NOT LIVE ANOTHER SIXTEEN months. By then a new President was in the White House, and he was resolved to right the wrong that history—and the publicity mavens of the Democratic Party—had done to Herbert Hoover. He also believed the country needed Hoover's talents as a thinker and manager of great humanitarian enterprises. "If you should be in Washington," Harry Truman wrote to Mr. Hoover on May 24, 1945, "I would be most happy to talk over the European food situation with you. Also it would be a pleasure for me to become acquainted with you."

I was a college student when that letter was written. One morning, as I hurried out of the White House, a tall, bulky man of a certain age came striding past me in the hall leading from the North Portico. He looked vaguely familiar, but I did not recognize him and he obviously did not know me. I watched with curiosity as he took the family elevator to the second floor. That evening I asked my father who he was.

"Go downstairs and look at the portraits hanging on the wall," my father said. He never missed a chance to make me do my own historical research. I quickly discovered the man was Herbert Hoover, and the reason I had not recognized him also became clear. His portrait is not full length and gives you little sense of his height and surprising bulk.

That visit marked the beginning of a friendship with my father that brought Herbert Hoover back to Washington to help feed more millions of destitute people at the end of World War II and, later, to reorganize the executive branch of the federal government. In 1946 my mother invited Mr. Hoover to the White House to help her unveil a lovely portrait of Lou, which should have been hung there years before.

By the time Herbert Hoover died in 1964, he had become a beloved elder statesman, restored to the list of great Americans. In 1962 he wrote to ex-President Truman: "Yours has been a friendship that has reached deeper into my life than you know.... When you came to the White House, within a month you opened the door to me to the only profession I know, public service, and you undid some disgraceful action[s] that had taken place in prior years."

I like to think that Lou Henry Hoover's spirit guided her husband's pen across the page as he wrote that letter—and her loving hand caressed his bowed head. It would by no means be the only example of the mysterious workings of the spirit in the history of the White House.

———

THE HOOVERS' STORY REMINDS ME OF ANOTHER WHITE HOUSE marriage between a gifted woman and a brilliant but rigid, driven public man. In one of the most extraordinary behind-the-scenes dramas in the mansion's long history, the relationship between Louisa Johnson Adams and her husband, John Quincy Adams, ran the gamut from love to loathing to redemption.

Louisa Johnson's father, Joshua, was a Marylander who flourished as a merchant in London before, during, and after the American Revolution. Louisa was born in England and was exceptionally well educated in French schools. A striking beauty, with glossy, reddish blond hair and large brown eyes, she played the piano and the harp, sang well, and wrote more than passable poetry. When she met John Quincy Adams, his father was President of the United States and he was the American ambassador to the Netherlands.

Each recognized the other was a catch. But something warned Louisa—and John Quincy—not to take the bait. Louisa seemed too forward to the proper young diplomat, and she was put off by his sloppy appearance, his stiff manner, and his fierce temper. When she urged him to wear more fashionable clothes, he complied, appearing at a Johnson family picnic looking like a veritable Beau Brummell. Later, he furiously informed her that no wife of his would ever tell him what to wear. Louisa advised him to find a more submissive spouse. When he proposed, however, she swallowed her misgivings and said yes.

Louisa was supposed to bring a handsome dowry to the union. But within months of their marriage, they discovered Joshua Johnson was bankrupt and the money would not be forthcoming. This alone was enough to give John Quincy negative thoughts about his new bride. Louisa did not help matters by talking back to him about everything from where they should live to how they should raise their children.

At times Louisa could be outright defiant. She and her husband began their married lives in Berlin, where John Quincy was sent as the first American ambassador to Prussia. The Queen of Prussia suggested Louisa wear rouge, which was very much in fashion in the capital. Her Majesty even presented her with a jar of the stuff, but John Quincy forbade Louisa to use it. To him rouge was synonymous with immorality. When Louisa applied it anyway, John Quincy scrubbed it off with a wet towel. A few months later, getting ready for an evening at the royal court, Louisa rouged her face again and absolutely refused to take it off. An infuriated John Quincy went to the palace without her. Far from being upset, Louisa felt she had won a moral victory.

Back in the United States, still more battles awaited them. Louisa found Boston's frigid winters excruciating and was even more pained by the chilly reception she received from her mother-in-law. Abigail Adams did not think any woman on earth was worthy of her eldest—and favorite—son. Louisa was soon telling friends that "hanging and marriage were strongly assimilated."

In spite of their quarrels, they were a well-matched marital team. Louisa was an expert hostess who invariably dazzled male guests. John Quincy's diplomatic experience, which included serving as his father's secretary when John Adams helped negotiate the treaty of peace that ended the American Revolution, made him an important personage. He had little difficulty winning a stint as U.S. senator from Massachusetts. But his heart was in foreign affairs, and he accepted an appointment as ambassador to St. Petersburg.

Pinched for money, John Quincy decided, without so much as consulting Louisa, to leave their two older sons, George and John, behind in Massachusetts with his parents. They would take with them only their third son, Charles. He did not even inform Louisa of this heart-wrenching decision until they were preparing to board their ship in Boston harbor. As America slipped beneath the horizon, Louisa asked her diary: "Can ambition repay such sacrifices?" She penned her own reply: "Never!"

Louisa Adams did not see her two older sons for eight years. Her bitterness toward her husband deepened after she gave birth to a daughter in Russia and the child died within little over a year. In spite of this searing loss, Louisa soon demonstrated a self-reliance which amply proved her contention that women are men's equals. While the Adamses were in St. Petersburg, the whole world went to war. Napoleon invaded Russia and simultaneously dueled England for global supremacy on land and sea. Meanwhile the British began slugging it out with the United States in what we call the War of 1812.

When Napoleon's Grand Army failed ingloriously and the Americans regained their fighting spirit after the burning of Washington, D.C., peace negotiations broke out. John Quincy Adams was appointed to head the American team of diplomats confronting some surly Britons at Ghent in Belgium. Leaving Louisa in St. Petersburg for the better part of a year, he successfully wrested a very advantageous peace treaty from the English, then casually ordered her to join him in Paris.

John Quincy apparently gave not even a passing thought to the dangers he was asking his wife to face. With her eight-year-old son Charles and three servants, Louisa set out in February across frozen Russia and Poland in a sled, braving desolate wastes and lawless guerrillas. In eight weeks she traveled a thousand miles and arrived in France just in time to encounter drunken French soldiers marching to join Napoleon, who had escaped from exile and was preparing for another try at *la Gloire.* The infantrymen took one look at Louisa's Russian-built carriage, remembered their humiliating retreat from Moscow, and decided to murder her.

Waving her American passport and crying "Vive Napoleon," Louisa coolly talked them out of their bloodthirsty inclinations and rode on to Paris. Far from being upset by his wife's ordeal, John Quincy made light of it, offhandedly telling his mother that the journey, which put her maid to bed with "brain fever" for two months, seemed to have improved Louisa's health.

Returning in triumph to the United States, John Quincy was summoned to Washington as President James Monroe's secretary of state. He saw the position as a stepping-stone to the presidency. If Bill Clinton was, as he claims, bitten by the presidential bug when he was sixteen, that insect must have zeroed in on John Quincy Adams in his cradle. From his earliest waking moments, his doting parents seem to have selected him to resume the family's tenancy in the White House.

Adams's chief obstacle to attaining this goal was himself. He spoke in a high, shrill voice and by his own admission was severely lacking in likability. "I am a man of reserved, cold, austere and forbidding manners," he confided to his diary. In a letter to Louisa, he confessed: "I never was and never shall be what is commonly termed a popular man.... I have no powers of fascination."

John Quincy's one and only hope of becoming President was Louisa. By now, she had been reunited with her two older boys and was more kindly disposed toward her husband. She went to work on his behalf in Washington, D.C., entertaining congressmen and their wives by the dozen, fascinating them with her tales of foreign lands. One of her guests called her "the most accomplished American lady I have seen."

In 1820 Louisa and John Quincy put almost every cent they had into an imposing three-story home on F Street, where they could entertain even more lavishly, as he launched his stretch run for the presidency. They added a twenty-eight- by twenty-nine-foot ballroom, in which guests could dance cotillions "with ease." Louisa also made numerous forays into nearby Maryland, where her relatives were "most respectable and distinguished," and succeeded in putting her home state firmly in John Quincy's column.

It soon became apparent, as the year 1824 dawned and President Monroe entered his final months in the White House, that the two men most likely to succeed him were John Quincy Adams and Andrew Jackson. At this point, Louisa pulled off the social coup that made her husband President. She decided to give a ball honoring Jackson on the tenth anniversary of his great victory at New Orleans in the War of 1812.

Louisa sent out nine hundred invitations, and not one was turned down. The only conspicuous nonattenders were President Monroe and his wife, who never went to private parties. Louisa, in a gleaming gown ornamented with cut steel, greeted General Jackson at the door, utterly dazzling him. He stayed at her side like a devoted suitor for the entire evening. The ball was the party of the decade in Washington and automatically elevated John Quincy to the same prominence as the hero of New Orleans.

The 1824 presidential campaign was a mess. With four major contenders, Jackson received a plurality of the popular vote—forty-two percent; John Quincy was second with thirty-two percent. But the General did not carry enough states to win a majority of the electoral votes, and the decision was thrown into the House of Representatives. There, with the help of another candidate, Henry Clay of Kentucky, who switched his support to Adams, John Quincy became the only son of a President to reach 1600 Pennsylvania Avenue.

He had achieved his dream, but it rapidly turned into a nightmare. Adams rewarded Clay by making him his secretary of state. Jackson's infuriated supporters—and a lot of other people—accused the President of making a "corrupt bargain" and coalesced against Adams's leadership. John Quincy and Louisa found themselves marooned in a virtually ostracized White House.

After having worked so hard to get there, Louisa soon came to hate the Executive Mansion. As First Lady, she was reduced to a mere ornament, and a pointless one at that, since her husband's administration was stranded. Moreover, the place lacked the comforts of "any private mechanics family." She told her son George it was impossible for her to feel at home in the house, "or to feel I have a home anywhere."

Not surprisingly, John Quincy was no help. When he relaxed and talked about literature or the arts, Adams could be interesting. (Henry Fielding's racy novel *Tom Jones* was one of his favorite books.) But most of the time he was a bore, prone to doze off in the middle of dinner. Louisa made no secret of the fact that she did not particularly enjoy her husband's company. One day she copied into her diary a bit of doggerel that had gotten into a capital newspaper:

> Asked by the Nation's chief to take my tea
> I hastened to him in surprising glee,
> But when I got there, all my treat, by God
> Was to watch his Excellency's Nod.

Before long the First Lady was deeply depressed. Her only relief was chocolate, which she devoured by the pound, without gaining an ounce of weight. Perhaps she was trying to cram herself with the sweetness that was so abysmally missing from her life. In 1825 Louisa decided to write her autobiography, which she titled "Adventures of a Nobody." Under the pseudonym Rachel Barb she also wrote a play about an aristocratic couple living in a great mansion. The main character, Lord Sharply, was "full of good qualities," but ambition "absorbed every thought of his soul." His wife, Lady Sharply, was, of course, miserable.

Inevitably, the frustrated President and his gloomy First Lady fell to quarreling. Their main bone of contention was the children. John

Quincy was always demanding impossible performances from his sons. Louisa was far more easygoing; she put happiness ahead of achievement. Hardly surprising, when she looked at her dour husband and saw the way a lifetime of parental pressure and superhuman striving had turned him into a virtual misanthrope.

John Quincy's presidency continued sinking into political oblivion. His party lost control of Congress, which went about their business as if the White House did not exist. Worse, his son John, who acted as his secretary, was a dilettante who spent most of his time chasing beautiful girls. In an inventory of presidential expenses, young John accidentally included the cost of a billiard table, which John Quincy had installed in the White House, mostly for his sons' amusement. The President's enemies leaped on this mistake, which was hastily corrected, as proof of his "aristocratic tastes" and indifference to setting a good example to the young men of the nation. In those days billiard playing was synonymous with strong drink, fast women, and sin.

The President vented his frustrations on Louisa and their oldest son, George Washington Adams. More Johnson than Adams, George was a dreamy, sensitive young man who wrote poetry and lived a vaguely bohemian life in Boston, trying to ignore the stream of angry letters his father sent him. Louisa defended George against the presidential wrath, thereby bringing not a little of it on herself.

By the summer of 1828, the President and his wife were barely speaking. Louisa spent as much time away from the White House as possible. When John Quincy wrote to her, he addressed her as "Mrs. Louisa C. Adams," as if they were divorced. He could not bring himself to write "Dear Louisa," any more than she could write "Dear John." Instead, she addressed him simply as "The President."

In Boston, George Washington Adams, struggling fitfully to live up to his Adams inheritance and his father's ferocious lectures, had gotten himself elected to the Massachusetts legislature and opened a law office. But he was defeated for reelection and few clients sought his legal services. He slowly sank into debt and squalor. Worse, he had an affair with a servant girl that produced an illegitimate daughter—a fall from grace which he managed to conceal from his parents.

Louisa made periodic trips to Boston to see George, who suffered from a variety of illnesses, some real, some imaginary. In 1827, on one of these journeys, she revealed once more that she, not her husband, was the politician in the family. She held a reception in Philadelphia at which the city's leading citizens all but threw themselves at her feet. Louisa promptly fired off a letter to John Quincy, urging him to visit Pennsylvania and other states if he wanted to get reelected. Too angry at her to take this excellent advice, Adams announced that when he began his summer vacation, he was going home to Massachusetts "as straight and quick as possible."

In a kind of counterpoint to John Quincy's presidency, George's fortunes continued to sink. He was forced to borrow a thousand dollars from a local tomb maker, and then had to reveal it to his father when he could not repay the debt. This triggered another spate of furious presidential letters, which did nothing but deepen George's overwhelming sense of failure. Meanwhile, as we have seen, Adams's political backers were fighting for his presidency by smearing Andrew Jackson's wife as a fallen woman. The filthy campaign could only have further convinced this emotional, despairing young man that he wanted no part of the world of ruthless ambition and raw power into which he had been born.

The year 1828 ended in total disaster for John Quincy and Louisa Adams. The President was routed at the polls by Andrew Jackson. For George Washington Adams, this only meant more trouble. Now a lame duck, John Quincy proceeded to concentrate all his fury on his eldest son, demanding this, condemning that, in another volley of letters that ended with a command to come to Washington at once.

George dreaded the thought of confessing his derelictions to his dour father face to face. As he prepared for the journey, he showed unmistakable signs of a mental collapse. He heard birds speaking to him from nearby trees, and his sleep was repeatedly broken by a conviction that burglars were prowling around his squalid furnished room. His younger brother Charles, who was in Boston setting up his own law practice, grew deeply alarmed at his conduct. Not knowing what else to do, Charles hoped for the best and helped George pack for his trip to Washington.

In Providence, George boarded a steamboat that would take him down the Rhode Island coast and through Long Island Sound to New York. All he could see as he gazed out at the water was his father's frowning face. Soon he began hearing a voice in the pounding steam engines, whispering, "Let it be, let it be." At 3:00 A.M. he rushed to the bridge to tell the captain he wanted to be put ashore immediately because the other passengers were conspiring to kill him. The captain assured him there was no danger on his boat, and George retreated to the open deck.

A few minutes later, a passenger heard a splash. He rushed to the railing in time to see George vanishing in the steamboat's foaming wake. "Man overboard!" the Good Samaritan shouted. The aghast captain stopped the ship; he probably knew he had just lost a President's son. He lowered a rescue boat, but all the sailors found were George's hat and cloak.

Two days later, the news reached John Quincy and Louisa Adams in Washington. Both realized that George had been sacrificed to John Quincy's ambition, in which Louisa had acquiesced. John Quincy was totally devastated—until he saw that Louisa was in even worse condition. For the first time in decades, they reached out to each other with sympathy and at least an approximation of love in their hearts.

John Quincy became "a ministering angel, always at my side," Louisa told one of her friends. She successfully stifled any impulse to blame him for the tragedy. They read comforting passages in their Bibles to each other. "We are in great distress," the ex-President wrote his son Charles. "But the first Shock of this heavy dispensation of Providence is past, and your Mother and myself, relying on him who chastiseth in Mercy, still look for consolation in the affectionate kindness of our remaining Sons."

When the family gathered to offer their sympathy, John Quincy asked Louisa to read the service for the dead from the Episcopal Book of Common Prayer. After decades of differences, he was finally trying to acknowledge her importance in their troubled partnership.

Their reconciliation deepened steadily in succeeding weeks. If they were apart even for a few days, he wrote letters to his "Dearest Louisa."

A few months later, an ex-President now, John Quincy walked through Washington's Rock Creek woods. He was still deeply depressed; he could not stop thinking of George. A rain shower forced him to take shelter under a tree. The downpour left the grass gleaming and filled the warm air with the scent of growing things. Life, hope, stirred in the dry husk that John Quincy's soul had become. Moments later, a magnificent rainbow arched above Washington, D.C. He told Louisa he felt it was a sign of God's mercy.

A few days later, Louisa picked up a copy of the *National Journal* of Washington and received an even more mystical surprise. The paper had printed a poem that George had sent the editor a few weeks before his death:

> There is a little spark at sea,
> Which grows 'mid darkness brilliantly,
> But when the moon looks clear and bright
>   Emits a pale and feeble light,
> And when the tempest shakes the wave,
> It glimmers o'er the seaman's grave.
>
> Such friendship's beaming light appears
> Through the long line of coming years.
> In sorrow's cloud it shines afar
>   A feeble but a constant star,
> And like that little spark at sea
> Burns brightest in adversity.

Louisa wept and showed the poem to John Quincy. She felt it was George's last message, telling them that in spite of the mistakes they had made as parents—especially the decision to abandon him for those eight long years of his boyhood—his love for them had remained alive in his troubled heart.

If readers require further proof that this ex-President and his First Lady had learned a profound spiritual lesson, they need only to look at the rest of their long lives. In 1830 John Quincy decided to return to Washington as a humble congressman. Louisa went with him and wholeheartedly supported the cause he soon embraced—the right of citizens to present protests against slavery to Congress. Dominated by southerners, Congress had passed a "gag rule" which enabled them to ignore the nation's mounting disgust with this blot on America's moral reputation. John Quincy soon won the title "Old Man Eloquent" for his struggle on behalf of this basic civil right.

One of their grandsons, Henry Adams, who would achieve his own kind of fame, remembered visiting John Quincy and Louisa in Washington as a boy. To him Louisa seemed "singularly peaceful, a vision of silver gray, presiding over her old President and her Queen Anne mahogany...an object of deference to everyone." Unlike Grace Coolidge, who was blessed with serenity from the start, Louisa Johnson Adams took several decades of turmoil to achieve it. In the end this star-crossed First Lady gave her driven husband a measure of inner peace in the bargain.

Chapter 21

—

THE

GLAMOUR

GIRLS

THE WHITE HOUSE HAS NOT ALWAYS BEEN DRENCHED IN TRAGEDY. Some First Ladies have been lucky enough—or clever enough—to escape—or at least transcend—tears. One is a relative of sorts, Julia Gardiner Tyler. The Trumans have long claimed her husband, President John Tyler, as kin. Another, Frances Folsom Cleveland, I had the pleasure of meeting when she was an elderly lady. She was as uncannily self-possessed in old age as she was when she married a bachelor President with an illegitimate child in his past and became the youngest First Lady so far.

When men praised Dolley Madison, they were complimenting her charm more than her looks. When they purred over Julia Tyler, they were complimenting both—with the emphasis, as the song from the musical *Damn Yankees* puts it, "on the latter." Many students of First Ladies consider Julia the most beautiful woman to have strolled the White House halls. Like Edith Wilson, she married a President who had lost his wife after he was elected. But that was only part of the role the Grim Reaper played in Julia's ascension to First Lady.

In one of those odd historical coincidences that give you the shivers, John Tyler, Harry Truman's putative kin, was the first vice president to move into the White House by virtue of a President's death. He succeeded a hero of the War of 1812, William Henry Harrison, when the old warrior died after only a month in office. Tyler was the first to encounter the animus that seems to greet every accidental President. Some critics even called him "His Accidency."

Tyler was a member of the new Whig Party, which had sprouted from the grave of the Federalists. But he was more interested in being President of all the people and declined to cooperate with the Whig congressmen and senators who had broken the power of the Democratic Party in 1840 with the first modern political campaign. The Whigs added Tyler to the ticket to help carry the South. He had been governor of Virginia, as well as a congressman and senator. They did not bother to check out his political opinions, beyond noting that he was not a Democrat.

The Whigs should have noticed that Tyler had independent opinions about everything and never hesitated to swim against the political tide. As President, he proved to be so independent, virtually his entire cabinet soon resigned and the Whigs formally expelled him from the party. Ignoring mobs of angry Whigs who threatened to burn down the White House and even talked of assassinating him, Tyler rejected so many bills from the Whig-controlled Congress he soon acquired another nickname: "Old Veto."

The President brought an invalid wife, Letitia, to the White House. Crippled by a stroke in 1839, she descended from the second floor's family quarters only once, to attend a daughter's wedding in 1842. A few months later, she died at the age of fifty-one. Early in 1843, when the official period of mourning for his wife had barely expired, President Tyler resumed entertaining at the White House, with a daughter-in-law as hostess. At one of the first parties, he met and was mesmerized by Julia Gardiner.

A smashingly attractive twenty-two-year-old brunette from Long Island, Julia was the daughter of one of New York's senators, David Gardiner. The President managed to kiss her on her second visit to the White House and proposed to her two weeks later at a

Washington's Birthday ball—ignoring her repeated murmurs of "No, no no!"

Such denials were de rigueur for young ladies in those early Victorian days. Julia was clearly entranced with Tyler—and with the White House. Born to wealth, she had displayed a fondness for the limelight at an early age. In 1839 proper New Yorkers had been shocked to open their newspapers and discover an illustration of nineteen-year-old Julia in a sunbonnet, urging readers to shop at a popular department store on Ninth Avenue. She told her mortified parents she had posed for the ad "for the fun of it."

The enthralled President bombarded Julia with flowery love letters, praising her raven tresses and snow white skin. She kept her fifty-three-year-old suitor at arm's length, though she was a frequent White House visitor—with her indulgent father as chaperon. At the same time she carried on serious romances with a congressman from South Carolina and a justice of the Supreme Court, using the timeless principle that nothing whets a man's ardor more than competition.

Then the Grim Reaper intervened once more. One chilly February day in 1844, Tyler invited Senator David Gardiner and his daughter for a cruise on the Potomac River aboard the U.S. Navy's new steam frigate, *Princeton*. The male guests went out on deck to see a demonstration of a new cannon, the Peacemaker. With a shattering roar, the big gun exploded, killing eight people, including the secretary of state, the secretary of the navy, and Julia's father.

Back at the Washington Navy Yard, a distraught President carried Julia ashore, almost falling into the Potomac himself when she awoke from her swoon and began struggling fitfully. Thereafter their tragedy-tinged romance progressed at a rapid tempo. In June the President slipped up to New York, eluding reporters, and married Julia in a private ceremony at the Church of the Ascension on lower Fifth Avenue.

When the news of this May-September union got out, some newspapers were pretty ribald. A pro-Tyler paper in Washington had described the President's departure from the capital as a vacation from his arduous duties. "We rather think the President's arduous duties are only beginning," chortled the *New York Herald*. Others made political jokes. One of Tyler's goals was the annexation of Texas, which had won its independence in 1836 and was eager to join the American union. The *Herald* referred to the President's marriage as a treaty of annexation "without the consent of the Senate." That was not far from the truth. Along with her beauty, Julia conveyed a handsome fortune to Tyler, who was, like many Virginia landowners, frequently short of cash.

Dolley Madison brought merriment to the White House; Julia Tyler brought zing. Impish, impulsive, flirtatious, she dazzled every politician in Washington, even congenital sourpusses like the South's champion, John C. Calhoun, who became Tyler's secretary of state. At one banquet, Julia reported to her mother, the captivated Calhoun spent most of the time whispering poetry "of infinite sweetness and taste" in her ear.

Almost every day was crowded with glamour and excitement in Julia's breathless reign as First Lady. When she was not presiding at luncheons, dinners, receptions, the new Mrs. Tyler dashed through the streets of Washington behind four snow white horses, finer than those of the city's preeminent connoisseur of horseflesh, the Russian ambassador. When she was not driving, she was cruising on the Potomac or picnicking in the woods around Rock Creek. Strolling, she was accompanied by an Italian greyhound, the favorite pet of fashionable ladies.

Even before she became First Lady, Julia was intensely interested in politics and had made a habit of visiting the House of Representatives to listen to the debates. There too she had worshipers, among them one of the many political bachelors of those days, a rather homely, bucktoothed character named Richard D. Davis from Saratoga County, New York. Whenever Julia appeared, he abandoned the issue of the moment and made a dash for the gallery to sit beside her. One day she appeared looking spectacularly beautiful in a huge flowered hat, which induced the panting Davis to break all previous speed records for getting to the gallery. A few minutes later, someone called for a vote on the issue under debate. When the teller got to

Julia Tyler looked–
and acted–like a
queen during her
whirlwind occupation
of the White House.
Men, someone said,
were so many notches
in her parasol.
*(White House Historical
Society)*

Davis, another congressman rose and announced: "Mr. Speaker. Mr. Davis has gone to the gallery to study horticulture."

Julia also charmed the press. The Washington correspondent for the *New York Herald*, which was well on its way to becoming the nation's most powerful newspaper, was so hypnotized, he volunteered himself as her press agent. He dubbed her "the Lovely Lady Presidentress" and never described her with fewer than two flattering adjectives. Among his raptures was the claim that Julia was superior to Queen Victoria and every other crowned head of Europe back to the consort of Louis XIV.

Not content with the fabulous notices she received in the *Herald*, Julia assigned her older brother Alexander to pen equally lyrical accounts of her parties for other New York papers. She was not above dropping her scribes saucy notes, asking why a recent White House event had not yet been publicized. Because she married Tyler when there were only eight months left in his term, Julia knew she had no time to waste if she wanted to make her mark as First Lady.

In the beginning, it looked as if her father's death might pose a problem; it was customary to mourn a parent or a spouse for a full year by wearing black and eschewing any and all kinds of revelry. Julia persuaded herself and everyone else that White House entertaining was not revelry but a duty. With advice, some say, from Dolley Madison, who had returned to Washington after her husband's death, Julia solved the mourning clothes dilemma by wearing black during the day and white, which was also acceptable, in the evening. Sometimes she combined the two colors, covering white satin or silk with black lace. Ropes of small pearls adorned her neck; on her forehead she wore a jewel cut out of black jet.

Determined to ignore her husband's unpopularity with the Whig half of Washington, D.C., Julia played her First Lady's role to the hilt. When it came to entertainment, her motto was "the grand or nothing." With lavish use of Gardiner money, she turned the White House from a "dirty establishment" (her phrase) into a shining model of contemporary good taste. In its spacious rooms she staged a succession of brilliant receptions, balls, and dinners that left staid Washington dizzy with delight.

With delicious daring, Julia introduced the polka at White House balls. This dance was considered so racy, President Tyler had previously forbidden his daughters (several of whom were older than Julia) to perform it. But he did not so much as peep when the First Lady pranced across the East Room in the arms of one ambassador after another. The dance soon became the national rage.

There was only one shadow on Julia's reign—her husband's jealousy of her long list of previous suitors. One in particular, the Supreme Court justice, still gazed wistfully at her whenever they met. One morning President Tyler refused to let her go to church because he feared the justice would be in a nearby pew with his eyes fixed on Julia instead of on the altar.

I must confess that even I, who have gone on record in favor of every First Lady following her natural bent, was somewhat taken aback by some of Julia's antics. She played the part of a royal consort a little too extravagantly for my down-home Missouri taste. She received her guests seated in a large armchair on a raised platform with a "court" of a half dozen or so ladies-in-waiting banked around her, all dressed in white. At times she wore a headdress of miniature gold bugles which resembled a crown. Only a President who was hopelessly in love—and knew he had no political future—would have tolerated such behavior.

In one of those unexpected twists that unsettle political pundits, John Tyler's embattled administration ended on a high note. When the Senate rejected the treaty of annexation he had negotiated with Texas, Tyler outfaked them. He argued that Texas could be added to the Union by a simple majority vote of both houses of Congress. Determined to get his way, the President used patronage and his not inconsiderable national following to pressure the opposition party, the Democrats, into making annexation one of the main planks of their 1844 platform. Thereupon he threw his support to the Democratic nominee, James K. Polk. When Polk defeated Henry Clay in yet another of the Kentuckian's many attempts to become President, Congress concluded that the people had spoken and voted the Lone Star State into the Union in the final week of the Tyler administration.

Many people think that without Julia's magnificent entertainments in the first three months of 1845, this happy event might not have taken place. Like Louisa Adams's ball for Andrew Jackson, Julia's galas made Tyler look irresistibly popular, even if he lacked the support of the two major political parties. Julia began her campaign with a New Year's Day reception that crammed two thousand people into the White House. One bemused reporter described the crush in verse:

> I beg your pardon General G
> For trampling on your toes,
> And Lady T., I did not see
> My hat against your nose.
> And Holy Jesus! how they squeeze us
> To that small room where he,
> Old John, attends to greet his friends
> This New Year's Day levee.

A week after this dazzling display of democracy in action, Julia switched to elitism, limiting the guest list to a ball so severely, there were cries of anguished indignation echoing all over Washington. For access to this fete, guests needed to have influence on the upcoming vote on Texas. Julia also politicked relentlessly for the annexation among her legion of adoring congressmen and senators. "Last night," she told her mother in one letter, "at least fifty members of Congress paid their respects to me." Even after her marriage, she remained a consummate flirt. Men, one historian has remarked, were just so many notches in Julia's parasol.

From New York City encouraging news about Texas arrived via Julia's brother, Alexander Gardiner. He reported that the city's Democratic Party had passed a series of ferocious resolutions, demanding an immediate congressional vote on Texas lest the British or the Mexicans woo the Lone Star State into their grasp. Julia decided to celebrate this good news with the ultimate gala. With the help of her sister Margaret, who functioned as the first White House social secretary, two thousand invitations went out to prominent Americans up and down the eastern seaboard and into the far reaches of the West.

An astonishing three thousand people showed up. They were somehow jammed into the bulging White House to ogle Julia and her court and a veritable roundup of other beauties she had corraled for the occasion. "We were as thick as sheep in a pen," Margaret Gardiner said. Julia, in a white satin dress embroidered with silver, covered by a matching cape looped with white roses, was at her zenith. The Marine Band in scarlet uniforms played polkas, waltzes, cotillions. Julia and Madame Bodisco, the Russian ambassador's equally beautiful wife, stopped the party when they joined in a cotillion with ambassadors from Austria, Russia, France, and Prussia. Eight dozen bottles of champagne were consumed, along with wine by the barrel. By the end of the evening, the huge chandeliers of the East Room had used up a thousand candles. Someone congratulated President Tyler on the sensational success of the affair. "Yes," he quipped. "Now they cannot say I am a President without a party."

Less than a month later, Congress passed the annexation bill, and Tyler handed Julia the pen with which he signed it as a testament of her role in the victory. She told her mother she would always wear "suspended from my neck the immortal gold pen with which the President signed my annexation bill." Note the personal pronoun. Julia had no doubts about who was responsible for this immense addition to the Union.

When my father carried Texas, a crucial state in his comeback victory in 1948, I like to think "Cousin" John Tyler and Julia were looking down, smiling. There is not much doubt that they were Democrats at heart, a fact that became dramatically evident in their post–White House years.

———

AT FIRST GLANCE, FRANCES FOLSOM CLEVELAND SEEMS TO HAVE been little more than a latter-day Julia Gardiner Tyler. In reality, there are so many differences between them, it would not be much of an exaggeration to say the only things these two women had in common were their youth and beauty. To begin with, their husbands were as different as two men can possibly be.

Geniality was the essence of John Tyler's southern style. Most of the time, Grover Cleveland was about as genial as a rudely awakened grizzly bear. His temperament seemed permanently chilled by the howling blizzards that frequently bury his native city of Buffalo, New York. A thick-necked, massive man who threatened the scales with his 250-pound bulk, he made his way in politics with blunt talk and unwavering, uncompromising honesty.

When he won the Democratic nomination for President in 1884, after a successful stint as New York's governor, his Republican opponents promptly nailed him with a smear that would have ruined almost any other politician. The would-be President had a ten-year-old illegitimate son. Republican flacks gleefully circulated a chant: *Ma, Ma, where's my Pa? Gone to the White House ha ha ha.*

Instead of issuing irate denials, Cleveland told his aghast supporters to admit everything. He had been involved with a New Jersey widow named Halpin, who apparently was also familiar with several of his married friends. When she gave birth, Cleveland, a bachelor, accepted responsibility to save his friends from embarrassment. He had supported the child and his mother with a monthly stipend ever since. The novelty of a politician so forthrightly telling the truth enchanted the American electorate. With the help of high unemployment and some blundering Republican remarks about Irish-Catholic Democrats, Cleveland won the election, entitling his gleeful supporters to throw the Republicans' campaign chant back in their dismayed faces.

During his first year in the White House, the bachelor President worked eighteen hours a day to prove to the American people that they had elected the right man. For formal state dinners and occasional lighter entertaining, he enlisted his unmarried sister, Rose, as his hostess. An intellectual who taught English literature and had written a book on the novelist George Eliot, Rose was an ardent feminist who was as blunt as her brother. Male guests left the White House reeling from lectures on the oppressed state of women. Aside from the opportunity to proselytize for her sex, Rose found the White House boring and spent her time on receiving lines conjugating Greek verbs in her busy brain.

Meanwhile, Cleveland was battling Congress over who was in charge of the country. Ever since the lawmakers almost impeached Lincoln's successor, Andrew Johnson, the legislative branch had assumed virtually total power in Washington. But behind and beyond the raging political warfare and the President's social isolation, romance was simmering. Again, the situation had all the ingredients of scandal. The young woman happened to be Grover Cleveland's ward.

Frances Folsom was the daughter of Oscar Folsom, Cleveland's Buffalo law partner. Cleveland was so close to the Folsoms, he had bought little Frances her first baby carriage. Oscar Folsom had been killed in an accident when Frances was twelve, and Cleveland had become the administrator of his estate. The welfare of Folsom's widow and daughter had been one of his major preoccupations ever since.

Only a few close friends and family members realized that the relationship between Frances and the forty-eight-year-old President had slowly shifted from the paternal to the passionate. Rose Cleveland later admitted she knew her brother's intentions even before he entered the White House. But Cleveland waited for Frances to graduate from Wells College in 1885 before formally asking her to marry him. His proposal was made by mail, but he later admitted that he had said some very romantic things to her in the East Room during a visit to the White House before he wrote the letter.

Frances said she would marry the President, but first she wanted to tour Europe. Cleveland acquiesced, though he grew a bit grumpy over her decision to spend nine months there. Such considerations were overshadowed by his desire to forestall ugly gossip and innuendo in the press by keeping their engagement a secret until the eve of the wedding. Cleveland was painfully aware that many people considered him a coarse, lumbering oaf, "a brute with women," as his predecessor Rutherford B. Hayes had indelicately put it during the campaign.

Secrecy almost unraveled when Cleveland sent Frances an affectionate bon voyage telegram and the Western Union operator slipped a copy to a reporter friend. But the reporter identified the object of Cleveland's affection as Frances's mother! With such rumors swirling, Frances herself was not exactly discreet. In England she wrote a friend, telling her she was engaged to the President; the friend opened the letter in a room full of people and became so excited she read it aloud.

Cleveland and his bride-to-be got a foretaste of things to come when Frances's ship reached New York on May 27, 1886. The President went up to greet her and incidentally review the city's Memorial Day parade. A small army of police was needed to hold back the crowds in front of Frances's hotel. The President himself was almost mobbed when he arrived to see her. But to Cleveland's immense relief, the popular mood was vibrant with approval. His tough stance as the people's spokesman versus a Congress dominated by special interests, his call for Congress to stop the exploitation of the working man by big business, had won him wide support and softened his rough image. The country was delighted that their forthright President had found a wife.

At the parade, the bands saluted Cleveland with specially selected tunes, such as "Come Where My Love Lies Dreaming." Toward the end of the march, one regiment's nervy musicmen swirled by the reviewing stand playing a song from Gilbert and Sullivan's new operetta, *The Mikado*, "He's Going to Marry Yum Yum."

The lucky few who attended the wedding got handwritten invitations from the President. Colonel William H. Crook, who had served as Lincoln's personal bodyguard, described Frances's arrival at the White House on the morning of June 2, 1886: "She tripped up the steps and swept through the great entrance like a radiant vision of young springtime... from that instant every man and woman [on the staff] was her devoted slave, and remained as such."

The White House was crammed with flowers from the conservatory—literally hundreds of potted plants on tables and mantels, plus ropes of fresh cut flowers draped along the moldings. At 6:30 P.M. the guests arrived, and at 7:00 every clock in the mansion began to chime, while across Washington church bells joined the chorus, and cannon in the Navy Yard roared a twenty-one-gun salute. The Marine Band, led by their eminent conductor, John Philip Sousa, struck up "The Wedding March," and the President and his bride descended the grand staircase.

Tall and full bosomed, Frances Folsom looked stunning in a dress of heavy corded satin, draped in almost transparent India silk, and fringed with orange blossoms. After a reception in the East Room and dinner in the State Dining Room, she and the President rode through cheering crowds to Union Station for a one-week honeymoon in Deer Park, in the mountains of western Maryland. There they soon discovered what would become the chief torment of their White House years—the prying eyes of the nation's reporters.

Cleveland already had a low opinion of the press. Early in his term, he had written to a magazine editor, declaring that in no other country in the world was "newspaper lying" so widespread. Now the reporters infuriated the President by camping around a perimeter of the honeymoon cottage and spying on the presidential couple with field glasses and telescopes. No detail was too small for their inquisitive eyes. They described every change of outfit by the First Lady and even checked out the grocery deliveries to give their readers imaginative descriptions of what the First Couple was having for dinner. The irate President raged that they were making American journalism "contemptible."

Returning to the White House to take up her official duties, the soon-to-be-twenty-two-year-old First Lady enchanted everyone. She never tired of standing in receiving lines and shaking hands with her guests. But she had to learn the hard way there was a limit to how much pressing the flesh could take. Massage and some tutoring in the art of the political handshake were necessary to keep her on the job. The stern, pugnacious Cleveland seemed to take on a softer aura in his wife's presence. He beamed as she melted roomfuls of visitors and told her mother in his gruff way that Frankie, as she was called, "would do."

Unlike the glamorous Julia Tyler, who adored playing queen in the White House and reveled in displays of presidential power, Frankie had no patrician pretensions. Instead of galas, she preferred simple receptions that were open to a broad spectrum of the public. One of her most popular innovations was Saturday afternoon receptions specifically for working women, who could not attend the weekday doings at the White House. Her popularity soared, and "Frankie Cleveland Clubs" sprouted in many urban Democratic wards. Soon her hair and dress styles were being imitated by women all over the country, and not a few manufacturers used her likeness in ads for their products.

Cleveland was inclined to denounce Frankie Clubs and, for that matter, every other kind of women's club; in his ultraconservative view, women should stay home and raise their children instead of running to meetings. But Frankie persuaded him to be more tolerant. Under her influence, his famous irascibility declined noticeably. She also coaxed him into shortening his eighteen-hour workdays and selecting more tasteful clothes.

The President remained at war with the press. Instead of staying in the White House, where privacy was practically impossible, he star-

tled everyone by buying a house on the Potomac, Red Top, where he and Frankie lived most of the time, commuting to the White House for public purposes only. (The area has since become one of the loveliest sections of Washington, Cleveland Park.) No one seemed to object to this idea, which strikes me as dreadful. The press, cut off from almost all access to the First Lady, had their revenge when Cleveland ran for reelection.

In the newspapers of this period, there was a notorious tolerance for "faking it," the term reporters used when they substituted fiction for fact. If the details were convincing, editors would run stories of heroic policemen subduing thugs, or firemen rescuing babies from burning buildings when nothing of the sort had happened. The reporters in the Republican-oriented newspapers began faking it about the Clevelands. Stories blossomed of a drunken President reeling around Red Top, clubbing the First Lady to the floor with a swing of his massive arm. According to another tale, Frances was supposedly thrown out of the White House in the middle of the night while her husband roared boozy insults at her. If any of this nonsense were true, I suppose Frances Cleveland would have been our only First Lady to qualify as an abused spouse.

The stories were too vivid to ignore. Frances finally wrote a letter to a woman in Massachusetts who had inquired if they were true. She said she hoped "the women of our Country" had husbands who were "as kind, attentive, considerate and affectionate as mine." The letter was given to the press and widely published in Democratic newspapers. But the smear campaign, which revived the image of the President as a brute, took its toll. Cleveland lost his 1888 bid for a second term to Benjamin Harrison, grandson of William Henry Harrison, the President whose death put John and Julia Tyler in the White House.

Other factors, such as Cleveland's refusal to play the patronage game with big-city Democratic machines, also played a part. But Frances Cleveland obviously felt she and her husband had been defeated by underhanded tactics, and she left the White House fighting mad. On inauguration day, as she went out the door, she told one of the staffers to take good care of the furniture and ornaments, because "I want to find everything just as it is now, when we come back again." The startled staffer asked when the Clevelands planned to return. "Just four years from today," Frances said.

That was exactly what they did, becoming the only President and First Lady to win a second term after a four-year hiatus. In American politics the feat is the equivalent of coming back from the dead. For this second White House tour, Frankie brought with them her first child, Ruth, who only escalated her mother's already tremendous appeal to the American people. During the 1892 presidential election, Frankie's picture appeared beside Cleveland's on many campaign posters. Although Cleveland still tried to discourage them, Frankie Cleveland Clubs multiplied across the land.

Yet Frances, for all her immense popularity, was totally nonpolitical. Cleveland was determined that she would never get "notions" like his aggressively feminist sister Rose—and she never did. She politely sidestepped the numerous causes she was asked to support and demonstrated, not for the first time, that personality is far more important than politics in determining a First Lady's popularity.

Little Ruth soon had a sister, Esther, the first President's child to be born in the White House. Like Jackie Kennedy in later decades, Frances vowed that the public would not have access to her children. She made this decision when she saw a horde of tourists snatch Ruth out of her nurse's arms on the White House lawn to get a better look at her. Esther's privacy was so severely guarded, the press were soon printing rumors that she was crippled or retarded. Frances ignored them.

The biggest test of Frances Cleveland's second term in the White House was the discovery that her husband was suffering from cancer of the mouth and only a major operation could save his life. Compounding the tension was the stark economic crisis that began with the crash of the stock market in June of 1893. With capital and labor almost at war, many members of the administration feared the country might collapse into anarchy if it were discovered that the President was mortally ill.

Working closely with Cleveland's aides, Frances went off to a summer vacation house on Cape Cod's Buzzards Bay. Meanwhile, Cleveland boarded the yacht of a millionaire friend in New York, ostensibly for a relaxing cruise before joining her on the Cape. The surgery was performed at sea. Almost half the president's jaw and much of his palate were removed. In two days he was strong enough to walk the deck, and he went ashore to join Frances at their vacation house without a word of the real story reaching the press. Can't you imagine how much the Clevelands enjoyed that? The operation remained a secret until 1917, when one of the surgeons told the story in the *Saturday Evening Post.*

For all her popularity, Frances could do little to help her husband cope with the public's disillusion with him when he proved unable to solve the nation's economic crisis. The Clevelands' last years in the White House were shadowed by political failure almost as stark as Herbert Hoover's. The Democratic Party deserted Cleveland virtually en masse. But Frankie's youth and gaiety remained an inexhaustible consolation for the often discouraged President. He left the White House a cheerful man.

If the glamour girls of the previous century have anything to teach us, it may be—a terrible thought for those Washingtonians who eat, drink, sleep, and breathe issues and crises—the ultimate unimportance of politics when issues and crises are competing with love in bloom.

Chapter 22

—

MATERNALLY
YOURS

THE LONGER I WORKED ON THIS BOOK, THE MORE CONVINCED I became that each First Lady should feel free to do what suits her. No matter what columnists, historians, and other assorted pundits say, there should never be a requirement that First Ladies fit into some sort of superachiever Wonder Woman mold. The ultimate proofs of this contention, in my not especially humble opinion, are two First Ladies who share a style that is the polar opposite of the political partner.

In 1901, when Theodore Roosevelt succeeded the assassinated William McKinley, Edith Carow Roosevelt came to the White House with the sort of catapulted feeling that wives of accidental Presidents know so well. She brought with her the largest family in White House history, six children, ranging from her obstreperous teenage stepdaughter, Alice, to her youngest son, Quentin, almost four. They in turn brought along a veritable menagerie, ranging from ponies to kangaroo rats. Whether she liked it or not, maternity was Edith's stock-in-trade. She not only liked it, she made it the symbol of the Roosevelt White House, with spectacularly popular results.

For Edith, maternity was closely allied with management, an absolute requisite in dealing with a family as rambunctious as her brood. She added to maternal management not a little ability at managing the White House—and her husband. An aristocrat who could trace her American lineage back to the great Puritan preacher Jonathan Edwards, Edith had an acquired ability to say and do the right thing in any and all situations. Frequently she exuded an almost preternatural calm, no matter how frenetic the atmosphere around her. Friends liked to say she had been "born mature."

Edith Carow's equanimity was an important factor in her marriage to Theodore Roosevelt. When Theodore went off to Harvard in 1876, he and Edith had an understanding that they would marry one day. They had grown up only a few doors from each other in New York City. But in Cambridge, Roosevelt met blond, beautiful Alice Lee and married her shortly after he graduated. Three years later she died of Bright's disease while giving birth to their daughter, Alice. After a period of mourning, Theodore proposed to Edith and she accepted him. Not many women could have coped so calmly and decisively with these unexpected turns of event.

Numerous surviving letters and reams of eyewitness testimony confirm that the marriage was remarkably happy. Edith gave Theodore the stability he badly needed; he had a tendency to ride off in all directions. He gave her the ebullience and excitement that prevented her imperturbability from lapsing into boredom.

Theodore Roosevelt had one advantage over previous accidental Presidents: he was already a national hero for his charge up San Juan Hill at the head of his Rough Riders during the Spanish-American War. Even without those still echoing shouts of popular acclaim, Edith and her husband both saw themselves as born leaders, ready and willing to run the country. While Theodore jousted with the encrusted conservatives in Congress, Edith reorganized the White House in a style that made her a truly pivotal First Lady.

Edith's two predecessors, Frances Cleveland and Ida McKinley, had both alienated the press, Frances by being virtually inaccessible, and poor, epileptic Ida by remaining virtually invisible. Instead of attempting to build a wall around herself and her brood, Edith decided to meet the reporters halfway—while insisting politely, firmly, that she would define "half." At regular intervals she released carefully posed photos of herself and the children. Edith's picture appeared on the cover of the *Ladies' Home Journal* and other magazines. But anyone who read the accompanying articles would have had to look long and hard to find any real information about her. Almost every word was about Theodore.

Edith also reorganized life in the White House in a way that left all future First Families in her debt. Until the Roosevelts arrived, the private quarters on the second floor existed in name only. The official or "state" rooms (used for entertaining) took up most of the mansion's first floor. The President conducted his business from an oval office on the second floor, with numerous other nearby rooms reserved for his ever-growing staff. This meant strangers were constantly invading the family quarters, making privacy impossible.

With six children and at least two maids living on the second floor, not to mention herself and her husband, Edith put herself vigorously on record in favor of an expanded White House. Fortunately, Congress and various architects and antiquarians had been debating this very question for several years. One group of experts recommended converting the entire house into executive offices and constructing a more private residence for the President and his family elsewhere. This was something the press-hating Clevelands would have warmly approved. But the Roosevelts, with their strong sense of history, firmly opposed the idea.

Edith, ever the manager, cut through the indecision by inviting the most famous architect of the day, Charles McKim, to come to the White House and tell her what could be done to make the place more habitable. The Clevelands and McKinleys had done little or nothing in the way of redecoration, and the old house was in another of its periodic phases of shabbiness—one senator called it "squalid." Aside from being unfit for family living, the cramped setup of the executive offices was out of step with the increased tempo of the modern presidency.

McKim recommended a bottom-to-top renovation, and with Edith's backing, Congress coughed up the money. The result was the most thorough overhaul the White House had received since the British burned it—and the creation of the Executive Office Wing, now called the West Wing—to provide working quarters for the President and his staff. The second floor thus became a private sanctuary for the First Family.

This was only the beginning of Edith's management. Her entertainments set a new standard for splendor and good taste. She achieved this with a minimum of fuss by hiring an outside caterer who handled all the formal banquets. To these Edith added a plethora of receptions crowded with artists and intellectuals. At one lunch in 1905, the guest list included Henry Adams, the country's greatest historian, Augustus Saint-Gaudens, its greatest sculptor, and Henry James, its greatest novelist. Even more popular were musicales, at which some of the world's best-known virtuosos performed. One happened to be a promising young Spanish cellist named Pablo Casals. Another, who won far bigger headlines, was the greatest pianist of the day, Ignace Jan Paderewski.

At all these events Edith presided with a charm that left everyone babbling superlatives. Not the least of her fans was her husband, who told one correspondent that she "combined...the power of being the best of wives and mothers, the wisest manager of the household and...the ideal great lady and mistress of the White House."

One of Edith's neatest gambits made me retrospectively envious— and I know my mother would have shared my sentiments. Instead of submitting to the perpetual hand mashing that other First Ladies have endured, Edith stood in receiving lines carrying a small bouquet— which of course relieved her of the necessity of shaking hands with anyone. She began this ingenious improvisation early in her White House career, and that was a good thing too. At their first New Year's Day reception, the Roosevelts greeted over eight thousand people.

Theodore (he hated to be called Teddy) was another large problem that Edith managed with a deft combination of bossiness, sarcasm, and

Here is Edith
Roosevelt early in her
White House career.
She all but exudes the
self-confidence that
made her one of our
most masterful
First Ladies.
(AP/Wide World Photos)

tenderness. When he worked past 10:30 in his upstairs study, Edith's foot would tap tap tap on her bedroom floor and staffers would hear her call: "Theodore!" He abandoned his desk instantly. At dinner parties, as Henry Adams loved to point out, Theodore had a tendency to dominate the conversation with torrential monologues. Edith stopped these, too, with a reproving glance—or a postprandial scolding. Politically, she was by no means out of touch. She read four or five newspapers a day and marked stories for the President's special attention.

Still another tactical triumph for this amazing First Lady was hiring the first White House social secretary, a shrewd Washingtonian named Belle Hagner, who dealt with the subtleties of guest lists and seating plans with an unerringly expert hand. Simultaneously, Edith took charge of yet another aspect of the social scene. Once a week, she met with the cabinet wives to coordinate their entertaining schedules. The goal was the avoidance of competition and/or duplication with White House events. It also was a discreet way of making sure the Roosevelts were at the center of the action all the time.

Unlike her successor, Helen Taft, who squirreled away a cool million and a half from her husband's salary, Edith and Theodore never stinted while they were in the White House. Compared with the Rockefellers and other megamillionaires, the Roosevelts were far from rich. In fact, Edith had worried about Theodore's plunge into politics because she feared they would go broke trying to keep up appearances for the benefit of the voters. But they both felt the President and his wife should put their best foot forward.

Ironically, the Roosevelts' superlative style eventually attracted critics. One newspaper attacked the White House "yachts," which now numbered three, the new presidential stables, which McKim had added to the grounds, and even the White House tennis court, which Edith had added to McKim's renovation to try to keep Theodore's weight down. Even harsher criticism was leveled at the lavish banquets. Edith toned things down a little while Theodore was running for election in his own right in 1904, and nothing came of the brouhaha. After they smashed the poor Democrats flat, Edith went right back to doing things as she pleased.

One of these things was the creation of a First Ladies' gallery in the corridor just beyond the South Entrance on the ground floor of the White House. Some people complained that the portraits should have been placed somewhere on the first floor (they are now in the East Wing lobby and are among the first things a tourist sees), but the wife of a Texas congressman congratulated Edith for rescuing "these admirable females from oblivion." I am happy to add my somewhat belated plaudits.

In her husband's second term, Edith Roosevelt's domestic management met a severe test. A crew of desperadoes took over the White House. They terrorized the staff, unnerved visitors, and even sabotaged the federal government. No one knew where they would strike next. The White House Gang, as they were called by insiders, were a rough bunch. They went by names like Slats and Sailor and Taffy. The leader was inclined to sign his name with a single, ominous letter: Q. He led them in swearing terrible oaths which always began: "By Buzzard!"

The leader, you may not be entirely surprised to learn, was Edith's youngest son, her "fine little bad boy," as she fondly called him— Quentin. He was, his father admitted, "a handful." He explored the White House with complete disregard for his own safety, crawling out on the roof and squeezing under the eaves in the attic, where he came face to face with several rats almost as big as he was. He also scaled the magnolia tree by his mother's window and wound streams of "official red tape" in and out among its boughs. He was equally unintimidated by reporters. One asked him for some details of how the President relaxed. "I see him sometimes," Quentin replied. "But I know nothing of his family life."

With Q in command, and Taffy (Charles Taft, son of William Howard Taft) as his right-hand man, nothing in the White House was safe. One of the gang's early triumphs was a shower of spitballs on Andrew Jackson's portrait, including a beautiful "gob" on the end of his nose. Another time, they used hand mirrors to flash sunlight into the windows of the State War Navy Building, completely disrupting two-thirds of the federal government until a sailor appeared on the roof and semaphored them to report to the President's office without delay for "Y-O-U K-N-O-W W-H-A-T."

Edith encountered the gang when she entertained an Italian diplomat, complete with a monocle, in a second-floor sitting room. The junior fiends climbed onto a skylight to examine their quarry, and Quentin began speaking in what he thought was Italian. "Quentin!" Edith called, glaring up at the skylight. The diplomat followed her gaze and saw six small boys, each with a monocle (improvised from watch crystals) in his eye, staring down at him. The astonished envoy's monocle popped out of his eye into his teacup.

Quentin collaborated with his older brother Archie for another coup against White House conformity. Eleven-year-old Archie was flat on his back, simultaneously stricken by measles and whooping cough, and mourning the death of his favorite animal, Jack Dog, a black and tan fox terrier. Quentin decided nothing would speed Archie's recovery faster than the sight of his calico pony, Algonquin. With the cooperation of a White House footman, he coaxed the 350-

pound creature into the elevator and down the second-floor corridor to Archie's bedroom. The invalid, it is claimed, made a miraculous recovery and was soon galloping around the grounds on Algonquin's back.

Other resident pets made the Roosevelt White House an unnerving place to work or visit. The Speaker of the House, an imperious Illinoisan named "Uncle Joe" Cannon, had his ankle clawed by Tom Quartz, the family kitten, as he descended the grand staircase. Kermit's kangaroo rat regularly came to the breakfast table and demanded lumps of sugar. Quentin wandered around with Emily Spinach, an emerald green snake, under his coat.

Edith's toleration of these antics is the best possible proof that her management of 1600 Pennsylvania Avenue was infused with genuine maternity. Earle Looker, who later became the chronicler of the White House Gang's exploits, opined she probably knew what they were up to almost every minute but let them get away with most of their dark deeds because she secretly enjoyed them. As the mother of four boys, I know exactly what Looker meant.

The offspring who put Edith's management skills to their ultimate test was not the White House Gang but her stepdaughter, Alice. An unabashed rebel, Alice made a specialty of doing what she hoped would upset her father. She spent most of her time with the 1905 equivalent of the jet set—the sons and daughters of the ultraconservative multimillionaires whom TR denounced as "malefactors of great wealth." With their encouragement, Alice smoked in public, bet on the horses, played poker, danced until dawn and slept until noon, and once raced an automobile from Newport to Boston unchaperoned. One member of her late mother's family characterized her as "a young wild animal that has been put into good clothes."

When someone complained to the President about his older daughter's behavior, TR exploded. "I can run the country or control Alice," he said. "I can't do both." Edith, keenly aware that she was only a stepmother, and that Alice was convinced her father did not care for her "one eighth as much as the other children," made no attempt to play the disciplinarian. She let Theodore handle that role—which he occasionally did in halfhearted fashion—while Edith persisted, in spite of frequent rebuffs, in being Alice's friend.

Proof of her success is a touching scene that I could never have envisioned for Alice Roosevelt. When I knew her in the late 1940s, she was all acid wit and sarcasm, an utterly delightful grande dame. It is hard, even now, for me to realize she was once as young as I was in my White House years. One evening in the fall of 1905, Alice followed Edith into the bathroom, waited until the First Lady was brushing her teeth (so she would have a moment to think before saying anything), and told her she had become engaged to Nicholas Longworth, the Republican congressman from Ohio.

Fifteen years older than Alice and already a bit bald, Nick Longworth had a reputation as a womanizer. Alice had spent four weeks getting up the nerve to tell her parents. It is not insignificant that she told Edith first. To her immense relief, Edith warmly approved the match. She knew Alice would never be happy married to some businessman. Politics was in her blood, and Longworth was considered presidential timber. Edith confided her doubts to a discreet relative. Love, she said, had "softened" Alice wonderfully, but "I still tremble when I think of her face to face with the practical details of life."

Alice's White House wedding became another of Edith's triumphs. Everyone who mattered sent presents and hoped for an invitation, but Edith limited the guest list to one thousand—coolly excluding some people who had hoped to buy their way into the ceremony with expensive gifts. One well-chosen guest was Nellie Grant Sartoris, who had been a White House bride herself thirty-two years earlier. Alice, resplendent in a princess-style gown, testified to her bond with Edith at the end of the ceremony. She walked over to her, arms outstretched, and kissed her twice.

—

EDITH ROOSEVELT LEFT THE WHITE HOUSE IN 1909 ARGUABLY THE most esteemed, beloved First Lady since Martha Washington. Eighty years later another First Lady, far more familiar to modern readers, duplicated many of her maternal triumphs, with a lot more irreverence and fun. In some ways, Barbara Bush faced a far tougher challenge. She succeeded a bone-thin First Lady who had been the essence of chic—and a favorite press target—Nancy Reagan. Before her had come Rosalynn Carter, the public partner who had her own problems with the First Lady watchers. Would the scribes do a similar number on Mrs. Bush?

Not to worry. Like Edith Roosevelt before her, Barbara Bush had thought out the role of First Lady from studying her predecessors' mistakes. No one would catch her playing uncrowned queen in the White House. Nor would she so much as hint at pretensions to being a coequal President. No, Barbara Bush decided she would just be herself, and that self flowed not only from her unique personality but from her age, her gray hair, her wrinkles, and her size 14 figure.

If Edith Roosevelt conquered the White House as everybody's mother, Barbara Bush, with five children in their thirties and forties and twice that many grandchildren, became everybody's grandmother. The role not only came naturally, it was shrewd, it was apt, it demonstrated once more the amazing range of choices available to First Ladies if they have the courage of their convictions—or, better, their predilections.

These days grandmother has more appeal than mother; grandmothers are those wonderful people who baby-sit for harried mothers and let the kids get away with murder. They are more lovable than mothers, who in my family at least are often regarded as the equivalent of Parris Island drill sergeants. Barbara Bush boldly made a virtue of her grandmotherly image. She not only declined to apologize for her gray hair and ample figure, she joked about these somewhat dubious assets.

The new First Lady said her mother told her she weighed a hundred pounds at birth. She grew up hearing her mother tell her sister Martha to eat up and then add "But not you, Barbara." She dyed her prematurely gray hair until she decided the hell with it in 1970—and "George never noticed it," she added acerbically, reporting on a phenomenon that sounded familiar to any number of wives.

Only in little flashes like these has the public gotten glimpses of Barbara Bush's truly wicked wit. One friend tells of sitting next to her at a rally in New Hampshire during the 1988 primary campaign while George Bush was on the podium taking questions. A woman asked him to explain his stand on abortion and added a virtual oration on her opinion of this thorny issue. Mrs. Bush leaned over to the friend and whispered in his ear: "Now there's a b.s. question."

Up on the podium, George Bush labored mightily to get on both sides of the dilemma with a series of convoluted on-the-one-hand and on-the-other-hand sentences. Mrs. Bush leaned over to the friend again and whispered: "And there's a b.s. answer."

When they were younger, Barbara Bush sometimes made her husband a target of her ego-deflating tongue—until one day he asked her in his offhand way to quit ridiculing him in public. She stopped, instantly and forever. She also did penance for another slip of her forked tongue in the 1984 campaign, when she remarked during the flap over Geraldine Ferraro's tax returns that the Democratic vice presidential candidate not only was rich but could also be described by another word that rhymes with *rich*. That crack got into print, and Mrs. Bush admitted to a relative that she cried for twenty-four hours and called Ms. Ferraro to apologize.

Both stories make it clear that Barbara Bush is a sensitive, deeply caring woman. As First Lady, she was also a political partner in ways that Edith Roosevelt never tried to be. When George Bush considered running for President in 1980, his wife sat in on the briefing sessions and shared the final decision with him. Together, she and her husband became one of the smoothest functioning teams in the history of the White House.

This is not entirely surprising, if we pause for a backward look. Barbara Bush has been at George Bush's side throughout his amazing Cook's tour of the American government, which took him from congressman to U.N. ambassador to CIA director to ambassador to China to vice president to president. If we combine these travels with his business career, which took him from the security of his upper-class Greenwich, Connecticut, world (and his bride from the nearby comfortable New York suburb of Rye) to the wilds of West Texas to learn the oil business, you get a woman who moved twenty-nine times in her forty-four years of marriage—and coped all the way.

Like Edith Roosevelt, Mrs. Bush has always been an impeccable hostess, who enjoys meeting new people and is unfazed by cultural and generational gaps. She especially liked George's tour as U.N. ambassador in New York City, where entertaining and diplomacy were closely intertwined. "I'd pay to have this job," she told one reporter. In Beijing during George's ambassadorship, she made a mighty effort to learn Chinese at the age of fifty so she could communicate with her hosts.

Pertinent as all this diplomacy undoubtedly was as a warm-up for the White House, it pales beside Mrs. Bush's toils during her eight years as the vice president's wife. She hosted a staggering 1,192 events at the handsome vice president's residence on Massachusetts Avenue and attended another 1,132 as a guest, frequently the guest of honor. She and George traveled to sixty-eight countries and four territories,

Barbara Bush proves she is a First Lady for all seasons, tossing out the first ball for the Texas Rangers.
(AP/Wide World Photos)

racking up 1,330,000 miles on Air Force Two—the equivalent of fifty-four times around the world. By the time the Bushes reached the White House in 1989, they had met almost every political leader on the globe.

This virtual on-the-job training may explain why Barbara Bush was probably our most unflappable First Lady. When reporters spotted her in slippers and bathrobe walking her dog, Millie, outside the family's Kennebunkport, Maine, compound, she struck them dumb with a terse "Haven't you ever seen an old lady walk a dog before?" Once Millie ran into the vice presidential residence with a saliva-drenched tennis ball in her mouth and tried to present it to Australian Prime Minister Robert Hawke. Mrs. Bush "gave her a clean one in honor of the PM," and the meeting continued as if nothing had happened. During her first months in the White House, she coped without blanching when her supersociable husband invited twenty people for dinner on two hours' notice and upped the count to forty the following night with the same amount of warning.

Some people have dismissed Barbara Bush's smiling serenity as a dividend of a privileged, affluent life. They could not be more wrong. She has come through one of the most awful ordeals a mother can face in this world—the loss of a child. Her first daughter, Robin, died of leukemia in 1953 at the age of four. That was when Barbara's hair turned prematurely gray. She sank into a depression in which, she "felt as if I could cry forever." She credits George Bush's optimism and energy and love for pulling her out of it.

Well before she got to the White House, Barbara Bush had decided to make children the focus of any cause she would adopt as First Lady. She soon refined this decision to focus on literacy and reading, partly because one of her sons had been dyslexic and she had seen firsthand the problems that a reading difficulty can cause. As the vice president's wife, she attended or hosted 538 events related to literacy. As First Lady, with money from her bestselling book about (or, as it said on the cover, "by") Millie, she created the Barbara Bush Foundation for Family Literacy, which disbursed her royalties to institutions and experts involved in the fight to improve America's reading skills.

Beyond literacy, Barbara Bush found time as First Lady to promote volunteerism in general. In Robin's memory she had long made a point of visiting hospitals to bring chronically ill children gifts and hugs at Christmastime. As First Lady she put on an apron in a mobile soup kitchen and took valentines to patients at a Washington old-age home. At an assembly in a de facto segregated Washington, D.C., school during Black History Month, she delighted the students by singing from memory all eight verses of "We Shall Overcome."

The Bushes liked living in the White House, in part for the historical setting. Mrs. Bush told me she particularly loved dining off the forty varieties of china now in the mansion's collection. She and George would kid about eating off Grover Cleveland for lunch and Abe Lincoln for dinner. She found she could wave to George in his Oval Office from her own office in the southwest corner of the East Wing—and she made sure he glanced up from his desk now and then to respond to her high sign.

Another reason why they enjoyed the old place was the First Lady's no-nonsense management style. When Nancy Reagan advised her not to let her children live in the White House, Barbara Bush crisply replied: "Don't worry. I haven't invited them." When grandchildren came to visit, there were no Amy Carter–like appearances at state dinners. The kids dined separately and undoubtedly had a much better time. They saw enough of the White House to say "I was there," but they never upstaged the adults. I am heartily in favor of this style of grandparenting.

On Mrs. Bush's side of the White House, things went so smoothly, it is hard to find anything that can be called a crisis. Perhaps the closest to one was the Wellesley flap, when a cadre of students at that eminent college protested the First Lady as their commencement speaker, because she had supposedly never accomplished anything as an independent woman. At the commencement, Barbara Bush replied for the millions of American women who have devoted their lives to husbands and children and volunteer work. She praised careers for women but ably defended those who chose to stay home and raise their children. It was, as one reporter said, "a job Wellesley done."

Most of the time, Mrs. Bush's profile as a political partner remained so low, it was practically invisible. But many people gave her credit for nudging George Bush's agenda toward a more caring administration. As someone else put it, she carried "the banner of compassion" in a presidency that was largely preoccupied with foreign affairs, from the invasion of Panama to the collapse of the Soviet Union to the Gulf War. In fact, it is no exaggeration to say that Barbara Bush was sending the public the signals they wanted to hear from George. Honesty compels me to add that when I interviewed Mrs. Bush for this book, she vehemently rejected this description of her role, saying George Bush did not need anyone, including his spouse, to make him more compassionate.

Nevertheless, the presidential election of 1992 was fought almost entirely on domestic issues. It was a tribute to—but also a liability of—Barbara Bush's determinedly nonpolitical style that in the final year of her husband's presidency, when his poll numbers began to sink, she remained at a stratospheric eighty percent approval rating with the American public. Another poll found her to be the world's most admired woman. But she was unable to transfer an iota of her amazing popularity to her husband.

Maybe that is a tribute to the good sense of the American people. For all the power and importance of First Ladies, nowhere in this book will you find me suggesting they should be on the ballot. The President is the man who is elected to the world's greatest political office. The buck will always stop in the West Wing of the White House, not in the East Wing.

Barbara Bush's White House success, like Edith Roosevelt's, suggests the American people are a lot more liberal about their First Ladies than many of the commentators on the subject. They have no strong preconceptions about how a First Lady should look or act. She is free to sell herself to them on the open market, using her glamour, her brainpower, her passion for politics, her love of beauty—or her maternal self. That too is the way it should be.

Chapter 23

—

NOW PLAYING: HILLARY AND BILL

WHEN I TOLD MY HUSBAND, CLIFTON DANIEL, I WAS ABOUT TO WRITE this chapter, he smiled somewhat sardonically, as befits an all-wise former managing editor of *The New York Times*, and asked: "Which Hillary Rodham Clinton are you going to write about?"

"The one we met—and liked," I replied.

Clifton's question has more than a little point, however. By this time a lot of Americans are undoubtedly a bit bewildered by the incredible outpouring of print and photographs and TV coverage of the current First Lady. There have been articles depicting her as a religious mystic, Saint Hillary in pursuit of the "politics of meaning"; as a cool, calculating lawyer with a hidden political agenda; as a crude opportunist with shallow ethics when it comes to making money; as a bossy, lamp-throwing termagant who really runs the White House; and as a clotheshorse who has fallen in love with high style.

I cannot recognize the Hillary Clinton I met in any of these capsule descriptions. In the hours I spent with her shortly after she and Bill moved into the White House, she was a warm, humorous, intelligent woman, completely at ease with her husband, keenly aware of her daughter's needs, and obviously enjoying life at 1600 Pennsylvania Avenue. But I would be less than honest if I did not note that Mrs. Clinton's first two years as First Lady have been fraught with controversy. When you view the verbiage from a historical perspective, however, a lot of it ranges from the same old stuff to downright silly.

Hillary is the real boss of the White House? People said the same thing about Abigail Adams, Sarah Polk, Helen Taft, Edith Wilson, and Nancy Reagan. The politics of meaning? Eleanor Roosevelt was repeatedly attacked for her crusades for social justice. A hidden political agenda? Rather like Rosalynn Carter, Hillary Clinton has been forced to deny she has a major role in shaping White House policy, beyond the one large task the President assigned her—the preparation of a universal health-care bill.

I decided to cut through the nonsense and asked Hillary Rodham Clinton face to face how she saw herself as First Lady after twenty months in the White House. Her answer revealed a calm awareness of the complexity of her job. She said she was doing her best "to fulfill the many different parts of the role" of First Lady. She was occasionally troubled by the way the press tended to see conflicts between the several sides of the job, announcing when she turned her attention to entertaining or redecorating that she was abandoning politics. "I've enjoyed the entertaining and the chance to contribute something to the White House," she said. "I've also enjoyed the chance I've been given to work with my husband on health care and other issues of interest to me."

In short, Mrs. Clinton sees herself as both a political partner and a traditional First Lady. She says she has read everything she could find about First Ladies and has concluded that almost all of them played some sort of political role in their husbands' presidencies. There is undoubtedly some truth to that observation. But emphasis is more important than mere numbers. A public political partnership is unquestionably the leading edge of the Clintons' White House image. This widespread impression is not entirely accidental. When I asked

Mrs. Clinton to name her most pleasurable moments as First Lady so far, she replied: "The passage of the Brady Bill. And the ban on assault weapons."

The Clintons were political partners long before they got to the White House. "My husband and I have always been each other's sounding boards," Hillary told me. "Even before our marriage, when we were students at Yale." In their years after Yale, Hillary became a lot more than a sounding board. According to many sources, she rescued Bill Clinton's career from collapse when he was defeated for reelection at the end of his first term as governor of Arkansas. She overhauled his entire political operation, got rid of do-nothing cronies, and put together the team that restored him to the statehouse and maintained the momentum that carried him to the presidency.

That is only the first of several large debts Bill Clinton owes his wife. During the 1992 primary campaign, a woman named Gennifer Flowers revealed that she and Bill had enjoyed a long-running affair. She had tapes of phone conversations in which Governor Clinton made some very compromising remarks. He was not the first presidential candidate to be embarrassed by such a story—Grover Cleveland, Woodrow Wilson, and Franklin Roosevelt come readily to mind. But in the aftermath of the way a similar story had destroyed presidential hopeful Gary Hart in 1988, the prospects for Bill Clinton were not promising. Until he and Hillary went on the TV show *60 Minutes* and she defused the ticking bomb by admitting that the Clintons may have had problems in their marriage in the past but they had worked them out.

No other First Lady except Rosalynn Carter has come to the White House with the ability to remind her husband that without her he would not be sitting in the Oval Office. I do not think Hillary has to remind Bill Clinton of this fact. On the contrary, it is part of the warp and woof of their remarkable political partnership. Does this give Hillary behind-the-scenes influence? Of course it does. But it is not, as far as I can see, the kind of influence that trivializes that word, or her role as First Lady. On the contrary, it enhances it, because few First Ladies have been more qualified than this Wellesley and Yale Law School graduate to play a public partnership role.

How successful has Hillary Clinton been as a public partner? Here the story becomes inextricably entangled with the question of how successful Bill Clinton has been as President. It seems to be the fate of public partners to rise or fall together—one of the risks of the high-profile game they choose to play.

Unquestionably, Hillary Clinton can look back on some successful moments as First Lady. She awed Congress with her command of the complexities of the health-care industry when she testified before them on the Clinton bill mandating universal care. A *New York Times* reporter cited her visit to Capitol Hill as "the official end of an era when Presidential wives pretended to know less than they did and to be advising less than they were."

Mrs. Clinton has been well received when she travels the country to speak on behalf of the administration—and she deftly handled several explosive questions about the Clintons' finances in a nationally televised press conference. But another *New York Times* reporter summed

Tape recorders whirring, I interviewed Hillary Rodham Clinton in the White House. Don't we look like we're taking this book seriously? *(White House photograph)*

up Hillary's dilemma in a comment on her campaign to rally support for health care. Both she and the issue were "linked to a President who is less popular—in some ways, much less—than either of them."

A few weeks later, a Times Mirror poll underscored this bitter point. The poll asked voters: "Of all the U.S. Presidents who have been elected since you started following politics, which has done the best job?" Bill Clinton finished seventh, behind George Bush. Ronald Reagan finished first.

Here is a painful example of what can go wrong with the public partnership approach to the role of First Lady. By identifying herself so resolutely—yes, courageously—with her husband's presidency, a public partner subjects herself to all the hostility a Chief Executive often arouses while struggling to fashion new domestic and foreign policies. She also exposes herself to the fallout from personal weaknesses which the merciless glare of constant press scrutiny may reveal in her spouse.

I have already expressed my respect for First Ladies who choose to be public partners. The women who espouse this rocky road deserve understanding and sympathy. In Hillary Clinton's case, some extra sympathy is definitely in order. Between my early White House visit with her and our interview for this book, first her father, then her mother-in-law died, and one of the Clintons' closest friends, White House aide Vincent Foster, committed suicide. Next, two other close friends of the First Lady, White House counsel Bernard Nussbaum and Deputy Attorney General Webster Hubbell, were forced to resign under less than auspicious circumstances.

Simultaneously, Mrs. Clinton herself became the target of some brutal personal attacks and prying questions from reporters that exceeded anything ever encountered by any other First Lady, including Eleanor Roosevelt. Along with the scandal of the failed real estate development, Whitewater, which she shared with the President, the First Lady has had the dubious distinction of having her own financial scandal to refute—the hundred thousand dollars she made from a one-thousand-dollar speculation in cattle futures early in Bill Clinton's political career in Arkansas.

After we finished working, the President popped in, cheered us up with some good jokes, and insisted we pose with him. *(White House photograph)*

I wish I could say Mrs. Clinton dealt with this matter effectively. Alas, instead of making all the relevant documents available immediately, and issuing a comprehensive statement on the whole affair, she or her press office mishandled it badly. They repeatedly changed—"clarified"—previous statements and dribbled out documents in a way that gave the impression they were being released under duress. As a result, the First Lady's adversaries felt free to sneer about the way the politics of meaning apparently did not interfere with making a quick buck.

The cattle futures inquiry paled beside the questions that Mrs. Clinton had to face about the suicide of her former Arkansas law partner and friend Vincent Foster. In the spring of 1994, in an interview for *Vanity Fair*, journalist Leslie Bennetts achieved a somewhat unenviable first when she asked the First Lady, with maximum bluntness, if she had had an affair with Mr. Foster. Hillary, according to Ms. Bennetts, almost wept, expressed a virtually inarticulate protest at the question, and finally said the rumor was "a lie." The First Lady then attempted to put the whole subject off the record, but Ms. Bennetts refused to do so.

Mrs. Clinton has admitted these experiences have made her first years in the White House somewhat less than wonderful for her. "It's broken my heart, in some ways," she told one journalist.

In my talk with her, she returned to this theme. "I have no quarrel with anyone who wants to criticize the President or me," she said. "I know it comes with the territory. I often think of what your father went through. But it's [been] very difficult."

I fear the White House has been almost as great a culture shock for Hillary Rodham Clinton as it was for Herbert Hoover. Mrs. Clinton has been used to success for a long time. Almost everywhere she has been a star. At Wellesley she was chosen to give the 1969 graduation address. She rebuked the guest speaker, Senator Edward Brooke of Massachusetts, for lacking confidence in her generation. *Life* magazine printed her picture and relevant paragraphs of her address. At Yale Law School she was an exceptional student, and she went on to a distinguished career as a lawyer, first in Washington and then in Little Rock. It has been upsetting for her to learn that braininess and hard work do not always solve problems in Washington, D.C.

The shock of being in the public eye has also caught Mrs. Clinton somewhat unprepared for a more traditional First Lady role, as a setter of styles. In the beginning, she seemed to personify the feminist claim that how a woman looks is unimportant. She readily admits that when she was young, she disdained makeup. "It wasn't just that I didn't wear it, it was a statement," she has said. As she grew older, she wore uninspired clothes from a dress shop in Little Rock, and in her first year as First Lady displayed little interest in fashion.

In 1994 she became a First Lady who suddenly put major stress on her appearance. She changed her hairstyle so often, it created bewilderment not only in the fashion world but among average Americans. She appeared in *Vogue* in a Donna Karan cutout evening dress, striking a pose sultry enough to win her a screen test. When she went to Europe with the President to celebrate the fiftieth anniversary of D-day, the First Lady's staff issued flowery press releases on her outfits. One gushed over the "lovely U-shape opening at the neck" of a "two piece fuchsia Noviello Bloom suit of linen blend."

Such a description of a Nancy Reagan outfit would have drawn no comment—and probably made it onto the style pages of many newspapers. But to hard-nosed reporters, this fervent prose seemed inappropriate to a publicly political First Lady. A few less-friendly types gleefully informed their readers that European fashion commentators had turned thumbs down on most of Hillary's clothes. "You're no Jackie Kennedy: Europeans Give Hill a Real Bronx Cheer" was the headline for one story in the New York *Daily News.*

Hillary is inclined to make light of the whole style flap. "Anyone who's looked at pictures of me, going back to when I was in high school," she told one reporter, "knows I change my hair all the time. I did that long before I was in the public eye. I try different types of clothes. I don't take it seriously.... I think it's fun."

Unfortunately, that statement does not jibe with her staff's intense effort to turn the First Lady into a clotheshorse and fashion exemplar. The stream of hyperbolic press releases did not strike reporters as "fun." Their reaction was, I fear, not fun for Mrs. Clinton either. Here, I think, was a case of a First Lady with no deep fashion instincts allowing her staff to push her in the wrong direction.

The fashion cross fire was intensified by the somewhat ambiguous position fate has assigned to Hillary Rodham Clinton since Betty Friedan launched the latest phase of the women's movement three decades ago. As the first First Lady to combine marriage and motherhood with a career before she reached the White House, she has had to pick her way through an emotional minefield. During the campaign in 1992, she stirred a storm with an offhand remark that she was not the sort of woman who stayed home and baked cookies. The uproar revealed the submerged hostility of many working wives and stay-at-home mothers toward higher-paid professional women who can afford domestic assistants and do not have to stretch themselves to hold down a job and simultaneously raise a family.

On the other side of the divide are feminists who rushed to Mrs. Clinton's defense when Michael Deaver, the veteran Reagan public relations adviser, offered his unsolicited opinion that Hillary's venture into *Vogue* was "kind of odd." Deaver wondered why, after Hillary had proven herself a tough, savvy political operator, she wanted to go back "to an image based on femininity." Supporters of the First Lady fired back, claiming she personified a new wave in feminism, a "spontaneous uprising" among women who are determined to define their sexuality without any interest in male ideas. "Female sexuality should no longer be perceived as undermining female authority, but as complementing it," declared author Naomi Wolf. She saw the many faces and hairstyles of Hillary Clinton as "a liberating affirmation of how multifaceted the female consciousness is."

With defenders like Ms. Wolf putting out stuff like that to boggle the voters, Hillary Clinton does not need enemies. There has been a tendency among some of her supporters to get carried away. One journalist called her "the icon of American womanhood...the medium through which the remaining anxieties about feminism are being played out.... Like Ginger Rogers, she will do everything her partner does, only backward and in high heels." Another reporter said she was "replacing Madonna as our cult figure." This is not intelligent thinking—or writing—about this embattled First Lady.

Hillary's stance as a publicly equal partner has unquestionably expanded the role of First Lady. As one astute Washington journalist has pointed out, she not only combined the independent spirit of Betty Ford, the shrewd femininity of Lady Bird Johnson, and the determination of Rosalynn Carter, she was *empowered* by the President to take charge of health care, the most important piece of legislation his administration undertook in his first two years in the White House. This empowerment was confirmed by a federal court, which described the First Lady as "a virtual extension of her husband" and "the functional equivalent of an assistant to the president."

This empowerment soon acquired a symbolic momentum, giving Hillary Clinton's political comments a weight and authority unmatched by those of any previous First Lady. When she said "we" would accept certain suggestions or alterations in the health plan, there was little doubt that she was speaking not only for her commission but for the President. Not a few people in Washington were upset about dealing with a First Lady with this kind of political leverage. They felt it was, if not illegal, at least unfair. Beyond Washington, it made people ask: who did we elect as President?

When Mrs. Clinton testified before Congress, the lawmakers, obviously flustered and awed, barely asked her a single serious question. A few days later, when Donna Shalala, the secretary of health and human services, testified on the administration's plan, she met a withering cross fire of hostile questions that more than made up for the solons' truckling before Mrs. Clinton. There were apparently many flaws in the health plan concocted by Hillary and her commission. But I wonder if subterranean resentment at her empowerment also played a part in the way Congress unceremoniously discarded it.

Empowering Mrs. Clinton has also aroused the ire of conservatives in the hinterlands. The right-wing think tank, the American Policy Center, has assailed the reign of "Empress Hillary," and the American Conservative Union announced the start of something called "Hillary Alert," a newsletter that will supposedly keep the nation up to date about the latest usurpations in the White House. Needless to say, these diatribes invariably end with a plea for donations to rescue the country from this horrendous threat.

The fusillades about the First Lady as a political partner have tended to obscure Hillary's role as President Clinton's wife. In December 1993, the nation got a stark reminder of this reality, when Mrs. Clinton demonstrated anew her readiness to defend the President's conduct and affirm her devotion to him. In a unique Christmas season press conference, Hillary denounced charges by Arkansas state troopers that they had regularly procured women for Bill Clinton while he was governor. Intermingled with her anger was an almost plaintive plea for the press to drop this unpleasant subject once and for all. "It hurts," she said. "Even though you're a public figure, which means apparently in America anybody can say anything about you. Even public figures have feelings and families and reputations."

One of the best comments on the First Lady's request for a moratorium on the President's sex life came from a Washington, D.C., psychologist. In biting terms, he noted that adultery occurs in at least fifty percent of American marriages, according to recent studies. The Clintons have been struggling to present themselves to the American people as a couple who have survived an adulterous episode in their marriage. But the press and public refuse to let them testify to this achievement because it upsets the primitive, idealized ideas that people have about First Families. Sadly, the adversaries who promote these sexual smears profit from this widespread mind-set—forcing both Clintons to fall back to defensive, angry denials.

Here, and elsewhere, I do not think this First Lady has received adequate credit for the way she has worked at traditional White House roles. At considerable cost in emotional stress, she was trying to protect her husband and her family from gutter tactics in the same way that Frances Cleveland responded to the fake journalism of her day. She was acting out of her deepest instincts as a woman, exactly as Edith Wilson did when she told Woodrow Wilson she would stand by him, not for duty, not for honor, but for love.

I saw further evidence of a traditional First Lady when I asked Hillary how their daughter, Chelsea, was coping with the White House. Her face came aglow, the bitterness that tinged many of her comments about her political struggles vanished. "She's a happy teenager, I think," she said, playfully rapping the table, as any wise mother of a teenager would do after making such a claim. "She comes and goes pretty much as she pleases, she has wonderful friends. We've kept the press out of her life."

With just a touch of ruefulness, the First Lady added: "That may be our only achievement so far."

Mrs. Clinton has also struggled to take charge of the White House and put her personal stamp on it. Here, too, she talked of difficulties, but they were less harrowing than her political travails. "Just finding your way around this house and knowing what is done, what's always been done, takes months," she said. "It was July of the first year when someone told me: 'You have to pick out a Christmas card by next week or we won't get it out.' I wish I'd known a little more about how things worked. We could have gotten up to speed a lot faster."

One sign of getting up to speed was a decision many other First Ladies might have hesitated to make—Mrs. Clinton fired the White House chef. She replaced the French-born incumbent, Pierre Chambertin, with a modernist American, Walter Scheib III, who specializes in "light" cuisine—a minimum of butter and rich sauces. When asked about the change, the President said he knew nothing about it. "I read it in the paper," he said, suggesting that, in some matters, the Clintons have an Eisenhower-like division of responsibility. Some people have speculated that getting rid of Chambertin and his rich sauces was a stealth attack on Bill's waistline. But I think it was largely an attempt to bring the White House in line with the ideas of Mrs. Clinton and her generation about healthy eating.

Chef Scheib and the First Lady teamed up for a resoundingly successful first state dinner for the Emperor and Empress of Japan in June 1994. Hillary decided to have it on the White House lawn, partly because the Emperor's father, Hirohito, had been entertained there in 1976. It was a brilliant idea, though a risky one—Washington can be very hot in June. But the First Lady equipped the huge white tent with air conditioners and hoped for the best. By 9:00 P.M., when the guests sat down to dine, there was a cool breeze and not a drop of perspiration in sight.

Since that big show, Mrs. Clinton has given state dinners for Russia's Boris Yeltsin and South Africa's Nelson Mandela. "I like working on these dinners," Hillary told me. "I worry about the flowers, the menus, about everything you have to do to make them beautiful."

Hillary has also played the role of presidential protector in the style of previous First Ladies such as Lady Bird Johnson and Bess Truman. Bill Clinton has a tendency to work into the dawn. Hillary frequently urges her President to take time off to golf. Also, "Every so often, we put a moratorium on [political] talk," she told me. "We say: no more. Let's play cards, go for a walk, go bowling—do something different."

Mrs. Clinton says she and Bill try to go out one night a weekend with friends, or invite friends to the White House to watch a movie in the mansion's theater. Bill has undertaken to teach Hillary how to bowl on the White House alley. She has an atrocious hook he is trying to correct.

Mrs. Clinton told me the White House experience has been "pretty positive" for the Clinton marriage. "As one of my friends says, it's like living over the store," she said. "We see each other during the day—and we have dinner nearly every night with Chelsea."

She paused for a moment and said one of the most profound—and touching—things I have heard from any First Lady: "It's more than being a political partner. I don't think there's any job like it in the world. You have to be a partner in the fullest sense of the word—someone who's trying to support the President in a personal way that's not available to him elsewhere."

On another traditional track, the First Lady has won high marks for her redecoration of the White House's private quarters. Typically, Mrs. Clinton read every book on the history of the mansion she could find before embarking on the project, which she knew could be politically explosive. The results show a side of this "now" couple that does not often come across in the heat of their political battles: their love of the American past. If it is true, as some psychologists maintain, that a woman reveals a lot of her personality when she decorates a room, Mrs. Clinton's changes suggest that behind her cool facade lurk a lot of strong feelings.

In the second-floor Lincoln Sitting Room, for instance, the First Lady replaced the subdued beige and rust color scheme the Reagans and Bushes had preferred with an array of more robust colors. Burgundy draperies with gilt decorations frame the two windows. The walls have been "ragged" in cream, and the window frames, chair rails, and cornices painted gold. The ceiling has been covered with a bold coffer-patterned paper. The red, green, and gold "Scotch" rug is a Smithsonian reproduction of a nineteenth-century American favorite.

For the Treaty Room, which President Clinton and several predecessors have used as an upstairs office, Mrs. Clinton decided to echo the days in the nineteenth century when it was used as the Cabinet Room. She added inlaid walnut bookcases and chairs upholstered in dark red fabric, ornamented with gold Napoleonic laurel wreaths.

New draperies in vibrant red and blue complement vinyl wallpaper simulating red leather.

It cheered me to see Hillary Clinton enjoying the traditional side of the First Lady's role. I suspect she is discovering there are a lot of satisfactions in it that often elude the practitioner of hardball politics. But she is not about to abandon her political partnership with Bill Clinton. She made very clear to me her intention to continue the fight for health care. She pointed out that Harry S Truman introduced health-care legislation in every session of Congress while he was President. "If we had done what President Truman wanted us to do back then, we would be a lot better off, both financially and in our ability to provide every American with health care," she said. "We've been struggling with this issue for fifty years. We're going to keep on trying to get it done."

I asked Hillary if she had ever considered running for public office after Bill Clinton left the White House. She shook her head and said: "I'm just trying to get through this experience, one day at a time."

Then she added some words that could become a guideline, of sorts, for American women. "I think women's role in politics will continue to grow," she told me. "I don't hold with the idea that women are better than men in public life, but most women bring different experiences into the public arena. I hope in the years to come not only will more women participate but women will try to change the content of politics so we will be more focused on what we can do for children, for instance, and win more support for families."

I left the White House with the feeling that I had talked to a First Lady who was growing as a woman and as a politician. I am confident Hillary Rodham Clinton will continue to do her very best to make a contribution to our American journey, in the White House or out of it.

Chapter 24

—

IS THERE LIFE
AFTER THE
WHITE HOUSE?

THE ANSWER TO THIS QUESTION IS AN EMPHATIC YES. A REMARKABLE number of First Ladies have had interesting and sometimes dramatic lives after they and their husbands retired from the presidency. Martha Washington, whose tenure preceded the move to the District of Columbia, expressed a sentiment many of her successors would share when she and George returned to Mount Vernon in 1797. "The General and I feel like children just released from school," she told one close friend.

But—another leitmotiv in the lives of many First Ladies—politics proved difficult to escape. The country almost went to war with France in 1798, and Washington found himself drafted as general in chief of a largely paper army, which nonetheless required backbreaking correspondence and ticklish diplomacy as old friends quarreled over appointments for themselves and their relatives. After the briefest of illnesses, George died at the end of the following year, leaving Martha inconsolable.

She remained the most famous woman in America and continued to entertain a stream of VIP visitors at Mount Vernon. She also remained a devoted friend to her successor, Abigail Adams. When Abigail moved into the unfinished White House in 1800, Martha sent her some venison, an invitation to Mount Vernon, and her love. After the Adamses lost the presidential election of 1800, Martha dropped her nonpolitical pose and startled some of her visitors by condemning President Thomas Jefferson and his embryo Democrats as national menaces.

Before she died in 1802, Martha demonstrated a very First Ladyish determination to preserve her privacy. She burned all of George's letters to her—an example my mother would imitate, without any need for a prior model. I can still hear my father saying: "Bess, think of history," and Mother replying "I am"—and throwing another letter on the fire. George was not around to say this to Martha, but I have a feeling he might have objected in the same pro forma way, and gotten the same answer.

Julia Tyler was one First Lady who played major-league politics after she left the White House. The advent of the Civil War catapulted Julia and her husband back into the national limelight. John Tyler was part of a 132-member "Peace Convention" that the politicians assembled in Washington, D.C., in February 1861 to see if some sort of compromise between North and South could be worked out before the guns began to boom. As an ex-President, Tyler had considerable prestige, and he conferred repeatedly with the lame-duck President, James Buchanan, while Julia wrote confident letters in all directions, assuring everyone that peace could be preserved.

From her suite at Brown's Hotel, Julia sallied forth to a round of parties, receptions, dinners, and balls. As one historian put it, "Washingtonians made one last effort to drown the throb of martial drums in a sea of alcohol and the swish-swish of dancing slippers." Julia was in her element and cut a stylish swath through the capital. Meanwhile, John Tyler was elected president of the Peace Convention and made a long speech urging compromise. The floundering Buchanan was so grateful, he called on Julia and her husband to thank them personally—a coup which left social Washington gasping.

It soon became apparent to many people that both Tylers were playing a very subtle game. While talking compromise, Tyler was secretly supporting resolutions within the Peace Convention that would have made the South a nation within the nation, with the power to veto all federal appointments within its borders and the right to secede from the Union whenever it pleased. Julia wrote candidly to her mother that she and the ex-President were basically playing for time, to give Virginia a chance to organize its defenses before seceding—and to persuade the border states of Tennessee, Maryland, and Kentucky to join her. "Very likely she [Virginia] will be able to draw off, which would be glorious, a couple of Northern states," she added. This ex–First Lady had become a secret agent for the Confederacy!

All these high-flying schemes came crashing to the ground when the President-elect, Abraham Lincoln, arrived in Washington and made it clear that he intended to enforce the U.S. Constitution in every part of the tottering union, and he was prepared to accept the South's challenge to open warfare to make good on his vow. John and Julia Tyler retreated to Richmond, where he made a speech calling for Virginia's immediate secession.

The next years proved to be anything but romantic for this quintessential glamour girl. John Tyler died in 1862 while war raged around their plantation, Sherwood Forest. Julia finally fled the carnage for the shelter of her mother's house on New York's Staten Island. But after the war she proved that the flair she had displayed as First Lady was no fluke.

With determination and guile, Julia regained ravaged Sherwood Forest and kept it going through Reconstruction and the depression of the 1870s, which wiped out much of the Gardiners' Northern fortune. She somehow managed to raise and educate seven children in the bargain—and demonstrated a positive genius for getting them government jobs, though they remained unreconstructed Democrats while the Republicans ruled the White House and Washington. In the late 1870s, she capped her career with a five-year campaign to win a federal pension for herself and other widows of Presidents.

Julia Dent Grant also remained immersed in politics for a while. Her post–White House years began with an absolutely fabulous world tour. Taking advantage of the fact that Ulysses S. Grant remained the most famous American of his time, Julia and a covey of Republican political bosses designed the trip as a covert bid for a third term. A small army of aides, servants, and reporters followed Ulysses and his First Lady for twenty-eight months, as they promenaded from London to Egypt to St. Petersburg to Tokyo, with innumerable stops in between. They dined with Queen Victoria at Windsor Castle and conferred with Pope Leo XIII in the Vatican. Their other hosts included Prince Otto von Bismarck, the famed "Iron Chancellor" of Germany, the Emperors of Austria and Japan, and the Czar of Russia. American newspapers were filled with drawings and stories of the Grants' royal progress.

The General maintained he was indifferent to whether he spent another four years in the White House. Not so Julia, who exuded the sort of determination that suggests she might have conquered the South more swiftly than her husband, if Lincoln had made her a general. On the eve of the 1880 Republican convention, Grant wrote a letter of withdrawal and gave it to his backers in case they needed it to provide him with a dignified exit. Julia exploded and ordered them "*not* to use that letter." She thereby set the stage for one of the forgotten dramas in the history of American politics, the die-hard stand of the Old Guard Republicans around their favorite candidate.

Julia urged Grant to do the unorthodox—go to the convention floor, where his fame would sweep the delegates into a stampede in his favor. Grant refused. In those days, it was considered undignified for candidates to admit they wanted to be President before they were nominated. The General was adamant in his refusal to go "hat in hand" to the convention and beg for the nomination. Julia regarded this as "mistaken chivalry" and urged him "for heavens sake to go— and go tonight."

The flabbergasted Grant, who knew his wife was headstrong at times, could only murmur: "Julia, I am amazed at you." He was probably more amazed to discover she was right. Grant led on the first thirty-five ballots, but he remained sixty-six votes short of the needed two-thirds majority for the nomination. The liberal Republicans finally coalesced around a personable vacuum named James Garfield, who Grant thought "had the backbone of an angleworm." Forbidden by Julia to withdraw, the Old Guard grimly cast their 306 votes for the General to the bitter end, leaving the Republican Party seriously fractured. The fissure widened after Garfield's assassination in 1881, enabling Grover Cleveland to win the White House in 1884 and restore the Democratic Party to respectability.

The widowed Edith Roosevelt remained aloof from politics until another Roosevelt reached the White House in 1933. Edith did not think much of Cousin Franklin. Any time a Republican newspaper wanted a blast against FDR, she was ready to supply it. She made headlines with her appearance at a Republican rally in Madison Square Garden in 1932. FDR, no slouch at this sort of game, wooed Edith's easygoing son Archie and was soon entertaining him aboard the presidential yacht. When someone asked Edith for an explanation, she said Archie had been seduced "because his mother wasn't there."

Eleanor Roosevelt's involvement in politics scarcely missed a beat after she left the White House. My father recognized her immense value as a symbol of America's global commitment to democracy and appointed her a delegate to the United Nations eight months after FDR's death. There she became a primary spokesperson for one of her favorite causes, human rights. Many people regard her as the guiding force behind the 1948 Universal Declaration of Human Rights, which to this day enables the U.N. to act on behalf of oppressed and deprived peoples.

Among the many former critics Eleanor beguiled in her post–White House years was the formidable Republican Senator Arthur Vandenberg of Michigan. When the Universal Declaration of Human Rights passed, the senator said: "I want to take back everything I ever said about her, and believe me it's been plenty. She's a grand person and a great American citizen." Few people know that part of the credit for this unexpected display of political harmony belonged to

Eleanor Roosevelt examines the United Nations Declaration of Human Rights. She was largely responsible for this historic document. My father appointed her U.S. delegate to the world body in 1946. *(Franklin D. Roosevelt Library)*

Harry S Truman, who had spent hours and hours converting Senator Vandenberg from the isolationism that typified the Republican Party of that era.

A few First Ladies have remained in Washington, or returned to it, and enjoyed the reflected glow of their previous fame, while serenely ignoring politics. The one who managed this difficult trick best was Dolley Madison. For nearly twenty years, she lived on her husband's Virginia plantation, Montpelier, hovering tenderly over her "great little Madison" as he slipped into a long, slow decline. When he died in 1836, Dolley headed back to the capital, where she reigned as a sort of queen mother for the next thirteen years. Presidents, congressmen, and ambassadors flocked to parties at her house on Lafayette Square. She was a virtual fixture at receptions in the White House as well. First Ladies sought her advice on matters of protocol and social diplomacy. Senator Daniel Webster declared she was "the only permanent power in Washington."

When anything important happened in the capital, Dolley was there, ready to lend the event her inimitable personal touch. In 1844, Samuel F. B. Morse, the inventor of the telegraph, gave a demonstration of his marvel. Dolley was on hand to receive the portentous message that crackled from Baltimore: "What hath God wrought." Morse asked Dolley what message she wanted to transmit in reply. She told him to send "my love to Mrs. Wethered," an old friend who was at the Baltimore end of the line.

Congress accorded Dolley a unique testimony of their near adoration of her. A North Carolina legislator moved that whenever she visited the Capitol, she should be seated on the House floor, instead of being forced to resort to the visitors' gallery. The resolution passed unanimously, and two congressmen were appointed Dolley's official escorts, to guide her to her seat whenever she chose to appear.

Edith Wilson spent her first three post–White House years caring for her crippled husband in a handsome red-brick Georgian revival house on Northwest S Street. (It is open to the public now and worth a visit.) After Wilson died in 1924, Edith devoted the rest of her long life to perpetuating his memory.

From the start, she nursed grudges and would brook no criticism of Wilson. Henry Cabot Lodge, the Republican senator who had led the fight against the League of Nations, was told he would be persona non grata at the funeral. Thirty-two years later, the *New York Times* columnist Arthur Krock spoke at ceremonies celebrating the centennial of Wilson's birth. He was generally praiseful—but he opined that Wilson should have done more to make his diplomacy a bipartisan effort by inviting a few prominent Republicans such as William Howard Taft to the Versailles Peace Conference in 1919. A few days later, Krock met Edith at another Washington affair and remarked on what a nice occasion the centennial ceremony had been. "Yes," Edith said. "It's too bad you could not have been *with* us."

Of Wilson's successors, the President who stirred Edith's greatest enthusiasm was John F. Kennedy, not because she agreed with his policies but she liked his book *Profiles in Courage.* Perhaps she felt the title implicitly praised Woodrow Wilson, although he is mentioned only in passing in the text. I remain fond of this feisty Democratic First Lady for an anecdote connected to her support for JFK. When a friend with a Nixon-Lodge bumper sticker on his car called on her in 1960, Edith told him *never* to park in her driveway again.

Readers may be surprised to learn Bess Truman almost settled in Washington, D.C. Most people assume it was Bess, the supposed non-politician, who could not get out of the capital fast enough. Actually, Mother was a nonpolitician the way the retired Joe DiMaggio is a non–baseball player. Politics fascinated her, and at first she could not bear the thought of leaving Washington for small-town life in Independence, Mo. For a while, Dad was disposed to humor her, and they actually made a few discreet inquiries about buying a house somewhere in the District.

But Dad, the supposed political habitué of the partnership, was the one who decided that an ex-President simply could not hang out in Washington, D.C. It would make the incumbent uneasy and might lead to unpleasant clashes. This was especially probable in the atmosphere of livid dislike and sneering superiority with which the outgoing Truman Democrats and the incoming Eisenhower Republicans regarded each other in 1952. For the sake of his blood pressure, as well as the dignity of the presidency, Dad decided Independence was the best—even the only—option.

Mother took the decision with good grace. But she had no intention of spending the rest of her days in Missouri. She had always had a yen to travel, and what better time to do it than in the afterglow of the White House? For the next ten years, the Trumans came pretty close to being globe-trotters, with trips to Hawaii and Europe (twice) and numerous hegiras to New York and, yes, Washington, D.C. They made no attempt to imitate General Grant and Julia, but they enjoyed spectacular receptions at several special habitats, such as Winston Churchill's spacious home, Chartwell.

The Trumans enjoyed all these expeditions immensely, even though the trips to Washington invariably ignited Dad's political fires and Mother occasionally had to do some emphatic stamping to put them out again. She finally convinced him that ex-Presidents only *think* they have power. If they actually try to throw their weight around, the results can be humiliating.

After Dad's death in 1972, Mother overruled my cogent arguments in favor of a move to New York and the proximity of me and her four grandchildren and elected to stay in Independence. She demonstrated everything I have claimed about her passion for politics by staying in close touch with the electoral scene on both the national and state levels. When Missouri's Senator Thomas Eagleton was massacred by the press for admitting he had a history of depression and had to step aside as George McGovern's vice presidential running mate in 1972, Mother wrote him one of her no-nonsense letters, telling him Bess Truman still admired him. When he ran for reelection in 1974, she endorsed him wholeheartedly, and the senator won, as they used to say in the Kansas City clubhouses, in a walk.

In 1976, operating from a hospital bed while being treated for arthritis, Mother demonstrated her local clout. She endorsed State Senator Ike Skelton in his race for Congress from Jackson County (which includes Independence). In the primary, Skelton had run poorly in Jackson County. With the support of the old pro from Independence, he breezed to an easy victory against a discomfited, unendorsed Republican.

Mother was amazed and not a little pleased by the upsurge in Dad's popularity during the post-Watergate years. Gerald Ford became the first of a long line of Republican Presidents who tried to claim similarities to Harry Truman. When the Truman Library dedicated a statue to Dad in 1976, President Ford was delighted to be the principal speaker. He and Betty Ford had a most enjoyable visit with Mother. She thought Betty was doing a wonderful job as First Lady— even though she said some things that left Mother gasping. "I like Mrs. Ford's *honesty,*" she told me, reaffirming her faith in that basic Truman trait.

It was Betty's honesty that rescued her troubled post–White House years. They began with a terrific struggle against the depression that had descended on her when Gerald Ford lost his reelection battle against Jimmy Carter in 1976. Try as she might to see the future in a positive light, Betty could not shake off her gloom. Her problem was complicated—perhaps even caused—by the medication she took to dull the pain of osteoarthritis. A further complication was a tendency to use tranquilizers and alcohol to control her anxiety and enliven her moods.

By the end of her first year in Palm Springs, which the Fords had chosen for their retirement home, Betty was in a daze most of the time. Her daughter, Susan, grew deeply alarmed and persuaded her father to convene a family conference at which everyone tried to awaken Betty to her plight and persuade her to get help. She resisted mightily at first, furiously condemning them for invading her privacy. Perhaps that was an inevitable reaction of someone whose privacy had been invaded so often in the White House. Eventually, Betty calmed down and realized her husband and children were motivated by love. She soon sought help at the Alcohol and Drug Rehabilitation Service of the Long Beach Naval Hospital.

Betty found it easy to admit that she had become addicted to medication but balked at confessing a dependence on alcohol. On this point, of course, she was imitating millions of other Americans who have the same problem. Denial is the alcoholic's first line of defense. Once more, Betty's innate honesty triumphed over her attempt at self-deception. She not only admitted she was an alcoholic, she accepted her doctor's advice and went public with the statement, to help others face the problem. Average folks do this at AA meetings. Ex–First Ladies do it on national television—one more testimony to the awesome power of their unelected office, even after they leave the White House.

With her life under control once more, Betty found herself almost as busy as she had been in the White House, coping with thousands of letters from people seeking advice or just eager to share their private tales of alcoholic woe. She hurled herself into campaigns to raise money for the National Arthritis Foundation and founded the Betty Ford Center for Drug and Alcohol Rehabilitation at Rancho Mirage,

California. The center rapidly became a national resource for people with substance abuse problems.

When I visited Betty Ford at her beautiful summer home in Colorado, she was still having a wonderful time being herself. She bubbled with opinions about the world around her, almost all of them positive. She was still deeply involved in fund-raising and other matters at the Betty Ford Center and repeatedly expressed her continuing concern for Americans struggling with addiction problems. She looks back on her twenty-eight months as First Lady without regret now, satisfied that she—and Jerry—have no reason to apologize for anything. They both take justifiable pride in having helped the nation recover from Watergate, our worse political crisis since the Civil War.

Lady Bird Johnson's campaign to beautify America did not end with her departure from the White House. After LBJ's death in 1973, she launched a program to plant wildflowers along hundreds of miles of Texas highways. She was also the prime mover in creating a beautiful park along the banks of Austin's share of the Colorado River.

On her seventieth birthday in 1982, Lady Bird founded the National Wildflower Research Center outside Austin. Here a staff of horticulturists study how to preserve and restore our native wildflowers, almost a quarter of which are in danger of extinction. Thousands of tourists and schoolchildren come to the center each year to tour the sixty blooming acres, which feature a reconstructed prairie with nineteen species of native grasses and more than seventy-five species of wildflowers that greeted the Texas pioneers.

When I visited her in Austin, Lady Bird, at eighty-two, was continuing to maintain a schedule that would intimidate most forty-year-olds. She still goes anywhere and everywhere to preach the gospel of beautification. She sits on boards and committees that promote this unimpeachable cause. On a visit to New York, she raced through a packed day with her staff panting in her wake. At 5:00 P.M. she confessed she was feeling a little tired. "Oh, to be seventy again!" she sighed.

Some First Ladies have preferred to emphasize the word *private* when they retired from public life. They not only avoided politics, they courted near invisibility. Frances Cleveland was one of these. She moved to Princeton, New Jersey, with Grover Cleveland and devoted herself to raising their family, which eventually numbered five children. When Cleveland died in 1908, Frances was only forty-four. In 1913 she married Thomas Preston, a Wells College archaeologist who soon joined the Princeton faculty.

When I met her in 1946, she was a gracious, self-assured woman of eighty-two. We were all attending a fete commemorating the founding of Princeton University. My mother, Eleanor Roosevelt, and Edith Wilson completed the plethora of First Ladies present. Among the other luminaries was General Dwight D. Eisenhower. Ike joined me and Mrs. Preston as we were discussing the renovation that the White House was undergoing at the time. Before I could introduce him, Ike turned to Mrs. Preston and asked: "Where did you live in Washington?"

"The same place Margaret is living now," she replied sweetly.

Only then did I manage to inform Ike that he was talking to Mrs. Grover Cleveland. His response was "It's time for lunch, Margaret." When a general is embarrassed, no one is more expert at executing a rapid retreat. I suspect that later in the day, some hapless aide got chewed out for not briefing his boss on Mrs. Preston's identity.

That sunniest of First Ladies, Grace Coolidge, also remained persistently nonpolitical—and virtually invisible—after her husband's death in 1933. Returning from a trip to Europe in 1936, when every Republican in America was girding for a titanic effort to defeat FDR's supposedly un-American New Deal, she was asked for a political comment. Grace coolly replied: "We are all interested in politics—we should be—but I am not actively interested."

Grace stayed far away from Washington, D.C., and generally eschewed the slightest attempt to get any mileage out of her previous fame. On the contrary, she did her utmost to disguise her identity whenever she traveled. One of her favorite stories concerned an incognito trip she took to Europe with a friend. Somehow the staff at one Swiss hotel learned she was the widow of an American President. While Grace was seeing to their luggage, the desk clerk asked her friend: "Would you sign the register for yourself and Mrs. Lincoln?"

Jacqueline Kennedy also largely eschewed politics—but she never courted invisibility. It would have been a waste of time. Thanks to TV and modern America's craze for celebrities, she remained one of the most famous, instantly recognizable women in the world. Jackie's post–White House years were divided into three oddly contradictory parts. For the first five years, she was a kind of secular saint, a status in which she willingly participated, building up the John F. Kennedy legend.

Bobby Kennedy's assassination in 1968 brought this phase of Jackie's life to a horrendous stop. Lady Bird Johnson told me that when she attended Bobby's funeral service in New York, she offered Jackie her hand and Mrs. Kennedy looked right through her, as if Lady Bird were not there. Mrs. Johnson, in her usual generous, understanding way, attributed this lapse to shock and grief. But something much more profound was happening in Jackie's soul. "I hate this country," she told a friend not long after the funeral. "I want to get out."

The result was a right-angle turn, from secular saint to fallen idol. Readers may remember that in the summer of 1963, Jackie had spent a controversial vacation aboard Aristotle Onassis's yacht in the Mediterranean, while JFK fretted and fumed in the White House. She had continued to see this unsavory but utterly charming Greek shipping magnate, and even before Bobby's death had toyed with marrying him. Now, the only Kennedy who might have stopped her was gone. Jackie accepted Onassis's offer, after he reinforced it with a ruby "the size of an egg"—and a prenuptial contract that deposited five million dollars in her bank account.

The dismay was global. Swedish newspapers cried: HOW COULD YOU? Bewildered Americans said they felt almost as bad as they had on November 22, 1963. The Roman Catholic Church tut-tutted that Jackie would be living in sin, because Onassis was a divorced man. But Jackie knew exactly what she wanted: money. Her presidential widow's pension of $50,000 and the $200,000 she received from a Kennedy trust fund were simply not enough to maintain her in the style she preferred—and perhaps felt she deserved. Occasionally she was defiant. She said she liked making people—especially politicians—squirm when they heard the name Onassis.

As Mrs. Onassis, Jackie spent Greek drachmas, French francs, and American dollars on a scale that staggered even a tycoon who maintained a staff of seventy on his private island of Skorpios. This led to violent quarrels and a growing coolness, which was exacerbated by the death of Onassis's son in a plane crash. Onassis began talking about a divorce so he could marry a younger woman and sire another male heir.

As one friend put it in a masterpiece of understatement, Onassis was "not kind" to Jackie in these later years. Another friend tells of watching him excoriate her for her sloppy clothes and unkempt hair when they went to lunch at the villa of one of his billionaire friends. Before he could subject her to the humiliation of a divorce, the golden Greek fell ill and died in a Paris hospital. His only heir, his daughter Christina, settled with Jackie for twenty-six million dollars.

Coming back to the United States, Jackie made another right-angle turn, into the sedate, respectable world of the very rich. Essentially, this was the milieu into which she had been born—but the Bouviers, their fortune shredded by the 1929 Wall Street crash, had found it anything but idyllic. Now Jackie triumphantly returned to it, her own woman, and concentrated on what mattered most to her—raising her children to be stable, intelligent adults.

This was the link that gradually enabled Jackie to regain her most admired status with American women. She lived on a scale beyond their dreams, with a fourteen-room Fifth Avenue apartment, a horse farm in New Jersey, and a 464-acre estate on Martha's Vineyard. But on this crucial family value of putting one's children first their lives and hers intersected.

In this most private phase of her public life, Jackie worked three to four days a week at a prominent New York publishing house, editing about a dozen books a year. The writers with whom she dealt testify unanimously to her intelligence, her wit, her remarkable breadth of knowledge about art and fashion and a host of other subjects that interested her. One fellow editor who knew her well has described these last fifteen years as the "most satisfying" part of Jackie's life: "It seems her happiness in that time quadrupled."

For a companion, Jackie chose an affable, worldly diamond merchant, Maurice Tempelsman. She presided serenely over her children's progression into adulthood. She loaned her name to various good causes, such as the preservation of Grand Central Terminal from the wrecker's ball, and to numerous fund-raisers and festivals for the arts. When she died of cancer in the spring of 1994, the outpouring of grief demonstrated how totally she had recaptured the world's admiration.

That other nonpolitical First Lady, Mamie Eisenhower, proclaimed herself a lost soul when Ike died in March 1969. Over the next ten years, however, Mamie showed more than a few signs of becoming a woman in her own right, outspoken and not in the least afraid of the limelight. She had no hesitation about comparing her home and mother lifestyle to the home and workplace of the feminists, and finding hers a better choice. She addressed the graduating class of Gettysburg College and paid several visits to the White House. On one of the last of these returns to Pennsylvania Avenue, she got on beautifully with Rosalynn Carter, the first of the public partner First Ladies. "I stayed busy all the time and loved being in the White House," she told Rosalynn. "But I was never expected to do all the things you have to do."

Some people see a sort of rueful confession in these words. I think they miss the basic satisfaction Mamie Eisenhower felt with her life. It seems to me she was telling Rosalynn, in a nice way, that if the First Partner wanted to work her head off and share the heart-palpitating heat generated by the Oval Office, that was perfectly fine—but you wouldn't catch Mamie Eisenhower doing it! She was too polite, of course, to point out which of them stayed way up on the list of most admired women during their White House years.

In spite of all the brickbats thrown at her and her husband by the press and biographers, Nancy Reagan emanated a quiet, even a triumphant, satisfaction when we met at the Hotel Carlyle in New York to discuss her White House years. In presidential terms, she and Ronnie "did it all." They won reelection, and Nancy left the White House far more admired than she had been when she entered it. We talked several months before doctors diagnosed Ronald Reagan as suffering from the early stages of Alzheimer's disease. But I have no doubt that Nancy will face this challenge with courage and devotion. It will be one more task in the major mission of her life: the protection of Ronald Reagan.

When we met, the only negative in Nancy's world was her continuing fear of an attempt on her husband's life. If anyone has any doubts about ex–First Families needing Secret Service protection, they will be banished by a story Nancy told me. A year or so after the Reagans returned to California, Nancy happened to glance out a window of their Bel Air home and saw a stranger wearing a T-shirt and overalls walking down a glass-walled corridor that connects the two wings of the house.

Who in the world is that? Nancy wondered. As far as she knew, there was no work being done on any part of the house. Before she could pick up the phone and ask her husband, who was in the exercise room, two Secret Service agents charged into the corridor. One of them jammed his gun under the intruder's chin. The man was a former mental patient who had scaled a wall and gotten into the house. He had no weapon. He planned to strangle Ronald Reagan.

For Barbara Bush, the most recent departee from the White House, life is still full of multiple satisfactions. When I talked with her at her summer home in Kennebunkport, Maine, she was entertaining seven grandchildren. She was writing her memoirs and was still deeply involved in supporting literacy programs and other causes in which volunteers play a major role.

Mrs. Bush also spoke with glowing pride about her sons Jeb and George, who were running for governorships in Florida and Texas. "Whether they win or lose," she said, "the mere fact that they have chosen to go into politics astounded me. It made me think maybe they didn't resent all those hours George and I spent away from home pursuing his career."

As for George losing the election to Bill Clinton, Mrs. Bush put it this way: "I didn't like it. But having said that, I think I've put it behind me. It's not my style to brood over the past—especially when the future is full of good things." Among the best of those things was the discovery when they returned to live in Houston that she could pick up with old friends after twenty years "without missing a beat." She says she and George have "yet to say no" to any board or committee in Houston that has asked them for help. It is part of their continuing commitment to the "thousand points of light," George's call for a massive outpouring of volunteers to help improve American life. "I still feel that is one of the most important things he said while we were in the White House," Mrs. Bush told me.

Her biggest surprise about her post–White House years was the discovery that "it doesn't stop." By "it" she meant being a public person. Her mail still runs to forty letters a day. Only a week before we talked, she had gone out for a sail with a grandson and stopped at a nearby town to pick up some groceries. People swarmed from all directions the moment she set foot on the dock. "We had to run a gauntlet from the boat to the store and back," she said.

With a few exceptions, such as Mary Lincoln and Pat Nixon, First Ladies have seldom evinced any major regrets when they look back on their sometimes agonizing tours in the White House. "I loved every minute of it," Barbara Bush told me. Rosalynn Carter said almost exactly the same thing. Betty Ford and Nancy Reagan, ditto.

Even Bess Truman, who sometimes claimed to hate every minute of it, confessed to a secret attachment to those tumultuous years. I once asked her if she missed anything about the White House. She sighed and said: "All that help."

Chapter 25

—

THOUGHTS AT
MY MOTHER'S
FUNERAL

On a sunny October day in 1982, Bess Truman was buried from Trinity Episcopal Church in Independence. It was the same small, brick house of worship in which she had married Captain Harry Truman, just back from the Western Front, in 1919. Determined to keep the service as quiet and private as possible—the way I knew Mother wanted it—I limited the guest list to 150. Only a few personal friends went back to her Washington days. There were far more people from Independence.

But I also knew that history could not be excluded from the ceremony. In spite of her fierce clutch on privacy, Mother was still a former First Lady, and Nancy Reagan, wife of the incumbent President, was on the invitation list, along with Betty Ford, the former First Lady she liked best. In a gesture that surprised me, Rosalynn Carter also flew to Independence to express her own and her husband's sympathy. Mother had declined to endorse Jimmy Carter in his run for reelection in 1980, although he and Rosalynn had kicked off their campaign in Independence in yet another presidential attempt to borrow some Truman magic.

The three First Ladies sat in the front pew, and one of the news photographers hovering around us begged me for permission to take a picture. I had banned all photography inside the church. After some urging from my newsman husband, who could not tolerate my inclination to ignore a historic moment, I relented and the picture was taken.

Now I am glad Clifton talked me into that picture. It has become a sort of touchstone to which I have returned more than once while writing this book. The seed for this book was planted at that brief, quiet funeral service, attended by those three very different First Ladies. They personified the amazing variety of talents and personalities who had held this unique unelected office. Then and there I decided I wanted to tell their story.

Here is the picture that partly inspired this book. Nancy Reagan, Betty Ford, and Rosalynn Carter sit in a front pew at my mother's funeral service. *(Bettmann Archive)*

Mother's life of course evoked other thoughts. At ninety-seven, she had become the oldest First Lady in American history. I remembered teasing her when Mrs. Wilson died at eighty-nine. I wondered if there was something in the air of the Big White Jail that contributed to longevity, little knowing I was talking to the coming champion. I thought of the staggering sweep of history that Mother's life encompassed. Born when Chester Arthur was in the White House, she had seen the nation through five wars and eighteen presidents.

Sitting there, listening to the hymns, I began to perceive in Mother's life what has since become apparent as I studied the lives of other First Ladies—their story transcends the politics of the moment and deals with fundamental things, above all faith and love. For Bess Truman—and for so many other of these presidential wives—faith encompassed not only belief in a caring God, even when life stirred bitter doubts, but the faith to endure, to go on caring about the people in their lives.

It was the strength, the duration of Bess Truman's caring that inspired affection in so many people. She shared that strength with her troubled mother, who never recovered from her husband's suicide, her often troubled brothers, her occasionally troublesome daughter—and above all her husband, especially during those eight years in the White House when he carried the future of the free world on his shoulders.

For Mother, faith also included a basic confidence in the huge, complex, ever-evolving United States of America. Disappointments and difficulties, public or private, never daunted her bedrock midwestern sense of America's immense potential, its endless capacity for change and renewal. Spiritually, psychologically, she remained close to those pioneer ancestors who had crossed the wide Missouri and gazed at the vast prairie's seemingly infinite distance, its promise of abundance.

Each of the three First Ladies in the front pew had attempted in her own way to forge a similar faith and offer a similar caring strength to her presidential husband. At the same time they sought within the context of their individual lives a way to find the White House role that best suited them as women. They recognized the symbolic power of the office of First Lady, and they struggled to cope with its multiple challenges—each choosing from a host of alternatives the ones that, in those wonderful words of Lady Bird Johnson, made her heart sing.

That last word may strike some people as a bit too extravagant for Bess Truman. For her, I would substitute "laugh." Mother had a wonderful eye for the absurdities, the follies of politics and politicians in Washington. In public, she usually looked solemn. But in private, she could unleash one-liners and sarcastic asides that reduced us to helpless laughter, with hers the heartiest of all. It was a priceless asset for any President to have in his White House.

All her gifts—of laughter, of native shrewdness, of caring, of faith in America—Bess Truman offered freely to her presidential husband. The other First Ladies did the same thing. Betty Ford's courageous candor, Nancy Reagan's protective devotion, Rosalynn Carter's fiercely energetic public partnership came with the same no-strings arrangement. That is where the faith that created these gifts crosses into love.

Love is the word which makes First Ladies ultimately important in the national scheme of things. Love has never been much of an ingredient in the politics of men. The closest they come to it is loyalty, which is an admirable virtue. But love goes beyond the boundaries of friendship and party; it evokes realities that every American can share in the framework of his or her individual life.

Unquestionably, there is something to the idea that the First Lady speaks to the nation's heart. A President has to do that too, but he represents other things—power, pride, policy—that can easily interfere with the unqualified caring the heart evokes. Simply by being there, creating, as Martha Washington did, the tone, the emotional aura of a President's administration, the First Lady reminds us that American politics has been different from the start. It has always recognized the need to win hearts as well as minds.

Whether First Ladies attempt to define this caring dimension or simply choose to personify it with a minimum of words, as Bess Truman and Jacqueline Kennedy and Pat Nixon did, in their very different ways, a loving woman is the ultimate role the First Lady plays before the American people. Thanks to the power of mass communication, she can now express many meanings of her love, she can reach out to a broad spectrum of causes and people. But she must remember—first, last, and always—she is the wife of a President who needs her strength and devotion as he struggles to lead America into an always unknown future.

INDEX

Page numbers in *italics* refer to illustrations.

Jaffray, Elizabeth, 108, 109, 237, 250
James, Henry, 308
Japan, 65, 75, 109, 331
Japanese Americans, 68
Jefferson, Thomas, 21, 26, 60, 90, 91, 93,
    95–96, 257, 335
Jenkins, Walter, 177–78
Jews, 151–52, 164
Jim Crow practices, 52
Johnson, Andrew, 72, 203, 207, 297
Johnson, Eliza, 203, 207
Johnson, Joshua, 277, 278
Johnson, Lady Bird, 5, 6, 13, 15, 39, 52, 85,
    134–35, 152, 154, 169–72, *172*,
    173–82, *182*, 183–87, 188, 189, 195,
    222, 328, 331, 344, 346, 354; beautifi-
    cation programs, 178–83, 186, 344;
    campaigning and rescue operations,
    175–78, 187; as a mother, 173, 183,
    185; political views, 173–77, 183–84;
    post–White House years, 344; rela-
    tionship with her husband, 170–71,
    174–77, 184–87; role as First Lady,
    169–87
Johnson, Lyndon B., 5, 15, 85, 135, 162,
    169–87, 198, 221–22, 344; 1964 cam-
    paign, 175–78; as Vice President,
    169–70; and Vietnam War, 183–87
Just Say No to Drugs, 158–59

Kansas, 272
Kennedy, Jacqueline Bouvier, 4, 6, 7–8,
    9–10, *10*, 30–40, *40*, 41–45, 155, 160,
    169–72, 195, 196–97, 303, 346–48,
    354; and assassination of her hus-
    band, 44–45, 169–71; cultural pro-
    gram, 37–38, 42; death of, 6, 7, 348;
    decoration of White House, 11,
    33–38, 190, 198; as a mother, 8, *40*,
    43; in Paris, 37–38, 39; polite brush-
    offs by, 39–40; political views, 42–43;
    post–White House years, 346–48;
    privacy of, 7, 8, 36, 40, 346–48; rela-
    tionship with her husband, 31–34,
    38, 39, 41–44; role as First Lady,
    9–10, 30–45, 169–72; sense of style,
    10, *10*, 30–33, 37–39, 43
Kennedy, Joe, 41, 60
Kennedy, John, Jr., 8, 32, 36, 39, *40*, 45,
    196–97
Kennedy, John F., 6, 9–10, *10*, 30–45, 114,
    169–71, 173–75, 180, 196, 218–19,
    220–21, 340–41, 346; assassination

of, 44–45, 169–70, 183; *Profiles in
    Courage*, 221
Kennedy, Patrick Bouvier, 43
Kennedy, Robert, 9, 32, 173–74, 346
Kennedy, Rose, 41
Kennedy Alliance for Progress, 170
Kentucky, 221, 222, 230, 261, 262, 336
Khrushchev, Nikita, 40
Khrushchev, Nina, 40
King, Martin Luther, Jr., 183, 186
Kiplinger, Willard, 63
Kissinger, Henry, 200
kitchen, White House, 9–10, 19, 21,
    69–70, 78–80, 170, 210–11, 215–17,
    331; *see also* food, White House
Knapp Foundation, 158
Kohl, Helmut, 164
Korean War, 34, 87

labor strikes, 125, 128–29
Ladies' Home Journal, 106, 307
Lady Bird Special (train), 175–77, 187
Lance, Bert, 153
Lansing, Robert, 128, 129
Lasker, Mary, 179, 181
Latrobe, Benjamin, 22
LBJ Memorial Grove, 135
League of Nations, 125–28, 238, 240
Lee, Robert E., 231
LeHand, Marguerite (Missy), 70
L'Enfant, Pierre Charles, 179
Leslie's magazine, 223
Library of Congress, 128
Life magazine, 78, 326
life span, presidential, 13
Lincoln, Abraham, 5, 11–12, 72, 101, 207,
    220–32, 318, 336; assassination of,
    209, 222, 232; and Civil War, 224–32;
    uncouth westerner image, 221–23
Lincoln, Eddie, 228
Lincoln, Mary, 11–12, 44, 168, 207,
    220–23, *223*, 224–32, 244, 251, 350;
    and assassination of her husband,
    232; and Civil War, 224–32; decora-
    tion of White House, 223–26; deteri-
    oration and mental illness, 228–32;
    as a mother, 228–30; political views,
    222–23, 227, 231; relationship with
    her husband, 222, 225, 226–32; role
    as First Lady, 220–32; sense of style,
    222, 223, *223*, 224, 227
Lincoln, Robert, 231
Lincoln, Tad, 231

ABOUT THE TYPE

The text of this book was set in Janson, a misnamed typeface designed in about 1690 by Nicholas Kis, a Hungarian in Amsterdam. In 1919 the matrices became the property of the Stempel Foundry in Frankfurt. It is an old-style book face of excellent clarity and sharpness. Janson serifs are concave and splayed; the contrast between thick and thin strokes is marked.